AF541739

THE INSIDE STORY OF INDIAN BANKING

THE INSIDE STORY OF INDIAN BANKING

SANDIP SEN

RUPA

Published by
Rupa Publications India Pvt. Ltd 2020
7/16, Ansari Road, Daryaganj New Delhi 110002

Sales Centres:
Allahabad Bengaluru Chennai
Hyderabad Jaipur Kathmandu
Kolkata Mumbai

ISBN: 978-93-90260-10-2

First impression 2020

10 9 8 7 6 5 4 3 2 1

Printed at Replika Press Pvt. Ltd, India

CONTENTS

INTRODUCTION

Writing the inside story of Indian banking has been as exciting as penning a thriller. It helped me explore innovative heists that overborrowed business barons have pulled off with the help of greedy bankers, bureaucrats and politicians, to defraud the banking industry. Had I not gathered critical feedback from bankers, data analysts and industry experts about frauds and defaults and how to counter them, written about bold reforms and the painstaking resolution of stressed assets, the merger of weak banks with the strong ones, this book could easily have been a potboiler.

But writing a non-fiction book about a moth-ridden banking system and the government's partially successful efforts to set things right in a society where corruption is still ruling strong is a work of some responsibility. So, I have preferred retaining depth of content over stylizing the narrative, and I have made every attempt to show the positive reform initiatives in a gloomy scenario of frauds and defaults.

The dismal story of bank frauds and failures is not new. It has its beginnings in the eighteenth century, when banks in India were largely run as private fiefdoms without any regulation. Banks mushroomed in the thousands and collapsed like nine pins in both British-ruled India and the princely states. While banks with Indian holdings, like the Allahabad Bank, founded in 1865 and Punjab National Bank, founded in 1894, have survived the test of time, we have not managed to reduce corruption and inefficiency in the banking industry. Keeping this background in mind, we look at events that have unfolded in the banking industry over the last 15 years, since 2005.

Some of the irregularities and crimes we talk about in this

book are public knowledge; others are not. In the case of the latter, this book will present irrefutable data to show that the frauds were indeed committed, even though action may not have been taken against the perpetrators for several reasons.

We talk of the unbelievable fertilizer import scam of 2007–09 and the nonviable and highly leveraged push towards sponge iron by the steel industry during 2007–11, which created the largest stressed assets of India. We talk of the strange new avatar of Infrastructure Leasing & Financial Services (IL&FS) after it was permitted to fund the Micro, Small & Medium Enterprises (MSME) sector, and the sudden rise of frauds involving the organization between 2007 and 2018 when it collapsed. We discuss the transformation of Dewan Housing Finance Corporation Ltd (DHFL) post 2010, when the second generation turned it into a high profile, low trust, debt-ridden unit, and the Housing Development and Infrastructure Ltd (HDIL)–Punjab and Maharashtra Co-operative (PMC) Bank nexus that led to one of the most audacious and brazen scams—all three under the nose of a sleepy Reserve Bank of India (RBI), compromised auditors and irresponsible rating agencies that lazily resorted to tick box supervision.

This book brings to you the interesting modus operandi of the diamond merchants pulling off Letter of Undertaking (LOU) frauds like Jatin Mehta of Winsome Diamond, Nirav Modi of Firestar Diamond and Mehul Choksi of Gitanjali Gems, and other foreign exchange frauds carried out by the likes of Nitin Sandesara of Sterling Biotech, all fleeing abroad with the loot before slow-moving enforcement agencies could nab them. We also talk of the Kingfisher Airlines fraud and the ICICI Bank fraud, the latter of which involved sweetheart deals its CEO Chanda Kochhar had with Essar Steel and the Videocon Group through their Mauritius-based holding companies.

We talk of the path-breaking reforms after September 2015 when the elaborate infrastructure of the bankruptcy courts was set up in less than two years' time. Thereafter stressed assets of over ₹3 trillion were identified and sent to the National Company Law Tribunal (NCLT) courts, a third of which were resolved within the time frame set by the newly legislated Insolvency and Bankruptcy Code (IBC), 2016. We also visit the chaotic period post September 2018 when the non-banking financial companies (NBFCs) started imploding with frauds, adding another ₹2 trillion to the stressed assets in less than a year. The NBFC reforms are just about beginning, and there could be more defaults on the way.

But the inside story of Indian banking is not only about juicy scams. It is also about the time-consuming battle of hard-fought reforms that is currently in progress. It is about lengthy court battles between the reluctant defaulter and a determined buyer, like the acquisition of Essar Steel by ArcelorMittal. It is about a 'work in progress' that may take another few years to succeed, if pursued diligently. It is about India's weakness of moving two steps forward and one step back on reforms. It is about fresh challenges being thrown up, as new frauds crop up even before the old stressed assets are resolved.

We talk of the silver linings of bold reforms among the dark clouds that surround Indian banking. The whiplash of bankruptcy laws causing widespread financial distress is not unique to India. Even developed nations like the US took a decade, during the 1980s, to find solutions. The disrupted credit lines and the pressure by banks on the industry to bring in more equity for the high debt they carry, the failed vendor payments of the 40 bankrupt giants that have hurt the cash flow of over 200,000 suppliers, and the deposits lost by lakhs of investors who invested in the NBFCs that defaulted have caused endless pain. This was the real reason why the economy tanked and would not have gotten back in shape anytime soon, even without the Coronavirus lockdown impact.

The current slowdown was partly due to a grossly over-borrowed industry downsizing and the loss of liquidity that the banking crisis has brought. But while the crisis was being tackled with some difficulty, the COVID-19 virus struck and paralysed the world. Indian political leaders and bureaucrats of the Centre and the states, cutting across party lines, took the safety first approach of lives over livelihood and went in for much extended lockdowns, halting all economic activity across the country. In the middle of lockdown 4.0, as I complete this book, I am adding a chapter that will discuss the possible aftereffects of COVID-19 and the challenges to be dealt with as industry lockdowns could lead to more debt and possible defaults.

Writing this book has been a learning process, as I spoke to many key stakeholders about both the problems and the solutions. This book could not be written without the feedback of over 60-odd bankers who are largely unnamed, as they wished to remain anonymous. The few who agreed to lend their names have been acknowledged. The bankers' feedback, given in almost every chapter, holds out critical advice and information from the banking community. There is also feedback from lawyers who practice in the NCLT courts and software professionals from my PAN IIT network who deal with banking software and fraud detection systems. I hope my readers will like this collective effort to convey this rapidly unfolding story of Indian banking.

SECTION I

THE TROUBLED LEGACY

ONE

THE ECONOMICS AND POLITICS OF BANK NATIONALIZATION

The banking sector in India, prior to Independence, was quite chaotic. India had many banks and frequent bank failures. The Bank of England was set up in 1694, and the British started developing their banking laws way back in 1708. However, they did not develop India's banking industry. They left the business of banking to the agency houses (companies) of Calcutta and Bombay.

While the agency houses set up their own banks in Bombay, Calcutta and Madras, a few Europeans and the leaders of the Indian nationalist movement realized that in order to benefit the population at large, banks needed to move out of the big trading centres and into the hinterland. In 1865, the Allahabad Bank was set up by a group of Europeans. It was the first joint stock bank where Indian ownership of stocks was permitted. Meanwhile, the Presidency Bank of Bombay failed in 1867 and most of the other agency house banks turned out to be short-lived experiments that could not survive the test of time.

After the initial failure, the presidency banks were revived as per an act enacted in the British Parliament in 1876, and were regulated by the Bank of England. The Bank of Bengal in India was consolidated with two other presidency banks—the Bank of Bombay and the Bank of Madras—to form the Imperial Bank, 50 years later. By the end of the nineteenth century, Allahabad Bank had opened branches in Kanpur, Lucknow, Jhansi, Bareilly, Calcutta and Delhi. This success of Allahabad Bank inspired a group of Indian nationalists and businessmen to set up the Punjab National Bank (PNB) in Lahore, in 1895. In 1905, Lord Curzon ordered the partition of Bengal, which led to the second Swadeshi movement (1905–15), led by the revolutionary-turned-spiritual leader Aurobindo Ghose and thinkers and freedom fighters like Bal Gangadhar Tilak, Lala Lajpat Rai, Bipin Chandra Pal, V.O. Chidambaram Pillai and many others. During this period, several other Indian banks were set up, including the Bank of India, Central Bank of India, Bank of Baroda, Canara Bank, Bank of Mysore and Indian Bank.

Banks Were Not Regulated before Independence

There were no rules or regulations for banking in India prior to Independence. Many wealthy people usually started their own banks with some capital, but in the absence of a regulatory authority, their accountability to the people could not be enforced.

Following a review of British India's banking system, the celebrated economist John Maynard Keynes wrote in *Indian Currency and Finance*, 'In a country so dangerous for banking as India, (it) should be conducted on the safest possible principle.' One school of thinking believes that the British did not want to transfer their good banking practices to India. They brought in know-how for creating physical infrastructure like railways, bridges and ports, because these helped them export goods such as tea, timber, cotton, gold and jewellery out of India. Developing banking offered no such benefits. Another school of thinking believed that the British did not want to tamper with the existing system that had been around in India for centuries. Banks in India used to lend at high interest rates against mortgages of land or gold. Some of the Marwari and Multani banks had their own money and did not even accept depositors' cash.

After the First World War (1914–18), there was an acute 'crisis of currency availability', following which several committees were set up. W.E. Preston, member of the Royal Commission on Indian Currency and Finance, set up in 1926, observed that, 'money lending activity in India could be traced back to the Vedic period, i.e. from 2000 to 1400 BC. The existence of professional banking in India could be traced back to the 500 BC. Kautilya's *Arthashastra*, dating back to 400 BC, contained references to creditors, lenders and lending rates.' At that time banking was largely based on trust and not on regulations, audits and compliance. Banking was fairly varied and catered to the credit needs of trade, commerce and agriculture, as well as to individuals in the economy. Preston went on to say that, 'it may be accepted that a system of banking that was eminently suited to India's then requirements was in force in that country many centuries before the science of banking became an accomplished fact in England.' By the late nineteenth century, it became profitable to invest in the business of banking. Despite many bank failures, investors often got away with profits. A well-known zamindar and his nephew, who were regular visitors at the Calcutta racecourse, were once heard to be animatedly discussing the huge profits being made by banks. The nephew was trying to convince the zamindar that banking was as easy as punting on the racecourse. 'After some initial investment the money will always come from the depositor,' he said. 'You would just have to know how to nurture the right horse to win.' He was planning to get some money out of his rich maternal uncle for a banking venture. But his uncle turned out to be smarter. Early next morning the zamindar sent him a rookie race horse with a note: 'It would be great to see you nurture this imported Egyptian stud and show me how to win.'

By that time, an extensive network of Indian banking houses had developed in the country, connecting all cities/towns that were of commercial importance. They had their own inland bills of exchange or 'hundis,' which were the major forms of transactions between Indian bankers and their transregional connections. A hundi is a bill of exchange or promissory note raised by the supplier for the purchaser at the time of supply of goods, defining the credit period offered, which was usually as long as three to six months. Hundis still exist as a medium of exchange in the Marwari community-dominated Barabazar area of Kolkata and Mumbai's Bhindi Bazaar, and even in many older companies set up by the Birlas, Goenkas, Dalmias and Khaitans.

The Reserve Bank, Initially a Currency Regulator

In the absence of a regulator, there were several bank failures before Independence. There was also an acute shortage of currency after the First World War in 1919. So, the need for a system, primarily to hold currency reserves, was felt. As per the recommendations of the Central Banking Enquiry Committee of 1931, the Reserve Bank of India (RBI) was set up in 1934 to address this need. It was initially a privately owned entity and based in Calcutta. It moved to Mumbai in 1937.

In its initial years, the RBI did not function as a bank regulator. Its primary task was to secure monetary stability in India and operate the currency and credit system. Its work could be classified into four broad categories: to act as a banker to the government; to act as a banker to other banks; to issue bank notes; and finally, to maintain the exchange ratio.

The original choice for the seal of RBI was the East India Company 'Double Mohur' with the sketch of a lion and a palm tree. However, when it created a controversy, it was decided to replace the lion with the tiger, the national animal of India. James Braid Taylor, who was the controller of currency at the mint before he became the second RBI governor in 1937, however, was not satisfied with the design. So he got the tiger photo reshot. The final result, though, was also not to his liking. The tree, he said, was 'all right', adding, 'But the tiger looks too like some species of dog, and I am afraid that a design of a dog and a tree would arouse derision among the irreverent...the tiger is distinctly good but the tree has spoiled it.'

The real problem was that the tiger was not in its natural

habitat under a palm tree. The palm tree was representative of the African desert terrain, and the lion was better suited to that environment. The tiger looked odd under a palm tree. However, the lapse was forgotten after Taylor became RBI chief and relinquished his seat six years later. The first two governors of the RBI were Englishmen, and C.D. Deshmukh, the first Indian governor, took charge in 1943. The RBI had much greater challenges to face over the next 70 years than just redesigning its logo. The flawed design, therefore, still remains.

There were more than a thousand banks in India before 1947. But in the absence of a regulator, nobody had a clue as to what they did. Quite a few of them were fly-by-night operators. The only distinction that depositors knew and could choose from was between the scheduled banks and the non-scheduled banks. Before Independence, the scheduled banks had a capital base of above ₹5 lakh, which was larger than that of the non-scheduled banks.

Between the two World Wars, each bank operated as it felt like. Each had its own set of rules and the laissez-faire policy permitted free entry and exit into the banking world. It also ensured that only the fittest survived. The situation was pretty grim, as the provincial governments did not really keep track of the activities or health of the banks, which were opening and closing frequently under the Companies Act. The bigger banks had branches in multiple provinces—both in Princely States as well as British-administrated territories—while the smaller banks were local.

Change in the RBI's Role

In 1939, soon after its formation, the RBI had suggested to the British government that they enact an independent banking legislation in India. However, preoccupied with the war, the government did not follow its recommendations and banks continued to remain under the Companies Act. In 1946, part of the concerns raised by the RBI was addressed by the promulgation of the RBI Companies (Inspection) Ordinance, 1946. So, at the time of Independence, banks in India neither had adequate legislation to govern them nor a regulator to ensure compliance with the law.

Between 1934 and 1947, over 900 banks failed despite the formation of the RBI, and banks continued to fail in large numbers even after Independence. This was the state of banking in India that we inherited from the British. From the regulatory perspective, it was absolutely ground zero in August 1947, from where we had to start and build institutions from scratch.

Banks failed en masse after the Second World War due to lack of liquidity and because they had mostly issued loans against land mortgages. When property prices crashed during the war, both the borrowers and the bankers vanished. It resulted in banks defaulting in large numbers, due to which thousands of depositors were left high and dry. In the early 1930s, there were 1,284 banking entities in 11 provinces of India, including the North West Frontier Province and Burma. Of these, 919 banks were located in Bengal alone. The maximum number of bank failures—as many as 70 to 80—took place in Bengal, specifically in the city of Calcutta.

The First Face-off between the RBI and the Government

The first confrontation between the RBI and the government of independent India occurred in the 1950s. As no legislation or code of conduct was available for the banks to follow, they essentially continued lending to organized trade. Soon after Independence, the government announced voluntary amalgamation of the thousand odd banks in the country. While the government strongly advocated for the measure and emphasized the need for consolidation, the amalgamations took place slowly.

A few years later, the RBI, prodded by the union government, decided that it would take up complete inspection of one bank every three years. This went on till the late 1950s, and the RBI maintained its right to independence and refused to accept any directive from the government to increase supervision. This was possibly the first serious confrontation between the RBI and the government, with the latter wanting greater supervision and inspection of all banks every year by the RBI. While the government was right in asking for this, India had over a thousand banks and it was not feasible for the RBI to agree to the request. It did not have the infrastructure or the qualified manpower.

Nevertheless, by the 1950s, the Government of India wanted to make qualitative changes in the banking industry. First, they wanted to reduce the number of banks. Second, they wanted to bring them under some supervision and regulatory control. Third, they wanted more credit from the banks for the manufacturing and agriculture sectors instead of just focusing on lending to traders. However, the government had not laid out any roadmap to make that happen. It took the next two decades for the necessary changes to take place.

In those days, when banks failed or there was a fraud in any bank, an ordinance would be issued by the government to tackle the problem. In 1949, these ordinances were consolidated into the Banking Companies Act, 1949, which was changed to the Banking Regulation Act, 1949 on 1 March 1966.

Bank Failures and Social Control in the 1960s

In August 1960, two large banks—the Lakshmi Commercial Bank and the Palai Central Bank of Kerala—failed in quick succession. The government realized that the large number of banks in the country needed to be pruned for any effective regulation. The then finance minister Morarji Desai was forced to take action. Consolidation and amalgamation were made compulsory instead of being voluntary. In the next three years, endless applications for consolidation were processed in the banking division and by 1964, the number of banks had been pared down to just 92.

Between 1960 and 1966, 48 banks went into liquidation. That is when the RBI was really pressurized to safeguard the depositors and check the accountability of the banks on a regular basis. The second amendment to the Banking Companies Act, 1949 came into force in September 1960. It was made to facilitate expeditious payments to depositors of banks that went into liquidation.

In 1963, during the Nehru era, an ordinance to nationalize five of the biggest banks was drafted at the behest of T.T. Krishnamachari, the then cabinet minister for economic and defence coordination. (The Sino-Indian War of 1962 had just taken place and India's defence preparedness was seriously questioned in Parliament. Therefore, a full-fledged minister was charged with looking after both economic and defence coordination.) Though Krishnamachari, who was in charge of economic affairs during both the Nehru and the Shastri eras, was a staunch supporter of bank nationalization, he could not convince any of the prime ministers or finance ministers to toe his line. The Congress party and the governments of the day did not officially support nationalization, despite pressure from the Left and the socialists within the Congress.

Despite the consolidation, banks continued to show weakness. Of the 92 banks, 20 banks were found financially unsound and unfit to be included in the RBI's Second Schedule (to the Reserve Bank of India Act, 1934 [Sections 2(e) and 42]). So, there started a debate in Parliament over how to make banks accountable and safe, and how make them provide credit for rural and industrial development. It was felt that social control of banks through a supervisory body was needed, to give the government powers to lay down binding directives for the operation of the banking industry. The Left parties were strong in the 1950s and the 1960s. They vociferously supported much stronger action and proposed bank nationalization. The then Finance Minister Morarji Desai was himself a great advocate of social control of banks. This gave his ministry a little more power to regulate them without actually nationalizing them.

The Politics of Bank Nationalization

The decision to nationalize banks in 1969 was sudden, but not unplanned. It was part of a strategy to establish Prime Minister Indira Gandhi as the sole and undisputed leader of the Congress Party. In the 1960s, the Congress had too many powerful senior leaders. They were not only old, conservative and ambitious, but also a politicking lot. The old guard of the party, popularly called the 'Syndicate', comprised of leaders like K. Kamraj, Moraji Desai, S. Nijalingappa, Neelam Sanjiva Reddy, S.N. Sinha, S.K. Patil, Atulya Ghosh, Veerendra Patil and a dozen others. They were known to be power-hungry, and many of them had not taken too kindly to the young woman who held the position of prime minister. While Indira Gandhi was the leader of the Congress Legislature Party in the Lok Sabha, the 'Syndicate' wielded power in the states as well as in the Rajya Sabha. They also controlled decision-making on political and economic matters. Indira Gandhi's fight with the Syndicate, which was more intense than her cabinet tussle with her Deputy Prime Minister Morarji Desai, was a fight for control of the Congress party and consolidation of power.

Bank nationalization became Indira's political masterstroke, consolidating her hold over the party. The turning point came with the unexpected death of President Zakir Hussain on 3 May 1969. Vice President V.V. Giri, a renowned trade union leader, was sworn in as an interim president as per protocol. The Syndicate wanted its own candidate, Sanjiva Reddy, to become the next president. That set the alarm bells ringing. Indira Gandhi was already hindered by the Syndicate's compromise formula that had made Desai the deputy prime minister and finance minister. Now, if the Syndicate candidate Sanjiva Reddy became the president, she knew that it would further curtail her autonomy and she would really have to become a 'goongi gudiya'—a moniker that had been used for her earlier.

On 11 July, the Congress Parliamentary Board met to decide

the presidential candidate. The Syndicate proposed Sanjiva Reddy, while Indira Gandhi wanted Babu Jagjivan Ram, a Dalit leader, to be the President of India. When Mrs Gandhi wanted to delay the selection process in order to arrive at a consensus candidate, S. Nijalingappa forced a vote in the six-member parliamentary board. Mrs Gandhi lost by four votes to two and Sanjiva Reddy became the official presidential candidate of the Congress party.

Mrs Gandhi had to find a way out in order to stay head and shoulders above the dual power centres within the Congress. So, she cut a deal with President V.V. Giri, which would help her decimate both Desai and the Syndicate. In short, the Bank Nationalization Ordinance would be signed by the Interim President Giri just before he resigned to contest the presidential election. In turn, she would informally support Giri, who would file his nomination as an independent candidate for the post of the president against the Congress's official candidate Sanjiva Reddy.

Thus, bank nationalization, which had been on the backburner for several years, suddenly came into the limelight. On 12 July 1969, in her address at the All India Congress Committee (AICC) Bangalore session, Indira suddenly pitched for bank nationalization and also submitted a note to AICC, setting off massive media speculation. However, nobody had the faintest clue that such a politically explosive ordinance would be pushed through within a week. This is because nobody expected that she would cut a deal with V.V. Giri to outsmart the Syndicate—a move that would split the Congress party down the middle a few months down the line.

Bank nationalization was the ace in the pack that would push out Morarji Desai and change Indira Gandhi's image to that of a strong and decisive leader as well. It would show that Mrs Gandhi could take bold steps to control the unwieldy banking sector. The state leaders—who, back then, had a decisive voice in any presidential election—would have to put their weight behind Mrs Gandhi's candidate, as people would love it. Besides, bank nationalization would bring the Left parties to support Mrs Gandhi against the Syndicate and ensure a win for her.

While what caught the imagination of the media about the coup was Indira's political win over her archrival, a deeper look at the history and the 'Haksar Papers', now in the Nehru Memorial Museum and Library (NMML), shows that there was much more to the exercise than just neutralizing Desai.

It all happened within a week. The political calculations were sewn up first. President Giri was scheduled to remit office by 20 July in order to submit his own nomination papers for the presidential elections. Parliament was to commence on 21 July. An ordinance could be passed only when Parliament was not in session. On 16 July, Indira Gandhi made the first move, stripping Morarji of the finance portfolio and assuming charge of the ministry. Desai threatened to resign from the cabinet. The fat was now in the fire. Indira Gandhi had to move speedily and get the ordinance passed in less than four days, while President Giri was in office.

Bank nationalization was a secret midnight coup that Prime Minister Indira Gandhi pulled off. Not only her cabinet, even the RBI Governor L.K. Jha and the Economic Affairs Secretary I.G. Patel, who was known to be close to Moraji Desai, had been kept in the dark during the drafting stage. This was a well-planned exercise masterminded by Gandhi's principal secretary and close confidant P.N. Haksar, during the third week of July 1969. It was executed with the help of A. Bakshi, the then deputy governor of RBI and a close friend of Haksar, and D.N. Ghosh, the deputy secretary of the banking division of the economic affairs ministry, a close friend of Bakshi.

On 17 July, Ghosh and Bakshi started working out the nitty-gritties of bank nationalization after a midnight call from Haksar. They found out that 14 scheduled Indian banks (deposit base above ₹50 crore) accounted for around 70 per cent of the total deposits and 60 per cent of the total advances of commercial banks. It was decided that these banks were to be nationalized first. The total amount of compensation to be given to the owners of the 14 banks was estimated at around ₹87.40 crore, which was more or less in line with what had been offered by the government during nationalization of the Imperial Bank to State Bank of India (SBI) in 1955. So, the compensation would be fair in the eyes of the Supreme Court, if and when challenged.

Next came the drafting of the legislation, which was done roughly on the basis of the 1963 Draft Ordinance initiated by Krishnamachari. That, too, was a midnight job. It was accomplished on 18 July with the help of Attorney General Niren De and his team. De was also handpicked by Indira Gandhi in 1967. He, like Ghosh and Bakshi, was a person with Left leanings. The cabinet accepted the Nationalization Bill immediately once it was ready. Left with no portfolio and outwitted by Mrs Gandhi, Morarji Desai resigned from the cabinet.

President Giri promptly signed the ordinance on 19 July 1969. The Lok Sabha passed the Bill on 4 August and the Rajya Sabha passed it on 8 August, with minor amendments. With the bank nationalization bill now done and dusted, Mrs Gandhi set about making her next bold move, which would either make her the undisputed leader of the Congress or drive her out of power for opposing the powerful Syndicate within her own party.

There was less than a week left for the presidential elections, but Mrs Gandhi refused to issue a whip to the members of the Congress legislature party to vote for the official candidate, Sanjiva Reddy. Instead, she asked them to 'vote as per their conscience'. This forced Nijalingappa to seek help from the Opposition—the Jan Sangh and the Swantantra Party—to cast their second preference votes for Sanjiva Reddy. It angered the rank-and-file of the Congress party, who were largely Nehruvian socialists. They now 'voted as per their conscience' on Indira Gandhi's call. V.V. Giri managed to scrape through, winning with 420,077 votes against 405,427 votes garnered by Sanjiva

Reddy. With this, Indira Gandhi went on to firmly establish her supremacy within the party. Later that year, the Congress party split and Congress (Indira) was formed, which eventually went on to become the official face of the Congress party.

The Economics of Bank Nationalization

According to D.N. Ghosh, the July 1969 bank nationalization, in fact, had three objectives. The first was to expand banking activities rapidly. The second was to turn its focus away from trade, which then accounted for two-thirds of banking advances, and instead focus on industry and agriculture. The third, of course, was Indira's political survival in her battle against Desai.

Bank nationalization was the first of many bold initiatives taken by Indira Gandhi after she came to power. She went on to make several game-changing moves thereafter, though not all of them benefited the nation. Her bold moves included removing privy purses, tightening the land ceiling act, nationalizing coal mining, nationalizing several textile mills, steel, copper, aluminium and cement plants, and introducing stringent licensing policies, bringing in the infamous licence raj. Many people associated with the banking industry, who were part of the ministry then, still vouch for it. We spoke to some of them, including those who did not have Left leanings and were not involved in the politics, and found many pro-nationalization voices. Even noted policymakers like RBI Governors N.C. Sengupta, M. Narasimhan, A. Ghosh and S. Venkataraman have gone on record to agree that it was an economic necessity of the day.

Statistically, a comparison between the nationalized SBI and other commercial banks at the time tells its own story. The Imperial Bank was nationalized and had become the SBI 14 years before other banks followed its path. It had grown thrice as fast as the private commercial banks during the period 1955–69. Besides, it had managed to penetrate India's hinterland and even opened branches in remote areas. With assistance from Industrial Finance Corporation of India (IFCI), which was set up in 1948, and the Industrial Development Bank of India (IDBI), which was set up in 1964, the SBI had started financing the industry sector. The public sector growth in the Nehruvian era was supported by the SBI. This was something that private banks failed to do, despite many commitments given to the government. These banks did business only with trade. This, again, was based on old practices picked up during their evolution.

Even today, 50 years after the bank nationalization of 1969, the topic elicits passionate discussion. A few economists believe bank nationalization to be the worst economic decision ever taken, while some others vouch for its positives. Besides the ideological divide of the Left and the Right, there were both political and economic compulsions behind the decision to nationalize banks.

Despite the large number of banks in 1947, their footprint was limited to a few big cities. During the first 20 years of Independence, there were only 1,443 rural branches, catering to over 70 per cent of India's citizens. Of these, more than a thousand rural branches belonged to SBI, which was nationalized in 1955. In the first decade after the 1969 bank nationalization, the number of rural branches increased ten-fold, to 14,171. Even urban branches witnessed a healthy four-fold jump to 32,219, as banking activities spread to the hinterland. Public sector banks (PSBs) delivered quantum growth within a decade that private sector banks had failed to deliver in the first two decades after Independence.

Most impressive was the rise of advances and deposits, which had previously dwindled largely because people did not trust private banks in those days. The belief that nationalized banks would not fail made deposits double every year. This enabled banks to give more advances to borrowers. Before the economic liberalization of 1991, the aggregate deposits of PSBs had grown to a mammoth ₹219,539 crore (₹2.19 trillion). Advances to agriculture had grown four-fold and those to the infrastructure sector had grown six-fold. Many bankers today feel that the role of financial institutions, namely the IFCI, IDBI and ICICI, was immensely helpful in the restructuring and growth of lending. These institutions helped banks understand the technology used by the industries and lend judiciously to them.

How Financial Institutions Assessed Industry Risks

In those days, the IDBI, the ICICI and the IFCI looked into every major proposal before loan was sanctioned to the industries. 'Banks did not have adequate specialists to understand business risks themselves,' says D.N. Ghosh. 'They took guidance from the financial institutions [that] would approve the project proposals before big loans were disbursed by banks. That ensured quick and relatively risk-free disbursement. So, post-nationalization, despite the prolific increase of bank branches, the number of bank defaults were minimal and even non-performing accounts (NPAs) were within control,' confirms Ghosh. Statistics show that banking grew rapidly and safely in the two decades (1969–91) between nationalization and liberalization. Despite the rapid growth, there was relentless pressure on PSBs to deliver quickly. There were long queues at banks for every activity—from cash deposit to pending loan approvals.

During the 1991 liberalization of the economy, the government of the day decided that bank privatization would be a priority, to improve service and delivery. Even financial institutions like IDBI and ICICI, which provided technical guidance to PSBs, were privatized and converted to Axis Bank and ICICI Bank respectively.

The absence of financial institutions was deeply felt some time after liberalization. The lack of technical expertise led to faulty loan approvals and bank NPAs rose, says a top banker. After the privatization of IDBI and ICICI, the PSBs were left on their own, to assess risks that had become more complex. From real estate to cement, steel plants to automobiles, the success of any industry started depending on the latest technology, and PSBs had literally no expertise to assess the same. According to these bankers, the spate of NPAs over the next two decades was largely because of lack of technical expertise to assess which industries had quickly upgraded their technology and which had not. But there are different opinions, and we discuss some contrary viewpoints from other bankers in the following chapters.

According to Ghosh, who was SBI chairman between 1984 and 1989, the PSBs have failed to keep up with client technology, which has quickly changed, and that, more than anything else, has led to improper risk assessment. As technology becomes more disruptive, Indian banks will keep feeling the pressure. His views find favour with most of the former top bankers. Morgan Stanley, Goldman Sachs and Credit Suisse have their own oil flow lines or mining strategies drawn out. Indian banks do not have technological expertise, and will witness more NPAs despite better regulatory oversight in the future. We find a lot of this to be true in our assessment of the failures in the steel industry, which we discuss in Chapter 3, which focuses on the infrastructure sector.

While the nationalized banks did have some very good effects on the banking sector, they were slowly corrupted by overborrowed business barons and vested interest, which led to the present banking crisis. We look at the problems in each sector, highlighting some critical concerns, major frauds and large bad debts in the subsequent chapters in section II, before we come to the solutions in section III.

SECTION II

THE PROBLEM

TWO

POLITICAL FIEFDOM: BANKS AND INDIA'S FARM SECTOR FUNDING

The Cooperative Credit Societies Act was passed in India in 1904. The passing of the act and the second Swadeshi movement (1905–15) together influenced the rise of cooperative banks in India. With their cause supported by nationalist intellectuals like D.G. Karve and Dhananjayrao Gadgil, rural banks opened up across India. A strong cooperative movement resulted in a virtual demarcation of territory, and the agriculture and rural sectors were earmarked as customers of cooperative banks. As a result, scheduled commercial banks did not expand their operations into rural India. A testimony to this is the fact that during the 1950s, two-thirds of commercial bank lending was to trade and one-third was to industry.

The cooperative movement, however, failed to increase rural credit after Independence. As a result, the RBI had to contribute to the funding of the cooperative banks time and again.

A top banker revealed,

> At that time, the RBI was playing the role of the lender of last resort for the cooperative banks. However, as the depositors were inadequate in the cooperative banks and credit needs were insatiable, it increasingly found itself being dragged into becoming the lender of the first resort.
>
> Cooperative banks often ran out of cash and increasing rural and industrial credit became very difficult, despite that being an objective of the state. It so happened that

> almost two-third of the funding started coming from the RBI, to keep operations meaningful. Saying No to the very influential co-operative banks was never easy.

The banker shared that he was once severely reprimanded by an influential Congressman with the words: 'Cooperative banks in India started not with the idea of making profits, but with the sole purpose of channelizing government money into the rural sector. So don't be a roadblock to a noble cause.'

To adequately meet the needs of the sector, the Agriculture Refinance Corporation (ARC) was set up in 1963 to work as a specialist agency for long-term and medium-term rural credit. Three years later, in 1966, the cooperative banks, which were initially under the control of state governments, were brought under dual control for better regulatory oversight. With this change, licensing, operations and interest rates were to be under the RBI's control, while registration, management, audit and liquidation were to be under the purview of the state governments. However, despite this move, cooperative banks kept failing to recover a large part of lending and soon became hotspots of bad loans, which had to be waived by political leaders from time to time.

The cooperative bank structure proved inadequate over time and National Bank for Agriculture and Rural Development (NABARD), an exclusive rural banking institution, was formed in 1982. It took over the functions of the Agriculture Credit Department (ACD), the Rural Planning and Credit Cell (RPCC) of the RBI, and the ARC. Eventually, NABARD became the key driver of rural credit.

It was evident that even after amalgamation and consolidation, the banking industry needed a further directional change to expand lending to the industry and agriculture sectors. But not much could be done, because commercial banks—which were in the private sector—could not encroach into the territory of the cooperative sector.

Cooperative Banks and Deep Stresses in Banking

The cooperative banks experiment created deep stresses in the Indian banking system. These banks failed with scandalous regularity across all states of the country. They duped the depositors, comprising largely of farmers or rural folk relatively lacking in education, who were attracted by the higher interest rates that these banks offered. There were too many cooperative banks to regulate. Most were poorly managed by their boards, packed with farmer politicians.

When a cooperative bank fails, it is placed under RBI jurisdiction and looked after by a disinterested administrator, who keeps the bank barely functioning. The bank is neither fully revived nor liquidated. The government pours in the taxpayers' money, time and again, to keep such banks barely breathing. It is akin to keeping a dying patient alive with a ventilator. The depositors—who are often lacking in education—get only 10-15 per cent of their deposit money back after a decade-long liquidation process. Often they only get ₹1 lakh each through the Deposit Insurance Guarantee Corporation (DIGC). According to Rajendra Phanse, director of the CKP Co-operative Bank, as many as 165 cooperative banks have been shut down in Maharashtra alone in the past 30 years.

Cooperative banks fail so easily due to lack of regulation. The rich farmer politician often grabs the benefits, while the poor and uneducated farmer foots the bill. There are many points of rupture: acute poverty and illiteracy in rural India, overdependence on agriculture as a driver of the economy, the need to produce enough food for a fast-growing population, and the local political class that virtually controls the village economy through the mahajans or loan sharks. It has brought about a system that creates rich and politically powerful farmers who control the banks and dictate their politics.

Rural poverty and dependence on farming for a majority of the population have made agriculture a priority sector. In voter-centric democratic politics, this makes it impossible for politicians to ignore the needs of the farming sector. A large part of the budgetary allocation is, therefore, always directed towards this sector. Farmers get special privileges like tax exemption, cheap loans, free electricity and subsidies on fertilizers and pesticides. These privileges, however, end up being enjoyed only by rich farmers and seldom reach the truly needy ones, due to which outcomes have been poor. This is largely due to the fact that several schemes have not been properly monitored. The funds have been misdirected and many grants are merely entries on paper. The risk to the farmer has grown, not fallen, with farm loans.

Political interference has only increased over time, despite streamlining, liberalization and increased supervision. Today, regulatory, bureaucratic, political and judicial interventions make the banking sector look like the proverbial caged parrot, unable to free itself and do profitable banking at an affordable cost. PSBs and co-operative banks are often given impossible targets by politicians, with little or no preparation time.

Ingenious Solutions to Meet Impossible Targets

A bank manager in a PSB told me the story of the innovative ways in which head office circulars are managed.

> I have a staff of six officers and have both rural and urban customers in the Gurdaspur district. Last year in the month of December the branches of our district got a circular that we have to disburse 6 lakh loans to marginal women before the end of the financial year 2018-2019. It is impossible to find so many women at such a short notice with our limited staff. So we went to the dealers of sewing machine and home appliances brands in our towns and struck a deal. These dealers would get women customers who would get the sewing machines without spending anything upfront. Rather they would walk away with additional cash on buying the equipment. The dealers immediately went on a

selling spree and I got my customers without moving from my office.

The branch manager added, 'I actually managed to meet my seemingly impossible targets easily. It was a win-win situation for all. Also, by this way, I knew that the end use of funds given to the borrowers was to some extent justified.'

It has long been known that rural development and farm sector loans benefit the product or the farm equipment supplier more than the rural borrower. The product supplier gets the payment for his equipment upfront from the bank. However, the entire liability to pay the bank back rests on the borrowers' shoulders. Similarly, while the farm equipment or fertilizer or pesticide supplier directly gains from subsidies given by the government, the farmer who invests in them has to do the actual hard work and produce and sell his crops and then pay back the loan to the bank. This is also the only way farmers or rural entrepreneurs can prosper.

Very early on, politicians and businesses discovered that the uneducated rural population could be easily hoodwinked, and the money allocated to the sector could easily be pilfered. As a large part of the funds failed to reach the people, the distress increased, and this ensured that there were more demands for funds. Moreover, the cooperative banks—and sector—were penetrated by political satraps.

Cooperatives Create Rich Farmer–Poor Farmer Divide

The case of farm loans and cooperative sector loans was similar to that of industrial loans. In each case, norms were flouted and banks continued to increase their exposure despite steady increase of losses. In many cases, politicians and farm lobbies devised multiple ways to milk the system. In the urge to derive maximum returns for themselves, they made the distribution of allocated funds opaque. Large-scale diversion of funds took place. Increasingly, subsides that were supposed to benefit the farmer were given to the suppliers of farm equipment, fertilizers, pesticides, seed producers and every other service provider in the farm sector. The problem was particularly severe before the introduction of Direct Benefit Transfer (DBT) in 2015; now subsidies are sent directly to the Jan Dhan accounts of beneficiaries.

The fertilizer sector has been able to exploit the farmer community the most. During the last decade, this sector has profited the most from subsidies. In 2012, a fertilizer dealer in the rural belt of western Uttar Pradesh (UP) used to illegally export his entire fertilizer consignment to Bangladesh, as a bag of fertilizer cost twice as much in that country. He also claimed subsidy on each of these bags of fertilizer, which he declared officially as local sales. Many businesses started manipulating the system individually, with support from politicians. One such large-scale manipulation involved some of the largest fertilizer producers in the cooperative sector.

Co-operatives Mint Money while the State Loses Out

Indian Farmers and Fertilizer Company Ltd (IFFCO), a farmers' cooperative, was set up with 70 per cent government equity and 30 per cent equity from 57-odd farmers' cooperatives. It had both urea- and ammonia-producing plants across India and, by the year 2002, had become a giant, with factories across north India and an annual revenue of around ₹6,000 crore. As IFFCO became profitable, many more cooperatives joined hands. Some of these cooperatives were real and some existed only as 'benami' or on paper, as there was no regulatory scrutiny for the sector.

The Multi-State Cooperative Societies Act, 1984 was amended in 2002, the last year of the Vajpayee government. The aim was to reduce government control and give greater autonomy to these cooperatives. This, however, gave rise to crony capitalism and allowed individuals to be in absolute control of a giant enterprise for their lifetimes. It allowed the 36,000 member societies (quite a few of them reportedly benami) to buy back the government's stake—amounting to just ₹115 crore—that year, at par and not at market value. If sold at the market value, it would have fetched the citizen taxpayer at least 30 times that value, as IFFCO had generated a revenue of ₹6,111 crore and had a net worth of ₹3,273 crore and a whopping profit after tax of ₹587.85 crore in the financial year 2002–03. If the shares of IFFCO had been divested by the government at the market value and not at par, the taxpayer would have possibly earned ₹3,450 crore instead of a paltry ₹115 crore. But this loss of a few thousand crores during the transfer of assets to the cooperatives controlled by rich farmers—with one lifetime managing director (MD) at its head—pales into insignificance if we see what happened in the next decade, during the UPA era.

It is important to note that at this stage, during 2002–03, India was self-sufficient in the production of fertilizer. Also, there was no subsidy on fertilizer till 2002. All that, though, was quickly about to change.

Not only did the government's stake fall to 41 per cent and the cooperatives increase their stake in IFFCO to 58 per cent that year, its managing director, U.S. Awasthi, in his mid-seventies at the time of writing this book, continued to hold the post permanently (and still does) as per special provisions. Interestingly, the company did not fall under the Companies Act or any other Act that had a regulator. The amended Multi-State Cooperative Act, 2002 gave the farm lobbies of India permission to create unlimited, unregulated wealth, which was funded by farm subsidies (from the taxpayers' money) but was clearly outside the purview of both the tax-man as well as the regulators. IFFCO became autonomous by 2004, with no government director on board. It subsequently bought Paradeep Phosphate from the Oswals for ₹2,180 crore and started investing in North America and the Middle East to become a major source of fertilizer imports to India.

As you can see, public wealth moved into private hands without paying a premium and the nexus of politics and business milked the economy on an unimaginable scale. This is just one example; there are several others across various areas of the cooperative movement, which has created India's great divide of the rich farmer and the poor farmer, and has systematically compromised its financial institutions.

From Self-sufficiency to 'Largest Fertilizer Importer'

The UPA government took two major policy decisions when it came to power in 2004. One was to increase the procurement of fertilizer through the import route, and the second was to subsidize fertilizer prices heavily, including prices of imported fertilizer. This higher subsidy policy resulted in the consumption of imported fertilizer rising sixfold (Fig 2.1) from less than 2 million metric tonnes (MMT) to over 12 MMT, between 2002 and 2012. The domestic fertilizer production, on the other hand, stagnated between 14 MMT and 15 MMT during the same period. Fertilizer importers began to make heavy profits during those years, as India became the largest fertilizer importer in the world.

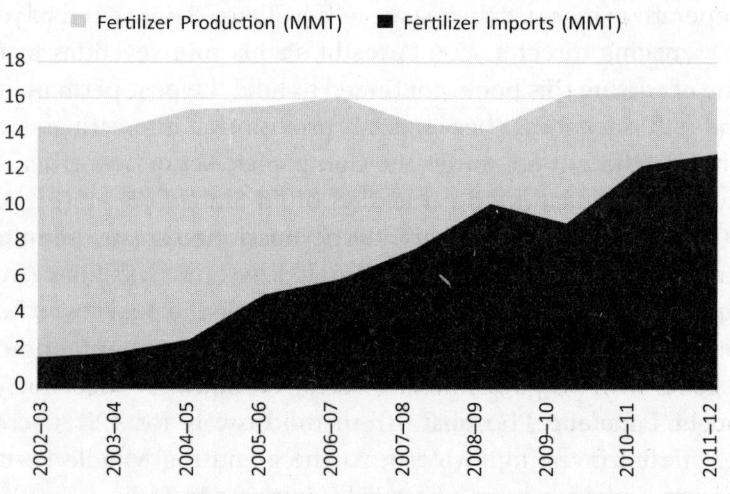

Figure 2.1 Fertilizer imports jump as domestic production stagnates

Data Source: Fertilizer Ministry

There was a five-fold rise in subsidies during the period 2007 to 2010, peaking at ₹67,200 crore. The entire banking system, and other financial institutions, were at high risk during this import spree.

Though India had two experienced state-owned importers in MMTC and STC, most of the importing of fertilizer during this period was done by the little-known Indian Potash Ltd (IPL), a private company in which IFFCO had 34 per cent stake. IPL had, on its board, several IAS officers, and like IFFCO, it had had one P.S. Gahlaut as its managing director for more than 20 years, well past any reasonable superannuation age. Apart from IFFCO, quite a few other fertilizer companies had minor stakes in IPL, which had a tiny equity base of less than ₹10 crore and a turnover of around ₹1,600 crore in the year 2004.

After the fertilizer policy on imports was modified, IPL aggressively stepped into the shoes of the state-owned importers, with political support. In May 2007, Dr J.S. Sarma, the then secretary in the Department of Fertilizer (DOF), issued two notifications to chief secretaries of states, to give 100 per cent advance for the import of fertilizers to IPL on top priority. The two orders made IPL a monopoly importer of fertilizers and armed it with huge advances, though fertilizers could be, and usually were, imported on Letters of Credit (LCs).

Between 2006 and 2008, IPL's loan funds grew tenfold, from ₹228 crore to well over ₹2,030 crore, and this debt was dangerously leveraged at an extremely high debt-equity ratio* of 15:1 (Fig. 2.2). The safe leveraging norm is usually 2:1. In IPL's case, its debt was 15 times its net worth during the period. Its auditors, Deloitte, Haskins & Sells, did not red flag it, and the debt doubled the following year. The operations put the entire banking industry at risk as the LCs were drawn on nearly half a dozen PSBs, with SBI, PNB and Allahabad Bank in the fray.

---

*Debt-equity ratio is the amount of debt a business can hold against the net worth, which is the promoters' equity and reserves.

Though such high leveraging is not permitted by the RBI, thanks to political patronage, IPL continued with high leveraging for several years—and this does not include the non-fund based borrowings.

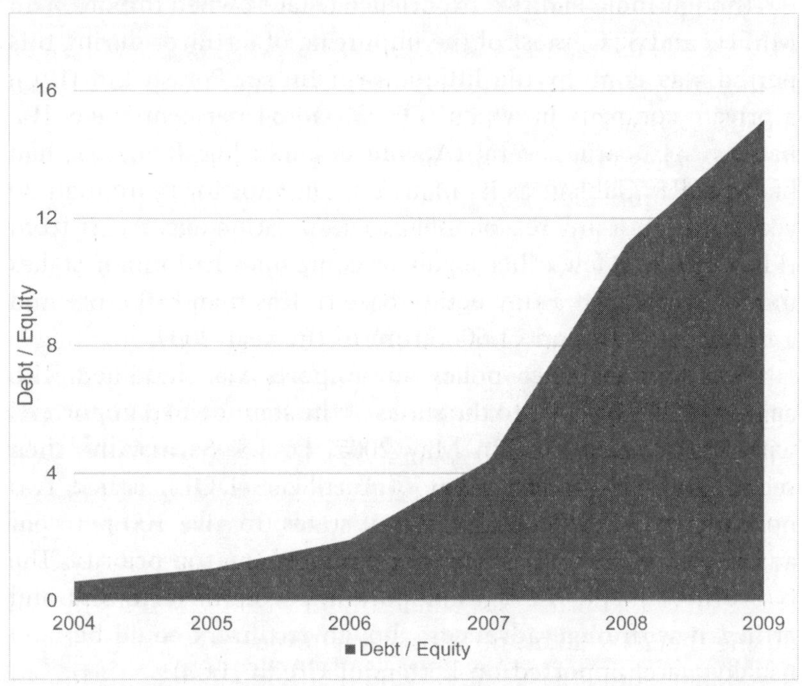

Figure 2.2: Thirty-fold growth in debt-equity ratio

Import Price Spike and Irregularities

International prices of Urea and Di-Ammonium Phosphate (DAP) rose to their peaks in 2008, as India became the largest global importer of fertilizers.

In 2002, India was a self-sufficient country with negligible fertilizer imports. After India opened imports in 2004, international urea prices jumped by 44 per cent in the year 2007, to $404 per metric tonne, while DAP prices jumped two and a half times to $790 per metric tonne. A report from the American Antitrust Institute stated that the profitability of American fertilizer companies went up by 300 per cent during 2007 and 2008, when all other industries were suffering from the banking recession.

This was the biggest spurt in fertilizer prices in four decades. Using round-trip trading and with the help of international fertilizer cartels, the prices of procured fertilizer kept on rising. The subsidies for the small farmer were usurped while the big fertilizer companies and importers got huge subsidies, which were borne by the taxpayer. The strong Indian demand made the fertilizer markets extremely volatile through 2009, despite a global slowdown.

As per the Comptroller and Auditor General (CAG), between June 2007 and February 2008, 17.58 lakh metric tonnes of DAP were imported in 43 shipments by IPL against 100 per cent advances from state governments, for which IPL failed to submit the requisite monthly sales reports even after two years. Imports of fertilizer through IPL continued and rose from ₹3,600 crore in 2006–07 to ₹32,600 crore in 2007–08. Despite CAG's censure on quantity and price mismatches in fertilizer purchases by IPL during the 2009 audit, no action was taken.

Looking into it in detail, we find that not only was the Indian buying volume huge, it had no relevance to market prices. The round-trip trading and over-invoicing theory also gains ground because the IPL balance sheets show several gross aberrations and undue risks taken, which, surprisingly, were not pointed out by its auditor, Deloitte, Haskins & Sells. Fertilizer subsidies, which were supposed to benefit the farmers, were usurped by the nexus of politicians, bureaucrats and corrupt businessmen who imported the fertilizers. Banks and financial institutions bore the risk as importers made hay.

This was one of the biggest scams in the last decade that went uninvestigated, despite the CAG flagging it. The mammoth subsidies from the taxpayers' money meant to facilitate the farmer, instead landed in the fertilizer importers' kitty, thanks to the politicians and bureaucrats who milked the system and also put the banking industry at risk.

Bankers' Response to Farm Loans and Waivers

There is another issue—that of frequent writing off of farm loans—that has often made the headlines. I asked several senior and middle-level executives in PSBs about how they perceived the situation.* The attempt was purely to try and look for solutions unique to the banks, and also to discover the problems related to political and bureaucratic interference in the decision-making of the PSBs.

The first set of questions was to the bankers who financed the agriculture sector and the small personal loans given to lower and middle-income groups, like the MUDRA loan.

A middle manager at Bank of Maharashtra explained that, 'IRDP (the Integrated Rural Development Programme) and KCC (the Kisan Credit Card) loans have historically been waived off by successive governments from time to time. Less than 25 per cent of these loans are repaid by farmers now as against 40 per cent a decade ago.' The decline in repayment could be due to adverse climatic conditions leading to crop failures, or simply because farmers know that these loans would be waived, if not repaid. 'However, many farmers maintain a regular liquid account in the banks and pay interests and capital back regularly. This is mostly true in Maharashtra, Andhra, Punjab and Haryana where the farmer is affluent and behaves more like a businessman. I have stayed in various rural districts where farm loan repayment was high as 80 per cent in good crop years,' he emphasized. 'I

---

*Nearly 60 bankers, along with a few software and legal professionals, were interviewed during the writing of this book. Some of the respondents agreed to speak on record while most insisted on anonymity, citing service conditions and fear of legal harassment. These individuals—a few named and most anonymous—contributed with their deep insights to the development of this book, particularly the part defined as 'Bankers' Response'.

know farmers who not only repaid farm loans regularly but also bought televisions, motorcycles and refrigerators with loans that they repaid on time,' he added.

Another bank manager said that some rural co-operative banks in the Vidarbha and Marathwada districts of Maharashtra sell off unpaid loans to loan sharks at a discount. In some cases, farmers are coaxed to take money from money lenders and settle bank loans at deep discounts. Each year, the finance ministry sets a target for rural loans to be disbursed under IRDP. This is conveyed to the bank headquarters, which has to meet the targets, irrespective of the financial viability of the loans. However, the execution is reported through the zonal managers, who hold the keys to disbursement of loans. To ensure responsible and uniform rural development across the country, every district in the country has one lead bank. The lead bank may vary between the districts; it could be SBI in one district and PNB in another.

The lead development manager (LDM) of the lead bank in every rural district, the key official involved in loan disbursement, is a very powerful person who, at times, is the contact point between the bank, the politicians and the administration. The MLA, MP or minister contacts the LDM for loan disbursement in his district. The LDM, with the local block development officer (BDO), visits the farmer(s) concerned, and ensures that the loan is disbursed once the farmer signs on the papers. 'At times, the loans are more than needed and around 10 per cent of the loan goes back through the BDO and the LDM to the concerned politicians and officials, ensuring that everyone gets a part of the pie,' the Bank of Maharashtra manager confirmed. 'The corruption has reduced, but not been eliminated, after the direct payment transfer into bank accounts have started,' he added.

A former general manager of PNB told us that 'for rural loans that are not repaid, legal cases are often registered. The paperwork has to be completed. The bank takes the farmers to the court and some repay under threat, while some commit suicide.

But there is usually no recovery in case of default. The paperwork comes handy because the debt is shown as "recoverable" and is not a "bad debt". Even if the court gives orders favouring the bank, there is no means to execute the order.'

Now, banks can take away the papers but not the land of a farmer, as taking land away or putting a farmer in jail for non-payment of bank dues can be politically disastrous. So, even if the bank book shows that a rural debt is recoverable, it is often actually not possible, except on paper. In effect, it is actually a non-performing asset (NPA), but one that will forever be in the bank books as a recoverable asset.

A very senior bank manager, on the condition of anonymity, stated that the writing off of loans by the state and central governments actually helps the banks clean up bad debts in the rural sector periodically. Under the current political environment, it is the only face-saver and must be continued.

Governments know that banks must get recapitalized by them with taxpayers' money. The 2019–20 budgetary allocation of ₹70,000 crore for recapitalization of banks sanctioned by Finance Minister Nirmala Sitharaman is in line with this thinking. In December 2017, the then Finance Minister (Late) Arun Jaitley had given a roadmap of ₹2.11 lakh crore for bank recapitalization, including raising bank bonds of ₹1.35 lakh crore. However, the current RBI Governor Shaktikanta Das firmly believes that a truly efficient bank is not one that gets recapitalized by the government periodically, but one that can access the capital markets.

Bankers' Feedback on How to Avoid High-risk LC Exposure

When asked how banks should avoid risks such as funding importers like IPL with high leverage, a senior risk manager and former general manager of PNB told me that the primary thing is paperwork: 'Personal guarantees and assets of the promoters must be pledged to the banks whenever exposure is high. So, in case of default, you have something to fight for. Vijay

Mallya and Nirav Modi are being pursued today only because of personal guarantees. The credit rating should be periodically done, and the leveraging criteria should be considered as a critical component.' He conceded that in most cases, defaults occur when the promoter's equity in a venture is low and the debt component is high. Any operation conducted with high debt equity is a risk to banks.

Bank officials, however, have little say in big-ticket loans, as they are political decisions wherein the sanction is given by the ministry. In such cases, senior bank officials are simply called by the minister or the secretary to his chamber and instructed to prepare and sign on the sanction letter.

'I have signed a dozen loan proposals in a single afternoon,' says the retired deputy managing director (DMD) of a PSB, surprisingly without remorse or regret, 'because the secretary had gone through it.' The loan proposals in such cases were regularized at the branch after the sanctions were given. The DMD relocated to Canada with his family in 2018.

The LCs or the LOUs for financing export consignments are inherently difficult to verify. Often, there are no assets commensurate with the additional loans given in case of restructuring or evergreening of old loans. When the credit officer at the bank has to prepare a proposal for an already sanctioned loan, he takes a personal risk. If he is cooperative, he stays in the chair for decades, as was the case for Gokul Shetty, deputy manager of PNB during the Nirav Modi case, where a fraud of ₹11,400 crore was committed.

'The key problem with LCs issued to IPL and LOUs issued to Firestar Diamond or Gitanjali Gems is that banks usually do not assess the risk properly. The banks only check whether the past LCs of the party are honoured, and whether the margin money and LC commission has been received. It is a very poor way of assessing a new risk, but that is what is done especially in case of exporters and importers,' points out one risk manager.

Often, the LCs are opened favouring associates of a promoter living in tax havens. The bank would be given to understand that it is a client account. The money comes back to the promoter once the cycle of round-tripping is complete through myriad benami firms, to camouflage the source of funds. Some of it he reinvests as fresh offshore equity. At times the bank also gets back its money, before larger LCs are issued. But the bank exposure is high during the interim period, when the funds are used for round-tripping and money laundering. Whether it is an LC or a demand note or a term loan or a cash credit limit, due diligence must be done before approving any form of credit as well as for use of funds after the credit is availed. This has been grossly lacking because of ad hoc decisions bypassing the laid down credit norms, and political interference at the higher levels in PSBs.

Next, we will take a look at the infrastructure sector, where the problems are similar but much bigger in scale. More than political interference, it is the highly borrowed state of the businesses that is of critical concern to the industry. This sector is the largest borrower from banks, if we consider the non-food credit segment. It accounts for 35 per cent of the total outstanding bank credit. It also has the largest stressed assets. We will take a look at some of these assets in the next chapter.

THREE

THE FAILURES IN THE INFRASTRUCTURE SECTOR

The banking sector, especially the PSBs, had been funding several large industries that had started incurring losses in the last decade for multiple reasons. As India did not have a bankruptcy law or any structured detection mechanism till the IBC, banks woke up to the losses too late in the day. Additionally, crony capitalism ensured that bank loans from PSBs were sanctioned to loss-making industries under the guise of 'restructuring' till they collapsed and defaulted.

The policy of 'evergreening' of loans by PSBs started during 2007–08 and continued till 2015. After it was discontinued, Kingfisher Airlines, Firestar Diamonds and Gitanjali Gems defaulted. Subsequent to that, Vijay Mallya fled the country in 2016, and Nirav Modi and Mehul Choksi did the same in 2018. The political backlash ensured that banking reforms were conducted in right earnest.

The major defaults, however, took place, unsurprisingly, in the infrastructure sector, with steel, real estate and construction majors failing to honour their debt commitments.

Topping the Default List: Steel Industry

Twelve companies were identified by the RBI as the biggest loan defaulters in 2017, with an outstanding debt of ₹253,712 crore. Of the 12 big defaulters, the five industries with the highest debt under the stressed assets resolution plan belonged to the steel sector. Bhushan Steel, Bhushan Power & Steel Ltd (BPSL), Essar

Steel, Monet Ispat and Electrosteel were identified as having a combined outstanding debt of ₹1.42 lakh crore as of November 2017.

Along with a banker and a steel industry specialist, we pored over the annual reports from the last ten years, of the five steel-makers who were India's largest stressed assets. The idea was to detect a trend and find the cause of ruin.

We found that while the capital-intensive steel industry was the largest contributor to NPAs, it was not actually sick. Most of the plants that turned unviable were those with expensive processing. Some of them had added electric arc furnaces and induction furnaces using sponge iron or direct reduction iron, and imported scrap as raw material. These were technologies brought about by circumstances that had now turned unviable, but were still being funded by the banks, leading to large-scale NPAs. Some of these plants, like Bhushan Steel, had even started depending on expensive diesel power because of inherent power shortage.

There is a technical side of the story that the reader must know, for without it they would be unable to understand how banks lost nearly ₹2 trillion from an industry that is central to the infrastructure sector and to India's growth story.

Did Technology Cook the Goose?

Till the late 1990s, steel in India was mostly produced in integrated steel plants. An integrated steel plant employing the Blast Furnace-Basic Oxygen Furnace (BF-BOF) route operated on a gigantic scale to produce steel efficiently and economically. Large plants like those in Bokaro and Bhilai, and Tata Steel, produced the best quality steel at the lowest prices, with very little environmental pollution.

At the turn of the century, electric arc and induction furnaces in India produced less than 2 per cent of the steel. They were used largely to produce small quantities of high-value special steel. They used the direct reduction process with imported scrap and/or sponge iron as raw material. Most such plants produced steel in smaller quantities, but at higher costs. As of 2002, India had just 23 sponge iron plants, producing a total of 6.97 MMT of sponge iron.

The country witnessed a mushrooming of sponge iron plants during the UPA regime due to several reasons. One, there was high demand for construction steel at that time. There was a massive housing construction boom in the US, with banks going on a financing spree to fund the sub-prime category, which eventually led to the global banking crisis in 2008. Moreover, with the Beijing Olympics scheduled to be held in the same year, there was a boom in construction projects across China. Most of the decade saw a massive rise in the demand and prices of steel. Indian steel producers wanted to join the gravy train of high profits, but there were two major problems: one, the shortage of iron ore, and two, the shortage of coking coal in the domestic market.

The public sector Bharat Coking Coal Ltd (BCCL) was in bad shape and coking coal production had been stagnant. There was an acute shortage of iron ore, as demand for steel was high. Both iron ore and coking coal were, however, key for an integrated steel plant. Moreover, setting up an integrated steel plant required huge investment and a very long gestation period of five to six years. So, India Inc. went all out to set up electric furnaces and induction furnaces.

During the decade from 2004 to 2014, a large amount of steel was being produced in electric furnaces using sponge iron or direct reduction iron (DRI) with imported metal scrap instead of the BF-BOF technology, which needed high-quality iron ore. This reduced both capital cost and time, and soon some of the big players, including Bhushan Steel, JSW, Monet Ispat, Essar and many others, also started producing 'hot and cold rolled steel' sheets out of steel produced in electric arc furnaces.

The integrated steel plants at Hazira with BF-BOF technology saw the addition of alternate gas based DRI technology and electric arc furnaces. Slowly, the beneficiation plants of the Bailadilla, Dabuna, Visakhapatnam and Paradip pellet plants ensured that Essar produced a large part of its steel through the DRI route. The profit margins in the industry were so good that Bhushan Steel even ran its Sahibabad unit with electricity from MAN diesel generator sets. Not only did it use a high-cost route to produce steel, even the route to produce power cost three times more than the conventional flue-gas-cum-coal-power route. As long as the sale price of steel was high in the international market, this was feasible, and these units kept on growing, with expensive technology and liberal funding from the banks.

The Rise and Fall of Sponge Iron

Twelve hundred induction furnaces and several hundred electric furnaces in India were installed within just a couple of years before the Beijing Olympics. The push towards steel-making through sponge iron proved disastrous for the environment, too, as India chose the coal-based sponge iron route instead of the gas-based DRI. The carbon footprint of coal is higher. Moreover, smaller plants did not treat flue gases and effluents adequately. By 2012, India became the largest global producer of sponge iron. Most of these supported small steel-making units, which were within the cities or in tribal areas of Bihar, Odisha and Jharkhand, and caused the skyline of North India to become permanently polluted.

In less than a decade, there were 450 sponge iron plants in India with an installed capacity of 42 MMT, producing 28 MMT annually.

Most of these units, other than those that have stuck to producing high-value special steel, have turned sick. The price of steel started stabilizing after 2008, and the high margins of previous years began to evaporate. The tough times for the electric arc and induction furnaces had started. As demand stagnated, they had to compete with the far superior and bigger integrated steel units, which produced cheaper and better quality steel. Even larger units, some of which had started out with integrated steel plants and had the cushion of high volumes, added electric furnaces later to enhance capacities quickly and cheaply. These units also could not compete in the global market as steel prices became increasingly competitive.

Electrosteel Castings, which was one of the largest global producers of spun cast iron pipes, commissioned its fourth coke oven battery to add capacities of 70,000 tonnes in 2009, when global prices started falling. In March 2015, the company reported an accumulated loss of ₹1,356 crore and an outstanding debt of ₹9,600 crore. Yet, in 2016, it debt financed a $6.6 million warehouse in Bahrain. In 2018, it went to the bankruptcy court. The unit had an outstanding debt of ₹10,273 crore. It is now being sold to a Vedanta subsidiary, promoted by the Anil Agarwal group, which has stated that the funds received from it as debt and equity will be used to fully settle the debts owed to the existing financial creditors by payment of ₹5,320 crore ($812.6 million), as per the National Company Law Tribunal (NCLT) order. The deal has been cleared by the National Company Law Appellate Tribunal (NCLAT), but has been challenged in the Supreme Court by one of the bidders, Renaissance Steel, who has raised objections to the eligibility of Vedanta.

After Essar Steel went to the bankruptcy court, its prospective buyers, ArcelorMittal, evinced interest largely in its 30 MMT per annum Hazira plant, which had an all-weather port and a natural gas plant. The Essar Hazira unit had installed a gas-based DRI at a low capital cost, with gas supplied from Essar Oil and ONGC offshore units. An interesting cost comparison by Nicky Mirchandani, an analyst at Bloomberg Quint, in October 2018 shows that the gross earnings of Essar Steel at ₹4,879 per metric tonne was much lower than JSW at ₹7,811 per metric tonne and Tata Steel at ₹10,865.

The ArcelorMittal deal left out its benefaction plants in Bailadila (Chhattisgarh) and Dabuna (Odisha) and pellet manufacturing plants in Visakhapatnam (Andhra Pradesh) and Paradip (Odisha). After the NCLT order in favour of the ArcelorMittal bid of ₹42,000 crore was given, a three-year bitter court battle ended in November 2019, when the Supreme Court ruled in favour of the takeover. We will discuss the huge debt pile of the Essar Group, its dubious financial transactions and the court battle to acquire Essar Steel in detail in Chapter 8.

Monet Ispat, which opted for the DRI route to make sponge iron-based steel, always struggled to keep its costs down. JSW, which acquired stakes in the company, restarted production in its two million tonne per annum pellet plant to reduce costs. This was a takeover without rancour or struggle, largely because Monet Ispat is run by Sandeep Jadojia, the son-in-law of (late) O.P. Jindal, while JSW is run by his second son, Sajjan Jindal. Though Sajjan Jindal is Sandeep Jadojia's brother-in-law, and as per the IBC guidelines, is thus not eligible to bid for Monet Ispat, the NCLT approved the ₹2,850 crore acquisition by Aion-JSW, possibly because it was the sole bidder. If JSW had not picked up the tab, the banks would have been left counting their losses. As it was, the banks took a huge haircut, as the outstanding debt to the banks as per the original 2017 bankruptcy filing was ₹12,115 crore.

All these steel plants were producing all, or part, of their steel through the DRI or coal-based sponge iron route. The consortium of banks, led by SBI, which lent money to all these steel plants, hardly understood the pricing dynamics of steel produced by this route.

Though capital cost was lower for steel produced through the DRI route, these plants were not competitive due to the higher cost of power, raw materials and operations, especially if they had to compete with conventional steel plants. The banks had no clue about the change in global steel prices, and India's massive push towards steel made through the DRI route continued. The banks kept on lending, even though profitability of the industry was no longer guaranteed. Manufacturers and consultants tried to cut costs, introducing low-grade ore that increased air pollution. In 2013, the rupee crashed and, as a result, electric arc furnaces that were operating on imported sponge iron and metal scrap started bleeding heavily. Banks kept on supporting the industry, which was moving fast into decline.

It so happened—and not by coincidence—that at the top of the NPA list were five steel plants. Till date, there has been no study done on why so many steel industries failed during the past decade. As a matter of fact, the National Steel Policy of 2017 proposes boosting steel production through the sponge iron/DRI route. This, despite the fact that the defaults largely happened with those producers who had installed electric arc furnaces or induction furnaces and used the direct reduction iron and imported scrap process to produce steel. They all went into the red. But there are 450 more sponge iron plants that, though smaller in scale and size, are sick and unable to pay back bank loans. The inability of India—with adequate iron ore and coal reserves—to set up integrated steel plants has today pushed the steel industry into sickness. But there is still no government policy on how to reverse the trend, revive the steel industry, set up more integrated steel plants and stop the industry from haemorrhaging.

Bankers' Feedback on Managing Technology and Investment Risk

D.N. Ghosh is possibly right when he says that Indian banks lack the requisite expertise to assess technology risks. He says that this has been increasingly felt with the PSBs after financial institutions like IDBI and ICICI were converted into private sector banks. According to him,

> Without knowledge about fast-moving technology, PSBs have no way to assess the risk adequately and hence end up giving loans that go bad. It is the single biggest reason of today's NPA crisis, far more responsible than corruption,

> political pressure or any other. This trend is set to accelerate, because banks are now exposing themselves to higher risk areas like Airlines which they do not understand.

All over the world, banks have cultivated industry expertise in fields where they have high exposure. At times, the knowledge is cultivated in-house; at other times, it is outsourced. JP Morgan, Morgan Stanley, Goldman Sachs and several other big global investment banks not only have loan exposure, but substantial investments in the metal, commodities and oil sectors. JP Morgan invested $1 billion in the London Metal Exchange in 2010. Goldman Sachs and Morgan Stanley were initially bankers to the European oil majors like Shell, BP and Total. Then they became trading partners of Big Oil and were a part of the trading cartel at the London Intercontinental Commodity Exchange (ICE). After the 2008 oil spurt, it was found that Morgan Stanley owns tank farms off the New England coast, which stores millions of litres of oil, and Goldman Sachs controls the valve trees that decide how the oil flows across Europe.

'There is possibly a need to create an investment institution (in India),' says one senior risk manager at Citibank who was previously with Bank of Baroda. He emphasizes,

> One bank which invests in the stock and future markets and also assesses the industry and advises all other PSBs to step up or slow down exposure in a particular industry. You get to know about the industry really well when you play the markets. Industry expertise needs to be cultivated, but that is no rocket science. When your own money is at stake at the stock or the commodity markets, you will make the effort to understand the industry. But before taking these steps, the government must disinvest its stake in these banks so that they become more accountable.

A former general manager of PNB has a different opinion on managing the technology risk. The problem is not with the technology, but with the intents of the borrower and the lender, he says. On the condition of anonymity, he shared,

> It is because PSB appointments at the GM level and above are done by the Ministry, that the problem has reached crisis proportions. Bankers try to please the officers at the department of banking and get into the good books of the Finance Ministry to secure a promotion. There is a price for each post and that is extracted by the politicians and the bureaucrats. A decade back, a bribe money of ₹2 crore was the standard requisite for the post of an executive director in a small PSB, while for a bigger bank it could be double that amount.

Former RBI Governor Urjit Patel admitted that the RBI was slow to take timely measures for managing the bad loan risks and shared revealing data about the banking industry being in dismal shape before 2014. At the Indian Economic Policy event at Stanford University on 3 June 2019, he said,

> Asset quality slippage can be traced to the 2006-11 credit boom, when lending grew at an average of over 20 per cent. The supervisor had failed to acknowledge and rectify the government banks' inability to identify poor performing assets; and restructure and react quickly to improve recovery and cut losses. The regulator failed in gauging when extant assumptions were getting stretched and needed revision.

IL&FS: The Largest Infrastructure Sector Default

India's largest infrastructure sector default surprisingly involved a NBFC and not a manufacturing or construction giant. IL&FS was a pedigree company created in 1987 for providing lease finance to infrastructure projects, with Central Bank, HDFC and UTI as co-promoters. It entered into a technical and financial collaboration with Orix Corporation, Japan, to bring international technology and finance to India. A few years later,

SBI and LIC also picked up stakes in IL&FS. The company did some notable work during the first decade of its operation, including lease financing the Delhi-Noida-Delhi (DND) toll road, the 9 km Chennai Nashri tunnel, the Patratu Ranchi Dam Road, and several other landmark projects.

Normally, IL&FS would work with state governments and union territories, funding their projects. So, despite delays, there were no bad debts initially. The problems started around 2007 when IL&FS moved into funding the MSME sector.

The MSME sector funding opened the gateway to the corrupt practices of the infrastructure finance company. Though the funding was small, below ₹25 crore, it was meant for hundreds of projects. The operations of the MSME sector are largely unstructured and so setting up fictitious non-existent MSMEs to launder and siphon off money was not difficult.

After 2007, apart from the governments of 22 states and eight union territories, IL&FS started lending to hundreds of MSME companies. It did not lend to all these companies directly. Instead, it created a complex structure with 24 direct subsidiaries, 135 indirect subsidiaries, six joint ventures and four associate companies, which are currently under the umbrella of the parent IL&FS. Such a complex structure of subsidiaries, with funds flowing from one company to another and coming from banks, SIDBI and international financiers, enabled the creation of opaque silos and the hiding of balance sheet losses. It also made routing money to fictitious benami accounts and money laundering easy.

Only a detailed investigation after the Grant and Thornton forensic audit of IL&FS accounts will uncover the route through which money was obtained and laundered by IL&FS subsidiaries. The preliminary investigations show that the senior management of the IL&FS, including its founder and chairman Ravi Parthasarathy—who quit the company in July 2018 on health grounds—and its Vice Chairman and Managing Director Hari Sankaran were involved, along with several former senior executives. The Serious Frauds Investigation Office (SFIO) in April 2019 arrested Hari Sankaran on charges of fraudulently lending money to entities that were not creditworthy or had already been declared NPAs. He has also been charged with fraud for capital market fund raising by IFCI Financial Services Ltd (IFIN), an IL&FS subsidiary.

Moreover, this has happened year after year, pointing to the complicity and connivance of the auditors and the banking rating agencies. While we will discuss the regulatory failures and how this very interesting mega-fraud happened in detail in Chapter 9, at this point the reader needs to know that even after the change of government, nobody could gauge what was happening as the IL&FS borrowings grew rapidly from ₹48,671 crore in 2014 to ₹91,091 crore in 2018—in just four years—and the interest payout nearly doubled to ₹7,922 crore.

All this happened because IL&FS funded the infrastructure business, and infrastructure lending, like agribusinesses, had become a holy cow, with priority sector lending earmarked for MSMEs. So, scrutiny was minimal and frauds happened. Even pumping money into IL&FS post default without basic restructuring was justified and done, because funding for MSME units in the construction sector became a priority. Needless to say, this leaves the door open for future frauds.

FOUR

HIGH-GROWTH RETAIL BANKING AND THE NBFC SHADOW

During the mid-1980s, the Indian consumer witnessed some transformative changes. The IT sector was just beginning with the advent of Infosys and HCL, which saw wages moving north. A new breed of employees called techies had emerged, who could afford a large surplus. Suzuki Motors had arrived in India, giving Indian consumers the option of a world-class product. The housing sector, too, was witnessing increased demand.

With the boom in the housing and automobile sectors, SBI realized the importance of retail banking. During the 1980s, SBI had little or no focus on profits. It was among the 50 largest banks in the world in terms of assets, but in terms of profitability it was placed a notch above 500. The bank's operations, even then, were modular and divided into 50-odd business segments.

The Housing Development Finance Corporation (HDFC) was one of the early NBFCs in the country. It started dealing with retail housing mortgage in 1977. Though it did not become a bank till 20 years later (HDFC Bank), it had already established a large, wealthy clientele, including thousands of NRIs. In 1986, SBI tied up with HDFC to set up Housing Promotion & Finance Corporation. This subsidiary, which was possibly the first retail banking effort by an Indian bank, failed to take off in a big way, as SBI did not give it their brand name. Later, in August that year, they set up the SBI Capital Markets to take advantage of the stock market boom. SBI moved early into the retail banking and mutual funds segment, but the PSB did not aggressively exploit the market till much later. It continues to retain the leadership position in retail banking, accounting for 28.8 per cent of the total retail loans disbursed in the country.

Private sector banking arrived in India in the 1990s, soon after the P.V. Narasimha Rao government made way for liberalization of the banking sector. HDFC got its banking licence and opened its first branch at Worli, Mumbai, in 1994. The financial institution Industrial Credit and Investment Corporation of India (ICICI) was permitted to set up the ICICI Bank Ltd as a wholly owned subsidiary the same year. The parent company was later merged with the bank and soon ICICI became the second largest Indian bank, while HDFC became the largest provider of retail loans to vehicle buyers across India. The private sector banks led an aggressive push in retail lending. The entire scenario changed, with the banker approaching the customer instead of the customer going to the branch, as was the case earlier.

Healthy Growth in Retail Lending

Retail banking has been expanding at a phenomenal pace of late. Between 2013 and 2018, it grew at a compound annual growth rate (CAGR) of 16.2 per cent, a growth rate higher than that of most sectors of the economy. This boom in credit-fuelled retail lending made India the fifth largest amongst emerging markets, behind China, Brazil, Korea and Thailand, with a total retail loan outstanding of $269 billion. Though the numbers are growing, they are still insignificant when compared to retail lending assets in China, which were 20 times higher at $5.8 trillion in 2017.

This is because India has traditionally been a 'debt-averse' nation, while Chinese borrowing habits changed rapidly after it became a global economic power in the 1990s. The CIBIL report of 2018, however, has identified a change of trend in India: 'In recent years, India has experienced a transformation of the consumer mindset from a savings-focused and debt-averse country to a more consumption-focused, leveraged economy.

The rate of change has been, and still is, significant, and is due to multiple factors: changing demographics, urbanisation, rising digitalisation and the subsequent rise of e-commerce, improved access to retail lending, and increased exports.'

There is another reason why retail lending has grown in the past decade. The rise of bad loans in the industry sector has ensured that banks have become risk averse to what was once the main customer base for the bank. In 2009, the credit given to the industry was 40 per cent while that to the retail sector was 21.5 per cent. A decade later, as growth slowed and industry defaults increased, the bank credit given to the industry has fallen to 35 per cent while retail credit has grown to 24.8 per cent. Banks are steadily pushing retail credit because the industry sector is still overborrowed and banks are reluctant to increase their exposure.

Retail banking in India grew through two different routes. One was the banking route, which was stable and largely regulated. Another was through the NBFCs, which has proved troublesome and high-risk. This, despite the fact that there have been several marquee companies amongst the retail NBFCs, like HDFC, Shriram Transport Finance, Muthoot Finance, Sundaram, and Bajaj Finance, which have led to rapid retail credit expansion. RBI's *India Trend and Progress Report*, released in December 2017, shows that NBFCs accounted for 55 per cent of the banks' retail lending, with a total outstanding loan worth ₹3 trillion. But after the IL&FS meltdown, the easy credit to the NBFC sector disappeared and the banks' credit exposure to the NBFC sector dropped by a massive 30 per cent to ₹1.96 lakh crore.

Three Pillars of Retail Banking

The three major areas where retail loans have seen a rise in India are home loans, consumer loans for automobiles, durables, etc., and the credit card business.

Mortgages have traditionally accounted for the largest segment of retail loans. As of March 2018, they accounted for

51 per cent of the total loans, down from 54 per cent in 2015. They are also the safest types of loans for a banker, giving steady and reasonably high returns and providing security back-ups. Home loans are the biggest segment among mortgage loans. According to RBI data, delinquencies in home loans in India are as low as 1.73 per cent, as against 3.03 per cent for loans against property. Home loans are usually taken by salaried employees, while loans against property are normally taken by small businesses.

SBI has become the largest home loan provider in the country, accounting for 32.1 per cent of total home loans as of March 2018. The bank is firmly focused on this segment. This can be deduced from the fact that home loans constitute 57 per cent of the bank's retail loans. Home loans grew by 13.26 per cent to ₹3.13 trillion during the year ending March 2018, giving a massive push to the affordable housing scheme under the PM AWAS Yojana. Nearly two-thirds of the loans given by SBI were in the affordable housing category, while it reported less than 1 per cent of NPA accounts.

Housing finance companies (HFCs) doubled their share in real estate builder loans to 23.81 per cent, while private sector banks too increased their credit share to 30.41 per cent. Credit from the PSBs was nearly halved to 24.34 per cent as banks turned risk-averse following the IL&FS crisis.

Apart from this, there are mortgage loans on movable items like automobiles. Here, the clear market leader is HDFC Bank, which saw its auto loan business double between 2013 and 2017 to ₹621 billion. SBI, with a business of ₹467 billion, and ICICI Bank, with an auto loan exposure of ₹255 billion, are way behind in this segment. Automobile loans (for four-wheelers and two-wheelers) have shown a higher growth of 20 per cent year-on-year during the year ending March 2018, as against 18.4 per cent for home loans. Moreover, the profit margins on automobile loans are significantly higher. Apart from automobile loans, loans against property and loans for consumer durables also jumped by 20 per cent during the same year.

According to Yogendra Singh, vice president of research and consulting for TransUnion CIBIL, 'Despite the significant growth in retail loans in recent years, consumers continue to do a good job of managing their debts.' Though the number of consumer loans rose significantly from 5.27 crore to 6.54 crore for the year ending December 2017, the exposure per consumer fell to ₹400,290 and the delinquency level remained fairly steady.

The third pillar of retail banking is the credit and debit card business. Once again, HDFC Bank is the clear market leader in this segment. It commands around 27.1 per cent of the market share with 12.48 million outstanding credit cards, against the second placed SBI, with 17.3 per cent market share and 7.9 million outstanding credit cards. According to CIBIL, during 2018, the credit cards and personal loans businesses in India rose by 28.3 per cent and 26.9 per cent respectively. Digital payments have grown, especially after the 2016 demonetization. One of the reasons for the growth of the credit and debit card business is the stagnancy in growth of ATM machines, which have remained at 2.2 lakh. The number of ATM transactions have grown by 15 per cent annually to 890 million. Meanwhile, debit card swipes have increased by 27 per cent, with 407 million transactions. According to RBI data, personal loans have grown steadily at a CAGR of 16.4 per cent over the last five years. The most popular segment is unsecured personal loans, taken by wealthy millennials for foreign travel and usually paid back in monthly instalments.

Not All Sunshine

Retail loans are, however, not entirely a sunshine industry. There are deeply troubled areas, too, in this segment. Most of the troublesome areas are the ones where NBFCs operate. They constitute a big operating part of the industry that is not directly supervised by the RBI or the stringent Asset Quality Review (AQR) norms that are applicable to the banking industry. The AQR, introduced in October 2015, makes banks review their own books and report the NPAs every quarter to the RBI. Thereafter, the RBI checks the figures and asks the banks to revise them in case of anomalies.

In the real estate sector, credit was sought by two borrowers: the builder and the house owner. While one of part retail loans, given by banks to home buyers, was transparent, another part, given to builders through NBFCs, was troubled. There are one too many NBFCs, and it is physically impossible for the RBI to regulate 11,000 of them. And all these entities are in the high-risk zone, as they cannot tap consumers through the current account savings account (CASA) route at low interest rates. They can raise money through several other instruments and tap foreign funds or even domestic banks for their fund needs, but all at higher costs. Hence, compared to banks, they are inherently high-risk entities.

Being unable to raise low-cost funds, NBFCs borrow from banks. The current exposure of domestic banks to NBFCs is ₹5.7 trillion (₹5.7 lakh crore). The RBI is contemplating introducing a system of risk-weighted credit from banks to NBFCs, so that banks can choose NBFCs as per their risk appetite.

The NBFCs are the middle layer of the lending pyramid. Their role was to spread credit to areas that banks failed to approach, but they have been unable to tap enough capital on their own steam. So, though they usually borrow at higher interest from banks, their inability to raise capital has made them overtly dependent on bank finance to manage their business. 'But you cannot borrow short term and lend long term,' says Aditya Puri, managing director of HDFC Bank. This is precisely what the NBFC sector was trying to do to shore up its profits. As a result, financial institutions like NABARD and SIDBI have funded two-thirds of the credit that NBFCs have invested in the markets today. And because the NBFCs have not invested judiciously, their stressed assets will ultimately reflect on the health of the financial institutions and banking sector.

The government has been proactive with legislation and

has put in new mechanisms to curb the rot. Probe agencies, including the Serious Fraud Investigative Office (SFIO) and the newly created National Financial Regulatory Authority (NFRA), have been active and fleet-footed of late. But now, it is time to not just deal with a fraud after it is detected, but to set up a preventive detection process to ensure that frauds do not happen at all, says a lead banker. This is especially important in the unwieldy and loosely regulated NBFC sector, where many small players exist. A senior RBI official, looking at the NBFC sector, once jokingly said that 'you don't have to create opaque derivatives in India for siphoning out money from banks. The probability that a bank fraud gets detected is always remote just because of the sheer numbers—can a few dozen inspectors ever check 10,000-plus NBFC accounts?'

The Elephant in the Room: NBFCs

The elephant in the room is clearly the large number of NBFCs in India vis-à-vis banks. The finance ministry has recently evaluated and found that of these 11,000 listed NBFCs, over 9,500 of them are high-risk. They have not complied with the law, wherein NBFCs are required to register with the Financial Intelligence Unit (FIU) and also file returns. The FIU wants to scrutinize their accounts under the Prevention of Money Laundering Act (PMLA). So, we will discuss the growth and challenges of the NBFC segment separately.

The NBFC sector has both retail and B2B players. Our focus will be only on the retail players, who account for nearly 55 per cent of the total retail loans, which amounted to ₹1 lakh crore before the NBFC crisis made headlines. As mutual funds stopped lending to NBFCs following the IL&FS default, banks had to fill in the credit needs, and their exposure by 2019 had reached a whopping ₹1.9 lakh crore. According to Aditya Puri of HDFC Bank, 'We feel that now that the banking sector problems have come out in the open, it can only get better.' He adds that the NBFC model needs to be redefined. It may be noted that

HDFC is the second largest player in the retail market, with experience in both the NBFC and banking sectors.

NBFCs have a big role to play in mopping up small investments. So, it is important that they stay and flourish without fraud or default. The health of the sector and the credibility of NBFCs are important. However, chit fund scams have been happening in India for ages. The modus operandi is simply to pool money from the poor and the uneducated, promising better returns, and then to siphon off the money.

But if you thought this was restricted to just the 11,000 NBFCs registered with the RBI, it would be a mistake. In a written reply to the Rajya Sabha during Modi 1.0, Nirmala Sitharaman, who was then the minister of state for corporate affairs, furnished a list of 34,754 companies that had enabling clauses in their memoranda of association for undertaking NBFC-like business ventures without valid licences from RBI. So, along with the 9,500 companies not registered with FIU, this additional number takes the total number of companies that are violating the ministry provisions to around 44,000. But this again does not include the lakhs of firms that are carrying on chit fund scams and other money-pooling activities at the micro level, which the government does not yet know about.

'Kitty' and Organized Chit Funds

The prime mover of the pooled money activity is the 'kitty', a small-saving activity amongst peer groups that collect household savings, usually on trust, on a monthly basis. The kitty gives each member a chance to carry home the monthly savings of the group, usually at a small discount. The one who collects the kitty last usually gets it with a small premium. The idea of the kitty is simply to offer a premium to the individuals who are saving, based on demand and supply. Now, kitties are usually conducted by a trusted community influencer, who is called the kitty operator. He or she acts like an unofficial bank, conducting the proceedings and keeping the money, the accounts and the monthly discounts, generated after distribution, in safe custody. Kitty as a form of saving is extremely popular with housewives and small businessmen, largely because bank services have been rare, bureaucratic and distant, especially in rural areas. The community influencers have earned the trust of their peer groups and advise households on how to save. These are honest savings at the micro level, successful due to community or peer pressure.

Chit funds are an equally popular method of small savings, but with higher risk. This is so because, unlike the kitty, which is a pooled saving scheme, chit funds mop up and deploy small investments in businesses. These businesses generate surplus, which are returned to investors. There have been thousands of chit funds, especially in South India, that have operated flawlessly for decades. Most of them are family owned, tightly managed and have subscriber bases of around 10,000 each, with each doing business of approximately ₹100 crore annually. Many of them have impeccable reputations and limited ambitions. The fund operators are only entitled to a 5 per cent commission (chit foreman's commission) and do not divert funds from the business.

Among the bigger and extremely successful chit funds are Shri Ram Chits, which has a subscriber base of 20 lakh, and Shree Gokulam Chits, with a subscriber base of 10 lakh, each with an annual turnover of ₹3,000 crore. Then there is Kapil Chits, with a subscriber base of 7 lakh and a turnover of ₹5,000 crore, and Margadarsi Chits, with 3.2 lakh subscribers and revenues of ₹10,000 crore. The Kerala government also runs the KSFE Chit Fund, with annual revenues of ₹20,000 crore. All these highly successful chit funds have been running successfully in the southern states for decades. More than 10,000 chit funds are estimated to be in operation today, and most of them are family-owned enterprises.

The chit fund scams are mostly connected to politicians, their relatives and other wealthy influencers. They usually invest a small amount of money in a scheme and ask their friends and followers to join, wherein they promise a higher interest rate, usually 3 per cent to 4 per cent above the bank. Then they appoint agents, who are authorized to bring in money in lieu of commissions. Each agent brings in at least ten more agents, who in turn tap more agents. Slowly, the Gram Pradhans, the BDOs and other quasi-government officials are co-opted into the chit fund scheme. They, in turn, convince the influencers who conduct the kitties and ask them to join with their peer groups in the chit fund, promising much higher returns than a kitty can give.

Relatives or associates of the politicians, who are the prime operators, also use their influence to convince people to invest in the chit funds. In turn, the influencers get small favours from the politicians. In a nation of red tape and bureaucratic licence raj, it is critical to be in the good books of the local politician. So, even without being directly involved in a chit fund, the local politician ensures that it operates at his beck and call. He also ensures that he gets his cut from the proceeds. It is a liberal cut, which the operator of the chit fund shares with his political bosses. As the pyramid of investors and agents grows, the chit fund prospers and surpluses are generated.

The Large NBFC Chit Fund Scams

Some of the chit funds are so voluminous that it is extremely difficult to track and trace their activities, especially because dealings are in cash. The chit funds grew more popular because saving in banks was difficult before the advent of the Jan Dhan accounts. You had to have a permanent address and two introducers to open a savings bank account. This was a difficult task for the poor and the lower middle class. Hence, small savers used kitties and chit funds, as they had no other outlet that gave them decent returns for their savings. The NBFCs cashed in on this. The Sanchayita group in the 1970s, the Sahara group during the 1990s, and the Sharada group in recent times have used the chit fund route to mop up money from millions.

Like in the previous frauds, the amounts involved in these chit fund scams are also mind-boggling. The only difference is that here, the money came not from the PSBs but from the uneducated rural population. The Sahara scam went on for decades till RBI stopped Sahara India Financial Corporation from raising fresh deposits in 2008. But Sahara, being Sahara, would always find a way, even if it was through brazen violations of law.

Soon Sahara floated two new infrastructure companies with a paid-up capital of ₹10 lakh each, and proposed to raise two Optional Fully Convertible Debentures (OFCDs) of ₹20,000 crore each. The Registrar of Companies did not file an objection against the Sahara issue, though the debt-equity ratio of Sahara would be 200,000:1 if such a high leverage issue was permitted. Further, as per the prospectus, these were to be raised through a public issue involving 30 million investors. Stopping public placement issues was outside the purview of RBI. However, Sahara tripped when it locked horns with K.M. Abrahams, a knowledgeable and honest Director of the Securities and Exchange Board of India (SEBI), over the three convertible debentures issued by it in 2008–09.

The SEBI expressed doubts about the veracity of the scheme and issued an order to Sahara to refund the money to the investors. This was challenged by Sahara in the Supreme Court. However, the apex court, on inspection, pointed out that there were absurd investment schemes for farming of Emu birds and goat-rearing that had raised hundreds and thousands of crores of rupees from the public. In each case, it was the nameless and faceless poor who would have suffered if the issue was permitted.

In 2011, the SEBI directed two Sahara group companies promoted by Subrata Roy to refund ₹24,000 crore to investors, collected against dubious hybrid schemes. The amount was raised in 2008 by Sahara Commodity Services Corporation and Sahara Housing Investment Corporation, violating security laws through the OFCD route. SEBI, interestingly, observed that Sahara claimed that it had raised the money from 6.6 million investors, when the largest company in India has an investor base of just 4 million.

After the SEBI directive, Sahara claimed it had returned ₹11,000 crore in cash to millions of investors. The Supreme Court found those names and addresses to be fabricated. On the Supreme Court's order, Sahara sent a truckload of documents for inspection. To illustrate its point, the Supreme Court stated that the typical investor, named 'Kalawati', apparently deposited ₹1,600 through a typical agent 'Haridwar', both of whose names and address were found to be incomplete and false. The top court came down heavily on the Sahara chief. It imprisoned Subrata Roy till he liquidated some of his overseas assets to deposit money with SEBI for returning to investors. Today Subrata Roy goes in and out of jail, often being out on parole, and is yet to be indicted on money-laundering charges.

Though Subrata Roy denies the allegation, it is widely known that Sahara not only took deposits from poor investors, but also converted cash-based black money into white money through the fictitious depositor route. It is believed that even black money from Iqbal Mirchi and Dawood Ibrahim was turned into white money by this route. Subrata Roy reportedly enjoyed political patronage from UP Chief Minister Mulayam Singh Yadav.

In case of the Sharada group scam, over ₹20,000 crore was collected from over 1.7 million rural investors in West Bengal in a mammoth Ponzi scheme. This money was collected through a consortium of 200 companies and thousands of agents. The investors were promised high returns but lost their money, and lots of agents bore the backlash and the investor wrath. When the company defaulted, the case was transferred by the Supreme Court to the CBI on grounds of international money laundering and complicity of top politicians belonging to the ruling party of West Bengal, the Trinamool Congress. The investigation has been slow and directionless, with politics entering the fray.

NBFC Credit Crunch in the Housing Sector

The housing sector grew phenomenally during the last decade due to easy credit availability. A lot of this liquidity came from unaccounted cash or black money. Most deals in the real estate sector had at least a 25 per cent cash component, some even more. In 2015, India's Black Money Act was introduced and the PMLA was amended by Parliament to close the loopholes and add more teeth. This made cash dealings a little more difficult and affected the easy liquidity of the sector.

Even where no black money deals were involved, cheque payment by the home buyer was only one part of the story. The second part was the loans taken by the real estate developer, both in cash and in cheque, from the financiers. While home loans were plentiful for consumers and defaults were minimal, that was not the case for loans to the builder. Due to lack of finance from the commercial banks, nearly 61 per cent of the sector's borrowings came from HFCs and NBFCs, at higher rates of interest.

Traditionally, a large amount of the money used to purchase land in this sector used to be in cash. This was because the stamp duties were high and income tax on short-term capital gains was exorbitant. So, value addition was done through cash deals, essentially used to reduce taxes. This became difficult after 2015, with the new laws and a vigilant and agile tax recovery mechanism put in place. However, the demand for better liquidity rose during that time, after the RERA Act of March 2016 made builders liable for delay in handing over possession to flat owners. So, real estate owners needed added liquidity to speed up delayed projects and avoid penalties. But just when real estate developers needed cash the most, the demonetization exercise slowed down investment in this sector.

The Case of Dewan Housing Finance Ltd

Just two months before the 2019 elections, the website *Cobrapost* accused Dewan Housing Finance Ltd (DHFL), a housing finance company, of a ₹31,000 crore scam. It claimed that DHFL's directors and key stakeholders, Kapil Wadhawan, Aruna Wadhawan and Dheeraj Wadhawan, used their proxies and associates to buy stocks in overseas shell companies. It also alleged that public money that DHFL had received as deposits had been laundered through loans and advances, given to shell companies in offshore tax havens for the Wadhawans to buy assets abroad. *Cobrapost* also alleged that donors linked to the Wadhawans had given donations of ₹19.5 crore to the ruling BJP, flouting Section 182 of the Companies Act, 2013, which governs corporate funding for political parties. Though a part of the pre-election political mudslinging, it had strains of truth, which sent tremors in the HFC market, coming so soon after the IL&FS collapse.

The DHFL directors denied the allegations and stated that the loans disbursed by the company were in compliance with regulatory norms, and that more than ₹17,000 crore had been repaid to investors in the last quarter. But, despite their stoic refusal of any wrongdoing, the stocks of the company tanked by more than 20 per cent. Soon, it became evident that there was some truth in the allegations, though not in entirety. The company was facing a liquidity crisis. It had been involved in siphoning money abroad. However, any default after the IL&FS saga would put the entire NBFC industry into an irreversible tailspin. Also, the Ministry decided that there would not be any takeover like with IL&FS. Instead, the Enforcement Directorate (ED) launched its own investigation into money laundering.

The promoters were to be allowed to run the company if they were able to manage the crisis, but there was a catch. Money needed to be infused into the company if it was to meet its debt commitments. The promoters were, however, not forthcoming. If retail investors and pension funds had to be paid off in full, the institutional investors needed to invest or take a haircut. It was widely believed that 65 per cent of DHFL's debt exposure was unsustainable. Whatever be the allegations of political connections, the banks and mutual funds (MFs) were required to take a call, and regulators like SEBI and RBI had to approve the deals. Also looming was an investigation by the ED that would eventually take its toll.

Among the institutional investors, SBI had the largest exposure—₹11,000 crore—of the total bank loans, which amounted to ₹35,000 crore (₹350 billion). Bond holders, including insurance companies, MFs and pension funds, had an overall exposure of ₹45,000 crore (₹450 billion). Leaving it to the investors would be a hands-off approach.

The MFs refused to take any cut, while the banks were ready. The restructuring would have the banks taking a haircut, in lieu of being handed more paper in form of additional equity. Such conversion of debt to equity was an added risk for the banks, primarily for SBI, Bank of Baroda and Union Bank of India, who had the largest exposure. Also, the proposal mooted that the promoters would continue to manage the company, and surprisingly there was no mention of forensic audits to probe the allegations. The financial institutions already had a majority stake in the company, so not much would change in terms of control. The deal proposed by the banks would only increase their exposure, without any gains.

It was easy to understand that through this bailout, the PSBs would not only take a large haircut, but also increase their risk and exposure to a business that was clearly not healthy. It was widely believed that bankers had not assessed the risk properly in case of DHFL and had readied themselves for a haircut. Now, it depended on the RBI and the SEBI to approve or reject this proposal given by the banks.

DHFL was a test case, as it was a financial company and not one with 'hard assets' like Bhushan Steel or Essar Steel. So, despite the AQR being applicable to all customers and the stressed asset identification now being compulsory, no such exercise had been undertaken for DHFL or any other HFC by the banks. The task was cut out, as the implications were huge for the RBI.

The termites had destroyed yet another room of the banking

industry. The NBFCs had always been treated separately, not facing the same scrutiny level as direct customers of the banks. They accounted for half the retail loan book of the banking sector. And retail business was the sunshine area for banks. Ensuring a high scrutiny level of the NBFC segment would not only slow down the loan books but also be an enormous task for the PSBs.

But on the other hand, if such practices continued, the PSBs could well be financing NBFCs that had high default potential—especially if they had political clout—and thus increase their exposure needlessly. Taking all these factors into account, the RBI finally took the decision to send DHFL to the bankruptcy court. NBFCs would get the same treatment as brick-and-mortar companies in case of financial emergencies.

This was a major victory for systemic checks and balances, and the RBI's landmark decision in the DHFL case removed any doubts of political favour or patronage being shown to the HFC. Meanwhile, the ED noose was also being tightened and the Wadhawans' endgame was all set to begin.

DHFL became the first financial services player to go to the NCLT. The RBI superseded the board of DHFL and appointed R. Subramaniakumar as its administrator.

Bankers' Response to NBFC Reforms and Restructuring

The bankers we spoke to are pretty dissatisfied with the way NBFC loans are being handled by banks. They say that despite the banking reforms, the financial sector remains at a high risk because the banks keep on lending to the NBFCs. These NBFCs are not closely regulated, and many have high leveraging and very poor loan recovery records in their retail operations. According to a former general manager of the Bank of Baroda, as long as the NBFCs are not reduced in number and regulated like the banking sector, they will continue to be high risk and will endanger the banking sector. He avers that the next set of reforms, therefore, should be directed towards the NBFC sector. Unless the long overdue reforms are put in place quickly, improvement in the health of the financial sector will be just a chimera. The senior banker adds,

> If a real estate company, or any other borrower, is highly leveraged and stops getting loans from commercial banks, they try and easily get their finances from any NBFC unit today, at a slightly higher interest rate. A loan refused by us could be granted by an NBFC funded by us, but without our knowledge. And once the high-leveraged, cash-short client gets funded by one NBFC he would have higher debt exposure and increase the risk of the parent bank.

Soon they move from one NBFC to another NBFC, with ever-increasing rates of interest. Money from one NBFC is used to pay off the previous lender. So, it is essentially a game of buying time. But, with the cost of funds growing, it makes the business more risk-prone and unviable. That needs to be stopped, says the senior banker.

It is very important to stop the debt component of any business from increasing beyond acceptable limits. Overleveraging of businesses simply through clever and diversified sourcing of funds by promoters needs to be stopped immediately. It has been universally found that businesses with high leveraging are more likely to go bankrupt. At the same time, when businesses go through the down cycle, they need greater liquidity to tide over the tough times.

Whereas the right way to increase liquidity in any business is to increase promoters' equity, it does not happen that way in India. Crony capitalism ensures that banks increase their exposure to save jobs, while promoters siphon out their equity and buy benami assets abroad, explains the senior banker. Banks cannot stand up and say 'no' to the Ministry unless they are autonomous. So, the key reform needed is to reduce government equity to below 50 per cent in all PSBs.

e-commerce: Fuelling Consumer Demand with Hands Tied

Ever since the 1990s, commercial banks and NBFCs have been at the forefront of rising consumer demand. EMI-based loans have ensured that the consumer is able to purchase capital goods that he would not be able to afford otherwise against small 'equated monthly instalments'. Vehicle advances, loans for white goods and other personal loans grew at an average of 20 per cent for most of the last two decades. The official season for such consumer loans starts with the festival season, commencing in September. Despite the very tight market conditions, the credit for consumer durables rose by 18.49 per cent between September 2016 and September 2017, and by 17.37 per cent the following year, ending September 2018. However, with demand for automobiles falling steeply, the high growth trend may be disrupted in the coming years. Also, consumers are veering towards new, innovative zero-interest loans being offered by business-hungry e-commerce majors, NBFCs and mobile wallet payment companies.

In 2013, the RBI banned banks from offering zero interest schemes against the purchase of consumer durables by households, stating that they vitiate the transparency in product pricing. It stated that fair practice demands that the processing charge and interest charge be kept uniform for each product or segment. But as the high street banks were driven out of that lucrative space by the regulator, e-commerce companies moved in and zero interest financing remained. Soon, the mobile wallet start-ups further upped the ante, promising not only zero interest buys but also 'cashbacks' on every purchase, just to keep the customer hooked on easy money. The RBI or the government could do nothing to stop this practice.

Regulators must understand that today there are many competing sources of finance available to the retail consumer, says a senior banker at Bank of Baroda. The rules must be the same for all financing companies and there needs to be a level playing field. PSBs can undertake the difficult business of growing credit in rural sector only if they can exploit profitable avenues elsewhere. Automobile and consumer durables financing were once high-growth areas for banks. The zero finance schemes offered by NBFCs tying up with consumer durable majors have taken over the bulk of this lucrative business. As per RBI, the banks' outstanding consumer loans have shrunk and now stand at ₹4,600 crore at the end of January 2019, as against ₹19,700 crore in 2018. SBI and some of the private sector banks have stopped erosion of their clients in this segment by ramping up credit card financing, but most others PSBs have not succeeded.

Card Business Shows Steady Growth

Less than 3 per cent of the Indian population use credit cards as against 75 per cent in Israel, 68 per cent in Canada, 65 per cent in the US, 27 per cent in Brazil, and 20 per cent in both Russia and China. As per RBI data, HDFC Bank was the market leader with 12.48 million outstanding credit cards, followed by SBI with 7.9 million, ICICI Bank with 6.4 million and Axis Bank with 5.7 million. While the HDFC credit card business grew by 18.41 per cent during the last year, SBI was able to increase its outstanding credit cards business by 31.8 per cent due to aggressive selling. The scope of growth in the credit card market is huge, but the consumer confidence is extremely low due to unstable and cyclic income patterns. In short, Indians shy away from using credit cards as against debit cards, the growth of which has been phenomenal.

This can be easily seen from the fact that there were 950 million debit card users by March 2019. The user base has more than doubled in the last five years. In 2009, the RBI asked the Indian Banks Association to create a not-for-profit debit card for domestic users. The card was launched in 2012. The Indian debit card market was then shared by the duopoly of Visa and Master Card, with RuPay debit cards being a marginal player, having just 0.6 per cent of the share in 2013. There were around

400 million debit cards in India at that time. Nobody expected RuPay to perform, as the foreign cards were long entrenched and technologically advanced players.

In 2014, the government decided to issue RuPay debit cards with every Jan Dhan account to enable rapid digitization. The RuPay cards issued by PSBs suddenly surged ahead. In the next five years, they were at the forefront of this growth, with 500 million RuPay card users and transactions, in excess of ₹16,600 crore (₹166 billion). However, debit card usage will see slower growth in the coming years as users are shifting to direct NEFT and UPI payment. There has been a rapid shift in payment modalities after the push towards digitization. Initially, debit card use and mobile wallets showed high growth, but now, the trend is direct bank-to-bank transactions through mobile phones using UPI.

FIVE

STRESSED ASSETS AND THE ROLLING OVER OF NPAs

I am sure that by now readers must have started making their own spreadsheets for the amounts lost by banks to financial frauds. Your spreadsheet must have added up to a few trillion. But do not panic. There will be more tremors on the way, and the part of the edifice that cannot stand on its own should be allowed to fall. All this may hold up the economic revival for a year or two, but for the next revival to be robust, the termite treatment must be completed. Banking reforms take their toll, and every country, even the US and the UK, have gone through this process. The termite treatment and liquidity crunch will hasten the collapse of the porous structure.

Let us now go back to the days before the evergreening era and see what the banking environment was like before the liquidity overdose. The Foreign Exchange–Balance of Payments (BoP) crisis of 1991, prior to liberalization, provided the incentive for subsequent reforms to ensure macroeconomic stabilization. The RBI, along with the finance ministry under Manmohan Singh, became the key drivers of this policy reform during the Rao era, both monitoring and maintaining, and also improving, the quality and quantity of reserves. The perimeter of structural reforms turned out to be much broader, transforming India from a relatively closed-door economy to a fairly open, robust one. There was an effort to attract non-debt capital flows. Also, a decisive move was made to shift from short-term foreign exchange external borrowings to long-term borrowings.

Among Narasimha Rao's key reforms, the least talked about are the banking sector and institutional reforms. The introduction of private sector banks and the power given to a number of regulatory bodies to streamline the service sector made the economy a responsive and performing one. Atal Bihari Vajpayee came in and reaped the benefits of Rao's liberalization, taking the economy forward. Both Rao and Vajpayee managed the economy tightly, without lax credit policies or freewheeling imports. As a result, the foreign exchange reserves grew and the Rupee achieved a semblance of stability.

Bypassing Standing Committee Reviews in Parliament

The last two years of the Vajpayee rule ensured high GDP growth of around 7.8 per cent, despite the reduction of fiscal deficit. The challenge then was to better the trend and try to reach the double-digit figure that China had consistently achieved for nearly two decades. In the first two years of its rule, the UPA government under Prime Minister Manmohan Singh was able to drive GDP growth to 9.3 per cent. But, despite the government's best attempts, it still was well short of the magic double digit mark. One way to try to unleash animal spirits was by liberalizing industrial credit. In 2006, the UPA government decided to push industrial credit and also liberalize the existing credit policy. Restructuring of loans of existing players struggling to complete projects was considered as a 'policy measure', to push investment in the infrastructure sector.

However, all such proposals would have to meet the scrutiny of the Parliament. The Budget session of the Indian Parliament has always been divided into two sessions, with a gap of several weeks between them. According to Rules of Procedure 272 and 331G, it was mandatory for demands of grants from ministries and departments of the government sector and PSBs and enterprises to be examined by the standing committees of Parliament. These standing committees, set up during the Narasimha Rao era, consisted of members of both houses of

Parliament. The objective was to examine the Budget grants in detail and hear and examine other witnesses, including experts and NGOs. The recommendations of these committees were often unanimous and non-partisan and usually adopted in the Budget proposal. It ensured transparency and discussion before major policy changes were introduced and expenses incurred.

On 18 March 2006, during the Budget session, the Manmohan Singh government surprisingly introduced a motion in Rajya Sabha for suspension of Rule 272 and subsequently Rule 331G in the Lok Sabha, without notice, and got it passed. This ensured that on 20 and 21 March 2006, the relevant credit revision bills that were introduced in both houses along with the Union Budget were passed without discussion, simply by a voice vote amidst a lot of uproar. The Opposition benches were unable to stop the moves of the government, due to lower numbers of members in the two houses. On 22 March, the houses met for half an hour amidst several disruptions and adjournments and got the annual reports of all the public sector organizations, outcome and performance budgets, and action taken reports passed. The afternoon session saw the adoption of the annual Budget without discussion or any kind of oversight.

Evergreening of Loans and Soft-handling Financial Sickness

One of the major moves after the 2006 Parliamentary coup was to take indirect control of bank finances and force them to expand credit. This was opposed by the RBI, which then had career bureaucrat Y. Venugopal Reddy at its helm. Industrial credit had never grown by over 20 per cent during the Narasimha Rao and the Vajpayee eras. Besides, foreign banks were kept in bay and though NDA had promised a reversal of policy, they did not implement it. In his autobiography, *Advice and Dissent: My Life in Public Service,* Reddy says, 'His (Chidambaram's) image as a reformer pushing for double-digit growth was, in his view, being dented by my caution to the extent of resisting some of his policies.' The then finance minister got his way and even extracted a personal apology from the RBI governor, on the advice of Prime Minister Manmohan Singh.

Once the RBI chief was browbeaten, the government then surreptitiously introduced a policy of evergreening of bank loans. The methodology adopted was very simple—and is still in practice today. It was a classic case of soft-handling of financial sicknesses for ulterior motives. 'I suspect that the soft-handling of the financial sickness in Jet Airways by SBI will result in transferring the ownership and control of [a] leading Indian airline to a foreign aviation company, at the expense of [the] domestic aviation industry...which is against both, the national interest and interest of shareholders,' says the whistle-blower of the ICICI case.

The situation is very grim across the industry. Banks have already exposed themselves dangerously by lending to a few hundred highly leveraged industries. Initially, it only happened to a few politically connected organizations in the infrastructure sector, but the combined greed of the bankers, bureaucrats, politicians, business tycoons, auditors/chartered accountants (CAs) and rating agencies has made it a regular feature for the banking industry since the turn of the century. Everyone had a share in the pie, and you could refinance your industry, irrespective of the losses, if you were ready to spend around 10 per cent to 20 per cent of the refinanced amount on slush payments.

Although we still cannot pinpoint why 2006–07 was the critical turning point for the once healthy banking sector, we suspect it was so because the government of the day discovered a way to bypass the Parliamentary Standing Committees and scrutiny and debate in Parliament. Success at bypassing the supreme institution of the country with ease gave them the confidence to overrule set banking practices with impunity. But that was not the only reason.

There was also the need to push industrial growth, which had started floundering. So, in the fiscal year 2006–07, the banks opened their coffers. As a result, industrial borrowings rose to an unprecedented 26.7 per cent (Fig. 5.1), which was twice of the previous year. The PSBs were literally pushed into providing this extraordinary credit growth, which later on turned into NPAs. This high credit growth started declining rapidly after 2012–13 and reached negative credit growth in 2016–17 after the banks started divulging the stressed assets and pulling back on debt to overborrowed industries.

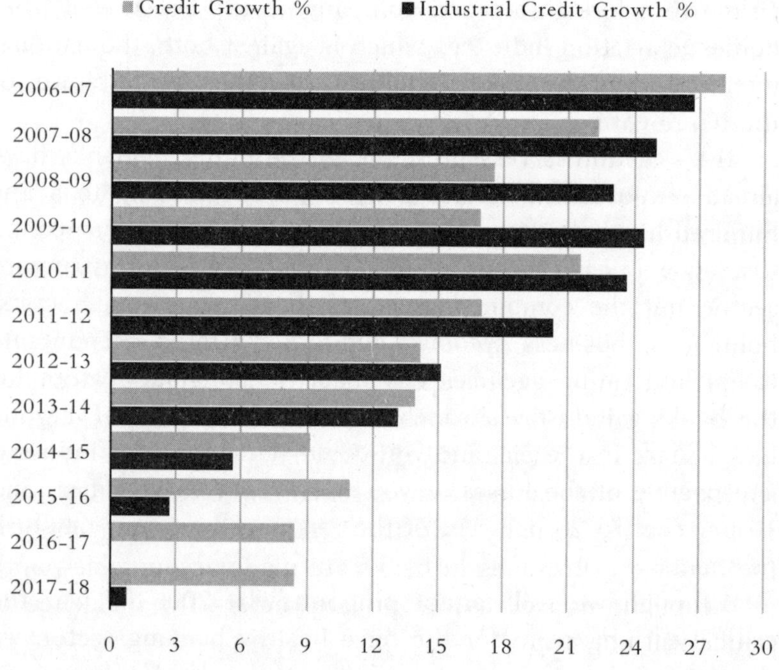

Figure 5.1: Credit Growth and Fall, 2006 to 2018
Date Source: RBI

After the collapse of Lehman Brothers and the global liquidity crisis, this massive credit expansion became easier to justify.

Also, nobody spent any time or effort in these years to check whether the credit was being rightly directed. Soon, it created a new crisis of bad loans across India that had no link to the US crisis.

Secondly, because of the easy credit policy in India, it ushered in a unique phase of crony capitalism that hurt the growth of the country. Troubled industrialists started getting easy access to high liquidity, which many siphoned off to offshore tax havens. The concept of restructuring the industry group, and not the industry, was in vogue, says a prominent former banker with PNB. So, in many cases, subsidiary companies were floated to bail out the industrialists and not the industries. They got access to this refinancing bounty, which was siphoned off. Thus, cash crunch remained across Indian industries, despite the apparent effort to boost the economy. This eventually led to highly stressed assets across the industry, as debt funds ballooned while the industries kept making losses.

A few years down the line, these accounts became non-performing, and we have been witnessing their steady rise in number for over a decade. Though the Stressed Assets Resolution Mechanism and the Bankruptcy Act have been put in place now, the effects of this decade-long abuse will take time to subside. This will also be because, though new laws are in place, the bad apples within the banking system remain, who will try new ways to defraud the banking industry. Unless those responsible for the massive loan frauds in banks are made accountable—both in the public as well as the private sector—the incidence of frauds will not stop.

ICICI: Sweetheart Deals with Stressed Assets?

It was not just the PSBs but also the private sector banks that propped up the stressed assets. Probes investigating the sweetheart deals that CEO Chanda Kochhar had with the Videocon group and Essar Steel are discussed later in the book, but investigations into ICICI bank deals showed that many more stressed assets were benefited during the Kochhar era.

Insiders in the bank allege that the problem was systemic and though Chanda Kochhar was the kingpin, the rank-and-file of senior managers under her, starting from the credit department and all the way to the bank chief, were involved. It was alleged that refinancing deals were widespread during that period (2007–13) and the share of the bank employees was around 5 per cent, with Kochhar's share being half. It was also alleged that in case of refinancing deals, around 20 per cent of the booty was kept for kickbacks, 5 per cent was the cut for the bankers, 10 per cent for the 'netas and babus' (bureaucrats and politicians) and 5 per cent for the officers of the income tax department. All this was facilitated seamlessly through CAs, auditors and tax consultants.

Though the probe into ICICI started hesitantly, and the bank initially denied the allegations, the issue has now gathered steam and could snowball. The ICICI Bank whistle-blower has listed 31 more corporations that were unduly favoured with refinancing during the Kochhar rule, and claims that the bank's checks and balances were routinely bypassed and risk management firewalls were porous. The Securities and Exchange Commission (SEC) of New York has launched an independent enquiry, as ICICI is listed at NYSE and any adverse findings could bring the stocks crashing at the global markets. But we will revisit the ICICI Bank lapses and the allegations later with circumstantial evidence, and presently return to the core issue of the extent of evergreening of loans by banks after 2006.

In March 2019, RBI started a fresh probe into the processes ICICI Bank undertook when it sanctioned loans to 55 entities, including Videocon Oil Ventures Ltd, Assam Oil Ltd, Shree Renuka Sugars Ltd, ABG Shipyard Ltd, IVRCL Ltd, Gammon India Ltd, Essar Group and Punj Lloyd Ltd, all of which were dangerously leveraged companies. These investigations, based on complaints by ICICI Bank whistle-blowers, relate to incorrect accounting of interest income and NPA recoveries as fees, illegal funding by bridge loans, and overvaluation of security for corporate loans. How loans from bank funds were given to overborrowed companies, whose promoters siphoned out the borrowed funds through a host of offshore shell companies and paid them back to their benefactors in the bank, is an interesting story. This is a pattern followed in many banks that carried the stressed assets. After all, ICICI Bank financed only a very small part of the Videocon and Essar restructuring package, and the PSBs that financed the bulk amounts must be held equally guilty.

The ICICI Bank money-laundering investigation is symptomatic of the problems of the banking industry. It is widely believed that Yes Bank, IDBI Bank, SBI, PNB, Oriental Bank of Commerce (OBC) and several other banks adopted a similar route to benefit large industrial houses with stressed assets. The companies where such banker–client connivances have been alleged are Essar Steel, Bhushan Steel, Videocon, Alok Industries, LANCO, Jyoti Structures, RComm, ABG Shipyard, DHFL, HDIL and IL&FS. We will discuss several other cases in the chapter on the promoter–banker nexus. It may take years to prove the allegations made against the banks and their executives, but we will discuss here the modus operandi of round-tripping.

At the core of the operations are nearly three dozen overborrowed companies, which accounted for nearly 80 per cent of the nation's stressed assets and are now facing bankruptcy. Videocon was only one of the many beneficiaries and ICICI, only one of the banks that actively propped up stressed accounts.

How Bankers Assisted Stressed Assets to Raise Benami Bills

Like in the Videocon case, most of the quid pro quo deals between the beneficiary promoters of the stressed assets and the banks were conducted in offshore tax havens like Mauritius. The sweetheart deal that ensured the ₹3,250 crore refinancing deal that ICICI Bank structured for Videocon Industries, as a part of the SBI-led consortium, saw kickback payments to Deepak Kochhar's Nupower Renewables in Mauritius. ICICI also funded the overseas arm of Videocon—a ₹660 crore package in foreign exchange, against which the Kochhars received kickbacks.

It is alleged that ICICI Bank issued LCs against fictitious bills to service a number of loans. These fictitious bills were raised by benami companies connected to the holders of stressed assets. ICICI officials did not perform due diligence while conducting KYC of these benami companies. They opened LCs without assessing the veracity of the bills raised.

The funds were raised repeatedly to falsely regularize a loan that would normally have defaulted. In one case, a ₹100 crore term loan was found to be serviced by three fictitious loans aggregating to ₹90 crore during a five-year term, with the connivance of the bank officials. The money was round-tripped at times through offshore accounts, and brought back as equity investment from Mauritius, the Cayman Islands or other tax havens. If proved, these charges would imply serious fraud, round-tripping and money laundering not only against the defaulting companies but also the rank-and-file of the bank that was surreptitiously involved in supporting those stressed asset holders.

Two officers of ICICI Bank who acted as whistle-blowers also alleged that,

> When a borrower didn't have enough balance available to make loan payments, temporary overdraft (TOD) was sanctioned to another borrower, to pay to the first borrower whose account needed to be saved from being impaired. In one instance, TOD was sanctioned to a service provider of a large borrower. This service provider had no borrowing arrangements with the bank. Unfortunately, the money could not be returned by the service provider.

The sources stated that the TOD became overdue and eventually an NPA, and they reportedly backed their statements with proof. They also alleged that the bank did not use FINACLE, the real-time core banking software used by the industry for term loans, but instead opted for an accounting software called SYMBOLS, which permitted the manipulation of end-of-day reports and allowed backdated entries. These are serious allegations and have caused the SEC to open investigations, as stated earlier.

The whistle-blowers alleged that in the case of Chanda's husband Deepak Kochhar, the support came not only from Videocon but also from Essar Group, another beleaguered borrower wrongfully propped up by ICICI Bank. Essar Steel Minnesota and Essar Oil (UK) allegedly received funding of $880 million (₹5,720 crore) from ICICI Bank.

The Ruias of the Essar Group allegedly used their son-in-law Nishant Kanodia of Firstland Holdings Mauritius (of the Matix Group) and nephew Anirudh Bhuwalka of AMW Motors Group for round-tripping funds via Mauritius to NuPower Group. The investment was allegedly done in the Deepak Kochhar company as a quid pro quo deal in lieu of ICICI Bank funding the cash-strapped Essar Group. Firstland Holdings allegedly invested ₹325 crore in NuPower Renewables through four tranches, even as ICICI Bank pumped in funds to Essar Global, an investment company run by the Ruia brothers and headquartered in Mauritius.

The allegations have been denied by Essar Group, which claims to have repaid the balance ₹12,000 crore debt to ICICI Bank, Standard Chartered and Axis Bank in January 2019. The Essar Group claims that repayment was done following the sale of Essar Oil to the Russian Oil giant Roseneft for ₹30,000 crore and it has ensured that 80 per cent of the group's debt to the Indian banking sector has been cleared. Essar Steel, another Ruia company, has already gone to the bankruptcy court.

Restructuring and its Correlation to Stressed Assets

While ICICI Bank is a one-off case of a bank propping up stressed assets, the case of stressed assets refinancing to shield NPAs happened in India across the board, with most banks. In case of PSBs, the investigations have been slow, because nobody wants to bell the cat. The above observation would, however, remain an unsubstantiated story, unless it was statistically correlated through evidence. So, we again looked up the RBI data for the entire decade of 2008–18 for proof (Fig. 5.2).

We found that restructuring or evergreening of loans as part of overall industry debt, which was already high at 3 per cent during the year 2008, rose progressively to 4.6 per cent in the financial year ending March 2012. It grew to 6.4 per cent in fiscal 2014–15, before the banks were forced to conduct the AQR by the RBI. It has slowly started dropping thereafter, but attempts are still being made to push in refinancing proposals for Jet Airways, IL&FS and DHFL, and some of these may eventually go through. If any such proposal goes through, it will create a precedence for restructuring and reviving an unviable industry. Whatever be the cause for the same, the effect will be disastrous.

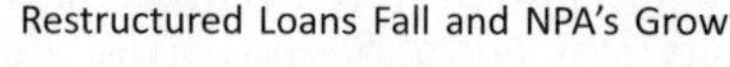

Restructured Loans Fall and NPA's Grow

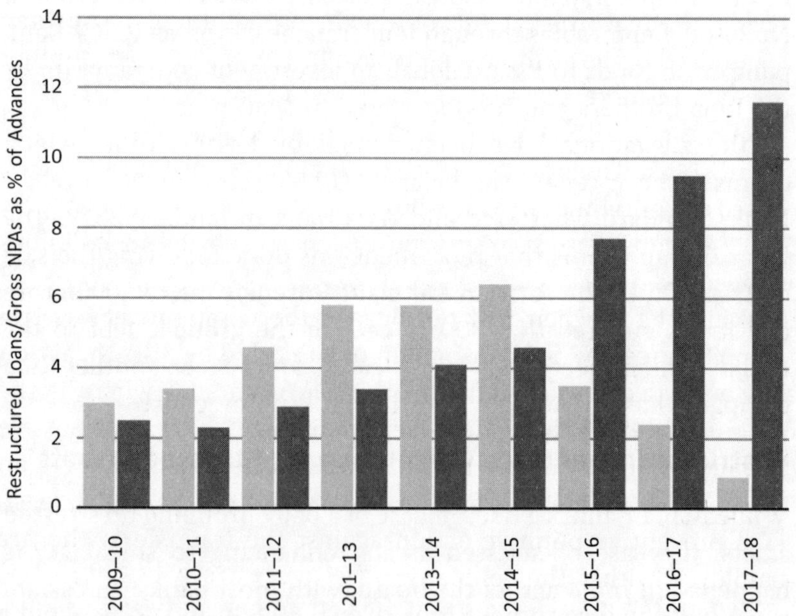

Figure 5.2: Restructuring of loans and rise of NPAs
Data Source: RBI

In fact, one restructuring proposal for a failed NBFC has already gone through. Yes, we are revisiting the case of IL&FS, a company with nearly a trillion-rupee bad debt. We must remind our readers that, after the Grant and Thornton forensic report, it was fairly clear that the company's balance sheet was fraudulent and cooked, and the money received by the NBFC from the banks was siphoned out of the system by its subsidiaries. Chapter 3, which gives the details of the IL&FS scam, shows that IL&FS did not lend to all these companies directly. Instead, it created a complex network of entities for round-tripping and money-laundering, with a web of 24 direct subsidiaries, 135 indirect subsidiaries, six joint ventures, and four associate companies that are currently under the umbrella of the parent IL&FS.

Here we examine the way IL&FS was allowed to raise finance for its stressed assets, and examine why the takeover of the organization may not have been a ideal solution—why IL&FS needs complete restructuring and investigation of more than a hundred senior employees to avoid a repeat of yet another default. Insiders say that this is only because the malaise in IL&FS is very deep-rooted and its operations are still opaque. Uday Kotak, who now heads the six-member restructured IL&FS board after preliminary inspection, has stated that IL&FS actually had 348 subsidiaries and not just 169 as reported in its books of account.

Much later, when RBI red-flagged the company, it was still being financed by the consortium of banks led by SBI. No action has been taken against the brothers-in-crime. So where is the accountability? When the government takes over the massive liability of any company that has little to no assets, it owes an explanation to the taxpayer. As a first step, it must, at least, take preventive punitive action against the fraudsters who are employed within the company.

When the government took over IL&FS, it did so to avoid a contagion crisis in the NBFC market, because IL&FS was funding major road sector and infrastructure projects. It also appointed a new board, but forgot to do two crucial things. It stopped short of dismantling and amalgamating the silo structure of hundreds of IL&FS subsidiaries, which left the door open for future frauds and round-tripping. Secondly, it stopped short of suspending all senior employees of IL&FS involved in round-tripping. The preliminary forensic audit report of Grant & Thornton red-flagged the areas where money laundering was done. Subject to final enquiry and conviction, these employees should have been suspended and Look Out Notices (LONs) should have been issued against them to stop them from fleeing the country. But nothing of that sort happened, leaving the way clear for future fraudulent transactions with the restructured funds after the government takeover, by the same employees through the same web of labyrinthine channels.

Bankers' Feedback: From Easy Credit to Credit Squeeze

The tell-tale RBI data also shows that NPAs rose when the restructuring of loans to the stressed assets was discontinued (Fig. 5.2). This was expected. If you stop the refinancing of bad apples, they will lack liquidity to pay interest and NPAs will grow. There was a lot of brouhaha in the media as NPAs rose year after year. By the year 2014–15, the gross restructured assets had reached an all-time high of 6.4 per cent. This meant that 6.4 per cent of the total assets were bad loans that had been kept from defaulting due to bank refinance. This dropped to 0.9 per cent by the year 2017–18. It was hoped that after the huge spike of NPAs, which rose from 4.6 per cent in 2014–15—before the AQR of banks began—to a high of 11.6 per cent in 2017–18, they would eventually fall. But the industry distress was still high and showed no signs of retreating. Why?

The RBI data (Fig. 5.1) also gives pointers to this distress. It also shows that the credit offtake to industries that had grown phenomenally during the UPA regime slowed post 2015 to near zero. The sharp drop in credit hurt liquidity and this was especially seen in PSBs that were pushed into restructuring.

There were other reasons as well for this industrial slowdown. In April 2014, the International Monetary Fund (IMF) had warned that a third of the corporate debt in India had a debt-equity ratio of more than three, the highest degree of leverage in the Asia-Pacific region. The easy credit policy of the past decade had ensured that the liquidity of corporates had been debt-driven and not through equity, raised in the capital markets.

Demonetization, GST and global trade wars did their bit to worsen the liquidity. The biggest reason of the industry distress, however, was the slowdown of bank credit and the disappearance of easy money. An assistant general manager of a PSB, who manages a large branch in a commercial district of Delhi with accounts of several medium and large industries, explained the phenomenon. 'We had four clients with borrowings of over ₹100 crore and nine national clients with borrowings exceeding ₹1,000 crore from the bank. Only one of these 13 clients had increased their gross borrowings during the five years from 2014 to 2018,' he said.

Before 2015, the branch manager was not even aware of the total amount of borrowings that each of his clients had. He was only aware of two clients, who were largely dependent on his branch for finance—one of whom had a total exposure of ₹86 crore, and another whose borrowings from his branch was to the tune of ₹37 crore. In 2015, he learnt that these two clients had borrowed from other banks too, and their gross exposure was around ₹130 crore and ₹150 crore respectively. The debt-equity ratio of the first party was 1.7:1, so things were not too bad, while the second party was 2.8:1. Incidentally, this was much higher than what the second party's balance sheet stated. All other parties were also highly leveraged with debt, well over three times the equity. As a matter of fact, the nine national account-holders were advised to reduce their borrowings and bring in more equity to meet the borrowing norms, as per an advisory issued by the central bank, RBI.

Of course, it was easier to issue an advisory than to implement it. Bankers could do very little to force the regularization of accounts. They could only stop lending, to put pressure on their clients. However, as expected, squeezing credit did not ensure results. Overleveraged clients did not bring in additional equity and recast their accounts. The tussle between the bank and overborrowed clients continued. The industrial situation worsened as the credit flow from banks slowed down.

The RBI kept up pressure on banks to conduct AQR stringently. Most industrial clients, especially in the infrastructure and manufacturing sectors, failed to live up to the set benchmarks. The automobile, power and telecom sectors proved particularly vulnerable. In a circular issued in April 2017, the RBI specifically red-flagged the telecom industry, and asked bank boards to review their exposure to the sector by 30 June and consider making provisions at higher rates. Now we know that more than one telecom major has not paid the AGR dues for over a decade and is on the brink of collapse. The Supreme Court has already turned down the appeal for a respite and the telecom majors Airtel, Vodafone and Tata Telecom have reluctantly started to pay up. Surely, the bankers will have a lot of bones to pick after the massive payouts. The RBI governor has already warned that the telecom companies may default on existing commitments to banks to meet the spectrum dues. A Bank of Baroda banker says,

> We at the Branch level knew very well that our clients would suffer, as the noose tightened first around the easy credit policy. Thereafter, the emphasis grew on identifying stressed assets.
>
> Every week, new procedures and guidelines were issued by our head office for early compliance. We realised that as per the increasingly watertight and well laid down RBI norms, nearly every asset financed by our bank was stressed. It was virtually impossible to hide these accounts as RBI

> called out banks who were not complying with the norms every quarter. There was surely no question of additional lending to these companies, which were already stressed. Any financial institutions or bank doing so, would earn the wrath of the regulator.

So, banks struggled to meet the new compliance norms, switching off the credit tap. 'The regulator was at a distance from the client and did not understand the distress of the industry—as the credit transmission slowed down to a trickle,' he emphasized. Also with industries being interlinked through the supply chain, the impact of NPAs and sick and bankrupt industries was felt across the industry. For example, one large steel industry that has gone to the bankruptcy court could leave over 50,000 of its vendors in the lurch, affecting their cash flow due to unpaid debts to vendors and sub-vendors. The tremor of the IBC has been felt far and wide and will continue for a few years. The effect of bank reforms—their fallout on the industry—is something that is not going to go away in a hurry.

SIX

BANK FRAUDS: GENESIS AND DETECTION

Bank frauds are not new to India. History shows that they have been causing bank failures since the 18th century. But bank frauds, post-millennium, are of a different genre. They are a result of a deep-rooted collusion or nexus between the lender, the borrower and the administration. Crony capitalism has led to these massive frauds. Many fraudsters have fled India with the money, and many are fleeing. The government amended the Fugitive Economic Offenders Bill in 2018, empowering it with powers to bring back those declared as fugitive economic offenders under the 2002 Act.

There is a real-time story of a fraudster trying to escape the Look Out Circular (LOC) that stopped him from taking a flight from Delhi to London. A month later he arranged a fake passport but was apprehended at the Biratnagar border with a gang of smugglers. Instead of escaping the country, he, along with four others, was arrested on multiple charges far grievous than wilfully cheating a bank.

The Crooks Are Fleeing, Frauds Are Ballooning

But while a few have been restrained, many have fled. In January 2019, the ministry declared the names of 72 financial fraudsters who had duped banks and fled the country since the banking reforms started in 2015. There is the case of Vijay Mallya, who has an outstanding amount of ₹9,000 crore against his name; Nirav Modi, Neeshal Modi and Mehul Choksi, with

₹13,000 crore outstanding; Nilesh Parekh, Kamlesh Parekh and Umesh Parekh, the Kolkata-based jewellers with outstandings of ₹2,600 crore; Jatin Mehta of Winsome Diamonds, who with his family fled to St. Kitts with outstandings of ₹6,800 crore; Nitin Jayentilal Sandesara and Diptiben Chetankumar Sandesara, who are reportedly in Dubai with outstandings of ₹5,000 crore; and many more.

There is a cat and mouse game being played out by the enforcement agencies and a powerful group of lawyers who defend the fugitives, and activists who claim to be fighting for transparency. Pune-based activist Vihar Dhruve filed an RTI petition seeking information on the number of people under the LOC scanner. In July 2019, the CBI refused to give details of orders. It cited Section 8(1)(h) of the RTI Act, which exempts it from disclosure of information that could adversely affect arrest or prosecution of an accused.

The noose around absconders is being gradually tightened. But the speed is slow and, typical of government action, the approach is leaden footed. As a result, the loot is still continuing and the fraudsters are still fleeing India.

The RBI, in another disclosure to RTI activist Saket Gokhale, confirmed that ₹68,000 crore of loan frauds had been written off by the regulator as of September 2019 from 50 top wilful defaulters, including Mehul Choksi (Gitanjali Gems), Jatin Mehta (Winsome Diamonds), Vijay Mallya (Kingfisher Airlines) and many others on technical/prudential write-off clauses. It was not clear whether these defaulters would be pursued in the courts for these amounts.

In February 2020, the Indian Government entered into a treaty with the UAE, permitting the UAE banks to recover ₹50,000 crore from fugitives who had duped them and taken shelter in India. The UAE government, in turn, have deported over 20 gangsters and economic offenders under the extradition treaty with India since 2015.

Most of the financial fraudsters get away from the scene

because the bankers are themselves not vigilant and enthusiastic about reporting a financial crime when it is happening. These frauds mostly happened because corrupt businessmen siphoned out bank loans given to industries. There were many bankers who were not involved directly, but they saw it happening and yet did nothing to stop it. And the fraudulent activities took place not over a couple of years but a decade. This was easy money and slowly, industrialists started siphoning off this refinanced capital to personal accounts in overseas tax havens.

As a result, the additional capital did not help the industries recover. Instead, evergreening of loans made them even more toxic. The effect of these toxic loan frauds is now threatening the banking industry. As the stringent AQR at the banks, introduced in 2015 by the regulator RBI, takes its toll, the frauds continue to be detected. As a result of this, NPAs will continue to grow.

Laws Alone Can't Stop Frauds, Regulators Must Act

There is clear evidence to show that lapses in detection and reporting of frauds by banks and regulators permitted the NPAs to balloon meteorically after 2015. Whether this was due to negligence or connivance or simply due to lack of the necessary skill set is still not known. Whatever be the reason, the RBI needs to take corrective action without further delay.

Over 49,000 cases of bank frauds took place between 2010 and 2019, amounting to losses of around ₹2 lakh crore (₹2 trillion) as per data received from the RBI. Fig. 6.1 gives the ten-year data and shows the sharp growth of bank frauds after the introduction of the AQR, from the third quarter of the financial year 2015–16.

The rise in bank frauds detected over the last four years has rung the alarm bells in the industry. But this is not a recent phenomenon. These frauds were taking place earlier as well; they simply remained undetected and away from the public glare.

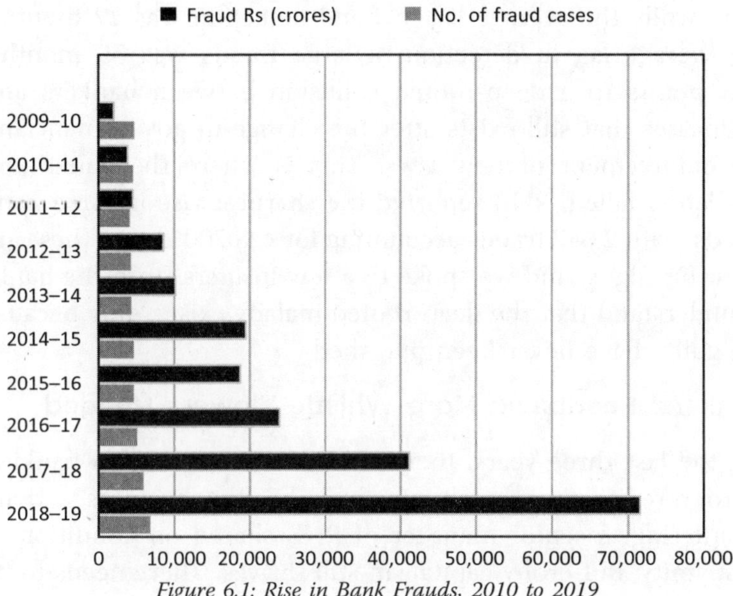

Figure 6.1: Rise in Bank Frauds, 2010 to 2019
Data Source: RBI

The AQR was like any deep-rooted surgery—it could not happen without much bloodletting. Headline numbers showed 70 per cent jump in frauds annually between 2017 and 2019. In the financial year 2016–17, there were 5,076 bank frauds worth ₹23,933 crore, while in the year ending March 2018, there were 5,916 frauds amounting to ₹41,167 crore. This further grew during the year 2018–19, and the number of frauds detected increased to 6,801, amounting to ₹71,542 crore. This is worrying not only because the detected bank frauds are increasing, but because a large number of these frauds ballooned in the last five years, even as the Modi government was bringing in regulation to tighten the banking laws. It shows that the noose is still not tight enough and the cleansing is still only a half-done job.

Additionally, a big leap has been detected in large frauds (₹100 crore and above), amounting to ₹52,200 crore. These constitute over three-fourths of the total frauds detected during the year.

Also, while the average lag in fraud detection was 22 months, the average lag in detection of large frauds was 55 months. This points to a deep-rooted collusion between bankers and businesses that still exists after the change in government and the enforcement of new laws. This is where the banks and regulators failed. PNB reported the sharpest rise in large bank frauds, with 2,047 frauds accounting for ₹28,700 crore. These are worrying signs, and we spoke to a few insiders from the banks to understand that the deep-rooted malady exists, only because the guilty have never been punished.

Bankers' Feedback: More Whistle-blowers Needed

For the last three years, there has been no growth in banking sector credit—as a result of which healthy business activity is suffering, a senior manager of PNB shared on condition of anonymity. But crony capitalism still thrives. There needs to be a thorough cleansing at the banks, with a criterion that weeds out the bad apples. It is not that the bank staff is unaware of the frauds that are taking place. But they remain silent because of deep-rooted organizational politics, which ensures that the guilty and the powerful are hand-in-glove.

Banks generally avoid transparency and open discussion on frauds. As of 2017–18, only SBI was transparent on this account, reporting 908 whistle-blower complaints—which was incidentally 21 per cent higher than the previous year. It was second only to Wipro on the complaint list and ahead of Tata Steel, Tech Mahindra and TCS. All banks must take a cue from SBI and try to frame a progressive whistle-blowers policy that is comparable to the best practices of blue chip companies in India and worldwide.

Whistle-blowers must be given protection and incentives to speak out and help detect ongoing frauds. The vigilance department of PNB is totally dysfunctional, and a lot of bribing takes place once a fraud gets detected. The growth and ease of bribing has emboldened the fraudsters, who expand their fraudulent business in connivance with corrupt bankers. You can see some of the bank staff working with corrupt businessmen to authenticate false business premises, create fictitious assets, regularize false invoices, generate bogus stocks worth billions of rupees, and so on.

Like small frauds, even big frauds have been detected in the last two years, claims the senior manager. The FINACLE 10 software's regulatory checks, which are currently in place, will usually start detecting anomalies and lead to trends that help identify any fraudulent transactions in two years' time. The software, developed by Infosys, is a globally accepted robust software used by most PSBs, including PNB. Hence it is quite normal that the average fraud detection time is 22 months. If fraud detection takes place within two years, and it is plugged in the next six months, the problem would be very much under control.

But these large frauds are allowed to grow, as someone is making big money while the fraudster cheats the bank. So, over the 55-month period—which is the average detection period for large frauds as per the RBI report—serious money has been siphoned out of the bank. Every zone in the bank has dozens of such accounts, and they are not really a priceless secret. Many senior employees of the bank know about them. But nobody speaks out, says the senior manager. If the government or the banking regulator introduces a whistle-blowers protection and incentive scheme, maybe the employees themselves will work to end the menace. Else, things look pretty grim at this stage.

Collusion between the banker, the businessman, the administrator, the regulator, the courts and the politician makes the frauds actually grow and become increasingly more ingenious and harder to detect.

Despite the change of government, the bad apples in the banking system continue to do fraudulent business without being purged year after year, and that has taken a toll on the employee morale at the banks. Nobody cares anymore, and at times one feels that everybody is keen to join in on the looting, says the senior manager. It was not so bad a decade ago, but things have gone downhill pretty fast. It is not only that PNB or the PSBs suffer from this malady. Some private banks, too, have this deep-rooted sickness.

Central Vigilance Commission Does a Deep Dive into Bank Frauds

The Central Vigilance Commission (CVC) did a detailed analysis on the top hundred bank frauds till March 2017, and came up with startling revelations. The report was released in October 2018.

It was found that the creation of fictional debtors was one of the popular methods adopted in large frauds. It was also found that delinquent borrowers often used massive over-invoicing to show assets, some of which did not even exist. Bankers and CAs helped such borrowers regularize and fund these assets. At times, old and junk machinery were painted and passed off as new. Imported second-hand plants that had been junked abroad were often bought and passed off as new machinery with bogus invoicing. Chartered accountants were even hired to access and manage the Core Banking System (CBS) during RBI audits.

The sectors that were looked into were gems and jewellery, manufacturing, agriculture, media, aviation and service sector. The report focused on the modus operandi of frauds, the type of lending, like consortium lending, individual lending and multiple accounts, as well as the common loopholes that help frauds. The report is important because it brings a fresh perspective from the non-banking sector on the vigilance needs for banking. It also bears a stark resemblance to the banking frauds committed by Nirav Modi, Mehul Choksi, Vijay Mallya and the Ruias. Unfortunately it does not name the parties involved in its case studies. The process needs to be continued every year, as fraudsters evolve and adopt new methods when the old ones come under scrutiny. It is also important to name the individual banks and the fraudsters, as definitive action can be taken by the investigative authorities based on the CVC report. The vigilance commission is constitutionally empowered to probe and report irregularities. The CVC report becomes weak and ineffective when the case studies are not identified with the names of the fraudsters.

Three cases were analysed in the gems and jewellery segment by the CVC. They bore resemblance to the frauds committed by Mumbai jewellers Jatin Mehta (Winsome Diamonds), Nirav Modi (Firestar Diamonds) and Mehul Choksi (Gitanjali Gems). The report, without naming the firms, cites instances where gold jewellery was imported by the jeweller but the antecedents of the supplier of gold jewellery or the verification of genuine gold and the invoice value were not ascertained by the bankers of the consortium, before giving advance. There were various points where the banks erred. Firstly, they financed the import of gold jewellery without verifying the antecedents of the party from which it was bought. Thereafter, the jewellers claimed additional finance to inset diamond jewellery, but the banks did not verify whether the work was done. Then again, the banks did not verify the antecedents of the party to whom the diamond inset gold jewellery was re-exported. The banks did not carry out due diligence on the parties; they did not check the value of the consignments exported nor the shipment papers. The details of receivables submitted by the borrower to the banks in order to avail credit facilities were found to be manipulated, false and fabricated. The fraud caused huge losses to the bank consortium, with zero salvage value. Though the CVC has recommended that appropriate accountability should be fixed in the chain of command, including sanctioning authority in the event of such frauds, it remains to be done. The people who have been investigated and arrested have mostly been lower functionaries. No directive has been given by either the RBI or the banks involved to fix the accountability of the senior management involved in the fraud. Even the ED investigation has left the top brass untouched.

Five cases were analysed by the CVC in the manufacturing sector, in the textiles, ferrous metals and pharmaceuticals products segment. In one case, nearly four of the five shipping bills that were financed by the banks were found to be forged. In another case, a bank financed ₹6,740 crore of purchases, of which ₹1,679 crore were bills of fancy shirting, all of which were false. The stock record showed that invoices did not have the name of the brand, the code or the sizes, and on investigation, the firm was even unable to confirm physical movement of the fancy shirting material.

In a third case, borrowers with multiple global offices in Dubai, Hong Kong and Singapore borrowed from Indian banks in one nation and sold to other bank borrowers in another. So, though invoices were submitted and finances availed, there were no business transactions.

In case of agro loans, the CVC report says that a company initiated an alternate procurement model whereby pre-harvest farm loans were extended to farmers through Village Level Aggregators (VLA), supported by Post Dated Cheques (PDC) as collateral security. After the introduction of pre-harvest financing, its impact was unknown. The traditional practices and controls of crop inspection failed, resulting in embezzlement of funds. Fake stocks were created through a collusion between employees and associates involved in procurement. The available stocks were misappropriated by the employees and the entire scheme of financing was supported by a consortium of banks, where the bankers were reportedly hand-in-glove with the borrowing farmers. In another case, the CVC report states that a company hugely inflated the cost of capital incurred on the building of a warehouse and got it financed by banks. In a third case, after taking a packing credit advance from a consortium of banks, the company spent the money but failed to execute the export business.

CVC Analysis of the Kingfisher Airlines Fraud

This is one of the most important parts of the CVC report, simply due to the scale and the audacity of the fraud. However, the CVC has cleverly hidden it at the end of the report, so that it does not become the banner headline of the report, and has not named the party involved. Though unnamed, the analysis of this fraud in the aviation sector by the CVC identifies it pretty clearly.

Kingfisher Airlines commenced its commercial operations in May 2005 and, at its peak, had both international and national routes. The company was promoted by another company, named United Breweries (UB) Group, which had a presence in several countries. It added a low-cost segment, called Deccan Airlines, which had 10 per cent of the market share just two years later in May 2007. At that time, Jet-Sahara was the market leader with 34 per cent market share. With the acquisition of Captain Gopinath's Deccan Airlines for ₹550 crore, UB Group's market share increased to 21 per cent of the domestic aviation market, and it became a close contender for the top spot.

Kingfisher Airlines was funded by a consortium of banks, led by SBI. It cheated the banks by suppressing facts in the financial statements and diverting the funds to related entities, for purposes other than those for which finance was disbursed. The banks failed to monitor the end-use of funds. Here, the intent was possibly to point to the diversions to investments made by Kingfisher in the IPL cricket franchise; Force India, the Formula 1 Racing team; and several yacht and luxury cruisers in Europe that improved the personal brand valuation of the promoter as well as the airline. The CVC report goes on to add, 'The Company ran its operations mostly on leased aircraft, for which an overseas entity (vendor) was created, which, in turn, created fictitious invoices with inflated bills. The money was transferred to it through legal means. Whatever the money the company owed to the leasing company would be disbursed and rest parked with the intermediate entity.'

The airline's balance sheet was never strong and its credit rating was lower than the minimum requirement for sanctioning loans. But Vijay Mallya was a Rajya Sabha member from Karnataka, whose candidature was supported both by the ruling Congress and the opposition BJP. So, in connivance with powers that be, the loans to the airlines were sanctioned and massive advances were given by the consortium of banks on its brand valuation, which was clearly illegal. For this, the company submitted valuation reports by two private entities, of which the consortium banks accepted the higher valuation figure, again in contravention of the law. Kingfisher was able to convince the bankers that advances and credit facilities should be sanctioned to the company on the basis of its brand name, which did not form any tangible security for the purpose of recovery.

The CVC has recommended that such practices should be discontinued in future. However, it has not investigated the nexus between business, banker and administration that caused these loans to be so easily disbursed. The vigilance department should probe into such a nexus and fix accountability, which is a part of its statutory duties. Moreover, it should help to set up a process, so that similar lapses do not take place in future.

The CVC, however, made some useful observations regarding the functioning of consortium banks that the government and the RBI need to heed. Banks lend to large borrowers as a consortium to reduce individual risk in case of a default. But the CVC says, this type of funding is actually increasing risks, because it is nobody's baby. The CVC report says: 'Multiple banking arrangements in large-value financing have done more harm than good to banks. This type of arrangement enabled corporates to secure multiple finances from various banks far in excess of their requirements. Funds raised were easily diverted through the company's accounts with various banks, in the absence of effective exchange of information between the banks.' It also categorically states that, 'Banks currently do not have a foolproof system of checking and confirming whether the company has actually been working on the contracts and whether the contracts were genuinely business based.'

Fraud Investigation Becomes Compulsory for NPAs

As the NPAs of banks rose, following the stringent AQR, the banks discovered a severe mismatch between assets and debt liabilities. For any recovery, the banks would have to take the business to the bankruptcy court. Here, the haircut would be decided, based not only on the books of the bank but also the verification of the value of the asset by third-party valuers of the interested bidders. Bankers also realized that the assets were of low value, largely due to serious frauds that had taken place where debt funds had been utilized inappropriately and had instead been siphoned away by the promoters. Many of the NPAs were not due to genuine business losses, but because of money laundering and serious frauds.

In February 2018, the government issued a directive to PSBs to examine all NPA accounts over ₹50 crore for frauds. The comprehensive and systemic checking of transactions of NPAs, along with legacy stock inspection, helped unearth a large number of unauthorized transactions and serious inventory mismatches. Identification of frauds in NPAs took place thereafter on a war footing.

As on 31 December 2018, around 204 borrowers had been reported as fraudulent by one or more banks. However, it was found that these borrowers were not classified as such by other banks having exposure to the same borrowers. This meant that red-flagged accounts of a few PSBs were operating as normal accounts in several other PSBs, availing more credit despite their default status in some banks. So, an exercise in sharing of information and consolidation of bank fraud data was initiated.

Sharing of Fraud Data

The sharp rise in frauds during the financial years ending March 2018 and March 2019 is probably a result of this exercise. The 70 per cent year-on-year rise was largely due to enhanced fraud detection. The RBI report of both years diagnosed that this was largely due to rise of loan frauds of above ₹100 crore. In this category, cash credit and working capital loan frauds dominated in the PSBs whereas retail term loans (non-housing) were a major contributor to the rise of frauds in private banks. It also pointed out serious differences in the fraud assessments of accounts by banks. Each bank had a different methodology and there was no standardization in the adopted procedures. So, new guidelines were issued to make the fraud-detection procedures uniform and more robust.

The entire exercise was also done to identify frauds in banks at an early stage. But the first two years of enforcement show that a key issue was a very high time lag of an average of 55 months in the detection of large frauds. Early detection of frauds was crucial for banks, but for that there was a need for advanced data management that could consolidate and cleanse data from internal and external sources for fraud analysis and investigation. So, we will look at the software readiness of the industry for the creation of early warning systems for frauds.

Fraud-Detection Capability of Banking Software

Even if banks detect fraud, they are unwilling to report the same. This is true for all banks, and hence it is not the technology constraint but the attitude and intent that matter. The mindset of 'no tolerance to wrongdoing' and thereby prioritizing safe and fair practices in banking needs to be inculcated.

In any modern-day banking system, customer records, banking transactions, loan approvals and disbursements, fund flow and transfers, and multiple processes are all recorded through a complex and robust software. The database design ensures that every table in the database must retain all information, not only of the borrowers but also of the bank branches and the bank officers involved, along with the lending process and the entire workflow. Besides, they are also equipped with fraud-detection mechanisms that analyse anomalies and data breaches and report the same.

All banks—public sector, private sector, payment banks and NBFCs—use multiple complex but standardized softwares approved by the RBI. A bank can be using one software for core banking, another for issuing LCs, another for NEFT payments, another for term loans, and yet another for SWIFT payments. All these softwares are equipped with Early Warning Systems (EWS) for detection of frauds, which are supposed to be reported within six months as per RBI guidelines. Of course, a bank that uses FINACLE 7 will be less equipped than one that uses FINACLE 10, but all have the basic capability to address the menace of frauds if the bankers are alert. All reports are available daily at the branch level and the circle, as well the centralized processing centre and the zonal office.

In case of frauds, there is a separate wing in most banks. For example, SBI has a chief general manager (frauds), who reports to the managing director (stressed assets, risk and compliance). Every bank these days monitors frauds at the level of a director or the managing director. However, in many cases, the guidelines for Red Flagged Accounts (RFA) are not uniformly applied by banks, leading to major frauds. The RBI report states that, 'In several cases, banks are unable to confirm the RFA tagged accounts as frauds or otherwise within the prescribed period of six months. As per central repository of information on large credits (CRILC) data, at the end of 31 March, 2019, the red flagged accounts reported by banks exceeded the stipulated six-month period in 176 cases.'

As of 31 December 2018, there were 204 borrowers who were red-flagged for fraudulent transactions by one bank, but were not reported by another. This showed that each bank was taking a different approach to recording and reporting frauds. The ED undertook enforcement action against 47 banks between July 2018 and June 2019, including against nine foreign banks, one payment bank and a co-operative bank. It imposed an aggregate penalty of ₹122.1 crore for non-compliance with and contravention of directions on fraud classification and reporting and violations of directions for Know Your Customer (KYC) norms and Income Recognition & Asset Classification (IRAC) norms, among others. But this was merely the tip of the iceberg.

The real elephants in the room were the large loans, disbursed to highly leveraged businesses that had first borrowed from and then manipulated the system with the help of bank insiders, to defraud the banks to the tune of trillions of rupees in the last decade. The reported reluctance of SBI to push DHFL to the NCLT court, despite payment defaults and the red flag raised by the RBI, points to a possible collusion between the banker and the borrower. The banker made repeated attempts to rescue the HFC from being sent to the NCLT court. In November 2019, the RBI overruled the lenders consortium and dismissed the board of DHFL. The HFC was send to the NCLT court, making it the first financial services company to be pushed to bankruptcy proceedings.

Bankers' Feedback: Swift Expertise in Auditors Lacking

In the case of Firestar Diamonds, Nirav Modi manipulated the banking system and defrauded banks through false LCs/LOUs placed on foreign banks. It is quite possible that he used generous bribes, and not political connections, to compromise the system. The bribe money from Modi and Choksi would, however, have travelled to the topmost executive of the bank, says a former senior general manager of PNB. Nirav Modi and Mehul Choksi had tapped into an infinite source of finance, provided by PNB. They had definite access to the bank's top management, a few (not all) of whom have been charged by the ED with conspiracy to cheat the bank. This, because the fraud was not reported for years and was covered up wilfully, despite RBI's warning to PNB.

Taking lessons from the fraud, banks have now started to link core banking operations with SWIFT. But they need to train and develop more executives who are experts in SWIFT operations. 'Many, many more,' says the senior banker. There is an acute shortage in PSBs of executives who can perform SWIFT operations, which is making the banks vulnerable and dependent on a few. So, new skills, and audit vigilance and monitoring techniques have to be developed, and internal auditors need to be adequately trained in foreign exchange operations.

However, there were many people involved in the Firestar International fraud, other than the bankers. In March 2016, one of the Nirav Modi companies had a net worth of ₹2,688 crore and was making a meagre profit of ₹185 crore. But it had bank borrowings of ₹3,509 crore and trade payables of ₹4,104 crore. Despite this unusually high leveraging, the Fitch-owned India Ratings gave it an Ind A rating, and banks kept open the credit lines to the highly overborrowed company. So, not only bank employees, but even the rating agency employees were either blissfully unaware of the wrongdoings, or deeply interested in giving Nirav Modi a helping hand. Another rating agency, CARE, raised a red flag in February 2016 and downgraded Firestar Diamond's debt instruments, worth ₹2,500 crore. Six months later, they withdrew the ratings, reportedly on receipt of a very unique no-objection certificate from banks.

Despite the weak financials, Nirav Modi had powerful contacts, leveraged the network of his high-profile CFO Vipul Ambani (first cousin of Mukesh Ambani), and kept up the facade of running a successful luxury gems and jewellery business. However, he could not convince investors and venture capitalists, nor get an IPO going, despite several attempts.

Nonetheless, Modi started rolling out his high-profile retail stores in New York, London, Paris, Hong Kong, Mumbai and New Delhi through 2015 and 2016, but could not ramp up his retail sales. Less than ₹500 crore of retail sales happened at Nirav Modi's glitzy stores, despite his presence in both Bond Street in London and Madison Avenue in New York. Already struggling, Modi's retail endeavour was hit by demonetization and nationwide IT raids thereafter. But he had his friends in the government, the banks and the regulator's office, who delayed all-out action against him till January 2018, giving him and his family time to flee India. While the technical aspects of the Nirav Modi fraud have been dealt with here, we will discuss the nexus between jewellers and bankers, and why the PNB top brass during the decade-long Nirav Modi Scam needs to be investigated, in Chapter 7.

SEVEN

THE NEXUS: BANKERS, BABUS AND PROMOTERS

In the last chapter, we discussed the CVC analysis of an aviation industry fraud. We also read the analyses of other bank fraud cases in the gems and jewellery segment. Now we will talk about a startling feedback from some investigation agencies and bank staff about the complicity of the bank chiefs, the bureaucracy and the politicians. Several other bank chiefs and promoters are also being probed, though the process is painstakingly slow. Also, not all those guilty are being probed. This is just the tip of the iceberg.

CBI Probes Mallya's Nexus with Bankers and Bureaucrats

Vijay Mallya's Kingfisher Airlines was already bleeding by early 2009. It had blindly acquired the ailing Deccan Airlines in 2007. The ₹1,000 crore outflow was financed by a SBI-led consortium of 17 banks. Why did they not insist on a third-party due diligence for the acquisition? Many routine procedures for the sanction of large loans were bypassed for Kingfisher Airlines. Besides, reports from some of the rating agencies, who had already red-flagged Kingfisher, were ignored.

Mallya had made a splash in the aviation industry with Kingfisher Airlines. He had targeted the high-end traveller and had quickly mopped up over 20 per cent market share. But he never made any profit. Kingfisher's balance sheet shows net losses in every year of its operation. Besides, Mallya had no clue how to run a loss-making low-cost airline like Deccan, especially one that operated in remote destinations with little commercial viability.

O.P. Bhatt was the chairman of SBI during 2006–11, when these loans were granted, while Amitabh Verma was the joint secretary, banking. Several e-mail correspondences between Verma, Bhatt and Kingfisher's senior management are being probed by CBI. Bhatt and Verma are reportedly under the CBI scanner for having granted continued financial support to the ailing airlines without any regulatory intervention. But, the investigation has been slow-paced and no chargesheet has been filed. Others at SBI branches in Mumbai and Bengaluru, such as the deputy manager, group executive, assistant general manager, credit analyst, and relationship manager, are also under the scanner.

There are, however, references to meetings held with political decision-makers, who gave permissions, and it will be interesting to see the minutes of these meetings in the 15,000-page CBI chargesheet to be presented in court. It will show us whether the case is substantiated with evidence or merely a political witch hunt, and will tell us if convictions can be got in the court of law.

The letters were written by Mallya to Kingfisher CFO Ravi Nedungadi. They cite meetings in February 2009 between Verma and Mallya, assuring government support to the ailing airline and specific assistance in the restructuring of debt. In his e-mail dated 18 February 2009, Mallya wrote, 'I am pleased to inform you that following my presentation, the Finance Minister has approved, in principle, the comprehensive financial restructuring package requested.' He further wrote, 'He has advised the Chief Economic Advisor, in the presence of Mr Pawar and myself, that (the) government will support Kingfisher and he has convened a meeting with the Secretary, banking and the Chairmen of SBI and PNB on Feb 25 and 26 in Delhi.'

In another mail, Mallya wrote: 'Amitabh called me to ask how the SBI meeting went, I gave him a detailed report and emphasized the urgency and criticality of getting an adhoc disbursement of ₹500 crore by March 31. Amitabh said he had spoken to Mr Bhatt and that this disbursement would happen.'

Chargesheet: Loans Sanctioned at Secretary Level

It is clearly evident from the CBI chargesheet that the Kingfisher Airlines loan was approved at the secretary level and passed on to the banks for execution. According to insiders, this trend has been common across India for granting bank loans over the last decade. While Verma was the key person in the Department of Banking, reporting to the finance minister, according to a senior official from the SBI he was not the only intermediary.

CBI has seized hundreds of hard disks from Kingfisher Airlines offices and Mallya's residences, containing more than a lakh of e-mails exchanged internally by Mallya with Verma and senior Kingfisher Airlines executives, including A.K. Ravi Nedungadi, Harish Bhat and A. Raghunathan. These e-mails, written between 2007 and 2013, also included references to discussions with the finance ministry, civil aviation ministry, petroleum ministry and the PMO, among others. The focus was largely on bank loans, and aircraft turbine fuel on credit supplied by public sector oil companies. The CBI would, however, have to find and track the money trail to prove conflict of interest or corruption before bringing charges before a court. That could be very time-consuming, because the payments made by the promoters were largely to offshore accounts of politicians.

In a separate case, the CFO of the now-defunct Kingfisher Airlines, A. Raghunathan, along with four other employees of the airlines, is being probed on charges of illegal funding of ₹900 crore to Kingfisher Airlines in 2010. None of these loans were awarded after assessment of creditworthiness by a third-party valuer. As a matter of fact, IDBI was fully aware that Kingfisher Airlines could not be given credit on its weak balance sheet—that it had always shown losses, and had a negative net worth and an accumulated debt of over ₹7,000 crores. It was known that these loans were granted without the backing of commensurate recoverable assets.

The CBI chargesheet states that a corporate guarantee from United Breweries Holdings and a personal guarantee from Mallya, stipulated for a short-term loan of ₹150 crore sanctioned on 8 October 2009, were required to be furnished within 15 days from the date of disbursement. They were submitted a year later. No independent verification was done on Mallya's statements of assets and liabilities, and his shareholding in the estates of United National Breweries (UNB), South Africa and VJM Resorts was not independently verified.

The IDBI chief was not the only banker who had gone out of the way to please Vijay Mallya. Dr K.C. Chakraborti, who headed PNB between 2007 and 2009 and then went on to become the deputy governor of RBI, and K.R. Kamath, who was PNB CMD from 2009 to 2014, are also under the scanner in the voluminous CBI chargesheet for loans given to Kingfisher Airlines, though no FIR has been filed against them.

The Nexus between Bankers and Jewellers

The PNB fraud was a slick operation where the big fish of the bank have got away. Whereas it was easy to get evidence of the nexus between Mallya and the bankers and babus, it will be extremely difficult to establish the nexus of Nirav Modi with the top brass, largely because Modi was a secretive operator.

We have discussed the Nirav Modi case from the technical complexity point of view in the preceding chapter, and shall also review it from the point of regulatory failures later in Chapter 9. Here we will examine it to investigate the nexus of bankers with the businessman, from the evidence gathered by the investigators. Is the evidence enough to get the required conviction?

The CBI chargesheet filed in the Mumbai courts in May 2018 names the managing director and the CEO of the bank, along with senior executives during the 2015–17 period, but not during the 2009–14 period, when the fraud started and assumed gigantic proportions. Perhaps a little more hard work is needed on the part of the investigative agencies.

It was apparently executed by two bank officials at the junior level: Gokulnath Shetty, who we have mentioned earlier, and Manoj Kharat, who operated the financial messaging system SWIFT, sending the documents to the international banks and crediting the money received in the companies owned by Modi and Choksi. Both have been arrested. But surely, this couldn't have been a two-man operation, if we consider the inherent safeguards built into the banking system. It is rather naive to claim that because the core banking software was not connected to the SWIFT network, a massive fraud could have continued for seven years with collateral-free debts in the form of LOUs of ₹13,700 crore. If bank management cannot sense outflows of such large amounts from the accounts of the bank year after year, it has to be either extremely incompetent or compromised.

The normal procedure of issuing such LOUs, LCs or credit guarantees would be to get a bank guarantee credit limit approved. For that, the companies that seek such bank guarantee limits would have to give margin money, which was usually 25 per cent of the limit sought. The bank guarantee would be a collateral in the form of verifiable assets, like property or fixed deposits, which had to be pledged to the bank. Usually, banks issue LCs when they have a credit-worthy customer, a viable lending proposition, the required collateral as bank guarantee margin money, and after checking that previous LCs have been repaid. None of the above was available in this case.

In PNB's case, junior-level officers had no powers to issue LOUs without a credit limit. They had no powers to waive or bypass collaterals or margin money. They had no powers to either create or raise the limits of borrowings. In this case, the LOUs raised each time were bigger than the previous ones, as they were used to repay past LOUs and also leave enough surplus for use by borrowers. No additional security was demanded for the enhanced value of LOUs. All these would have been approved or intentionally waived off by the branch manager or at the general manager level at the Brady House Branch of PNB. The branch manager would have access to the concurrent audit reports where the core banking accounts and the SWIFT transactions had been looked into. The senior management, the executive directors and the chairman of the bank would know about the entire operations—and not only because Modi and Choksi were prized clients of the bank till 2017.

The investigation into the nexus between crony capitalists, corrupt bankers, regulatory authorities, bureaucrats, and politicians, in the case of Nirav Modi and Mehul Choksi, is in progress. It is, however, not comprehensive. One bank chief, Usha Ananthasubramanian, has been booked, but it is not that only she would have overlooked indiscretions of the Modi–Choksi duo during two years as the PNB managing director and CEO. Every PNB bank chief between 2010 and 2017 would have done the same, say people in the know. The CBI chargesheet says that in 2016, a fraud at the Indian Overseas Bank in Chandigarh had come to light in which a PNB branch in Dubai was one of the banks to have issued fraudulent LOUs. Many LOUs had been raised from the PNB Brady House Branch to overseas branches of Indian and foreign banks, which were found to be fraudulent.

The RBI had woken up to these frauds and issued circulars in 2015 to banks to avoid issuing such LOUs. Anathasubramanian was booked, along with General Managers Nehal Ahad and Rajesh Jindal, because she had overlooked the indiscretions by the Modi–Choksi duo and misreported the non-compliance of RBI guidelines in granting loans. But this misrepresentation of facts had been happening all along. K.R. Kamath was the PNB chairman during 2009–14, when the issuance of fraudulent LOUs to Modi–Choksi duo really flourished. Jindal was the general manager at the Brady House Branch of PNB in Mumbai just for two years, and Ahad for another two years. There is no reason that top officials like Kamath should be spared along with other senior managers at Brady House and the Zonal Offices involved in supporting the Modi–Choksi companies during the seven-year period.

A bank fraud as large in scale as what happened in the Nirav Modi case simply cannot be done without the involvement of senior officers. So, every senior officer of PNB during that seven-year period—the chairman and managing director, the EDs and the general managers—must be probed. True, some of them would be clean and would have only supported the operations considering that the business was growing. Not all would be guilty. But there would be some who would have knowingly and actively shielded the fraudulent transactions.

Gokulnath Shetty has testified that the general manager of the branch, Rajesh Jindal, asked him at first to prepare the fraudulent LOUs in 2010. At whose behest did Jindal make this request? Thereafter, Shetty says, he was threatened and blackmailed by Nirav Modi and Mehul Choksi that he would be exposed unless he kept issuing such LOUs. This was quite possible, especially if the senior management of the bank was in league with the concerned businessmen. Who were the seniors backing Modi and Choksi? The employee, in this case Gokulnath Shetty, would have no recourse to stop the LOUs, complain about the fraud, or even get himself transferred from that position without support from seniors. So, the system, once compromised, grew to be one of the nation's biggest frauds. Could all this happen without the approval of the top management of the bank?

The Rise and Fall of DHFL

DHFL was a 20-year-old HFC with a conservative balance sheet, with an annual loan disbursement of ₹2,266 crore in 2008. Till 2008 its loan book showed cumulative disbursement of just ₹9,348 crore. It serviced a steady client base of middle- and low-income (sub-prime) home buyers with an average loan ticket size of ₹7.5 lakh, promoted and nurtured diligently by its founder Rajesh Kumar Wadhawan.

After his demise, the company was run by his sons Kapil and Dheeraj. By March 2011, DHFL became the fastest growing Housing Finance Company. Under the second-generation leadership of Kapil Wadhawan, disbursements jumped suddenly by 68 per cent to ₹6,505 crore and the overall loan portfolio went up to ₹14,111 crore. Three years later, in the year ending March 2014, the yearly disbursement was ₹16,647 crore and the cumulative disbursement was a mammoth ₹58,810 crore.

DHFL, during the financial year 2013–14, had a tiny equity of ₹128 crore, along with reserves and surplus of ₹3,446 crore. But the borrowings from National Housing Bank and other financial institutions and banks were ten times as much, at ₹36,891 crore.

This trend continued for the next five years without the regulatory rap, largely because it was an HFC dealing with priority sector housing and low-cost slum development. In the year 2019, before its default, its secured loans were ₹93,707 crore against a net worth of ₹8,102 crore. It showed net current assets of ₹98,490 crore, which was largely unverified. How was this permitted? Why did the lenders or the regulators permit such high leveraging of funds without verifying their use? There are serious questions about the end use of the funds. Part of the borrowings was used by DHFL for the acquisition of the home loan division of ING Vyasa Bank, and later Deutsche Postbank Home Finance, to increase its client base. Part of it was to lend to developers in the realty sector. A large part of it was siphoned to overseas offshore tax havens, where the domestic HFC had no reason to send funds. Besides, the unusually high leveraging of funds was a sure-fire recipe for disaster. But the RBI and the lenders to DHFL, as well as the rating agencies, had their eyes closed. Was it due to a nexus between the lender banks, the borrower and the regulator?

This trend continued despite a new government taking charge and banking laws being tightened in 2014. As a result, four years later, the situation had deteriorated further. DHFL soon realized that it could no longer operate as a niche player, with high-cost funds from banks. The retail market for housing loans had become competitive. It could not compete with SBI and other PSBs in the consumer housing loan segment, as after the change of government, the banks were now targeting the low- and middle-income segment with attractive interest rates. The only option was to give credit to builders who were facing a liquidity crisis and were perpetually in need of funds. So, DHFL borrowed from the banks at moderate interest rates, and lent the money at high interest rates to real estate developers. It was a high-risk strategy, but developers were ready to borrow at a high cost. It increased the margins as well as default risk for DHFL.

DHFL was a prominent player in the sub-prime retail segment. After Kapil Wadhawan took charge in 2011, it was in a hurry to grow. It started exposing itself to the builders and real estate developers in the sub-prime first-place category, who had poor or no credit history and little financial muscle. There were many property developers in that segment, who would borrow at high interest rates of 2 per cent per month or more. DHFL even loaned vast amounts to organizations linked with Iqbal Mirchi, who was the prime accused in the Mumbai bomb blast case. DHFL's book was slowly filled with loans to shady real estate developers, but the risk was not appropriately priced. The demonetization drive of 2016, the shortage of liquidity following the slowdown of bank credit, the vigorous enforcement of the money laundering act by the IT department in 2015 and the RERA order against 2,000 builders, many of whom have been arrested, and the prolonged slowdown in the real estate sector, further worsened the situation.

But DHFL continued to lend aggressively and grow dangerously on borrowed funds. As of March 2019, it had 31 banks in its lending consortium, with Union Bank of India as the lead bank for credit facilities aggregating to ₹32,955.94 crore. It had also raised other forms of debt both from India and overseas, such that its debt-equity ratio had climbed to 10:1, five times higher than the safe norm. Besides, the consortium of PSBs kept on lending to and keeping alive this HFC tottering on the brink of collapse since 2011.

It is obvious that the Wadhawans had friends amongst the bankers, bureaucrats, regulators and all major political parties of Maharashtra. While Kapil Wadhawan's group DHFL was reportedly close to the BJP and the Shiv Sena, Housing Development Infrastructure Ltd (HDIL), a company promoted by Kapil Wadhawan's uncle Rakesh Kumar Wadhawan, was close to the Nationalist Congress Party (NCP). Both the Wadhawans, till recently, were part of the Mumbai cocktail party, jet-setting glitterati circuit.

So, it was not surprising when the SBI-led group of bankers forwarded the 'Trust Proposal' to refinance DHFL by converting debt into equity, while keeping Kapil Wadhawan as the CEO. SBI is the lead banker of the Trust Proposal and its interest in refinancing DHFL and converting its loan into equity is particularly suspicious. It is quite possible that bankers were guilty of collusion and did not want DHFL to default, only because it would have immediately triggered fraud investigations by SFIO as per the 2018 finance ministry directive to banks to investigate all NPAs above ₹50 crore. But can DHFL be shielded?

Terror Financing Probe Trips DHFL

In all possibility, DHFL cannot be and will not be shielded. Investigations by the ED reveal that DHFL had started financing Sunblink Real Estate, a firm promoted by Dubai-based gangster Iqbal Mirchi, accused in the Mumbai bomb blast case, in 2010. The loans grew over the last nine years and Sunblink's accounts show that DHFL had cleared the consolidation of outstanding loans worth ₹2,186 crore in July 2019. The money was laundered and used for terror-financing operations by the gang, which is closely associated with Pakistan-based mafia boss, Dawood Ibrahim.

The company admitted in regulatory filings in August,

'Given the ongoing discussions on the resolution plan with the lenders who have signed the ICA (inter-creditor agreement), the company believes that its payment obligations falling due in the immediate future, may not be met as per their existing schedule.' This was largely because the repayment plan included securitization of bundled loans that had no buyers. DHFL posted a quarterly loss of ₹2,224 crore in the last quarter of the financial year 2018–19. Besides, one of its statutory auditors, Deloitte Haskins & Sells LLP, has resigned and the demand for forensic audits of the company accounts are growing with each passing day.

Money Laundering by Wadhawans Needs Investigation

Worse still, HDIL was advanced large sums of money with little or no verifiable security. In January 2013, the Wadhawan family had started an exercise to reduce cross-holdings among the family members of Rajesh and Rakesh Wadhawan. Kapil and Dheeraj (sons of the late Rajesh Wadhawan) stepped down from the board of HDIL while Rakesh and Sarang stepped down from the board of DHFL. This was done to reduce scrutiny by regulators on loans to its own directors and their enterprises by NBFCs, HFCs and other financial companies.

However, DHFL's financial troubles were being deftly managed, as banks continued to finance its risky loans. After IL&FS defaulted in 2018, various DHFL papers, like its medium- and short-term funds, were subject to several downgrades by rating agencies. The HFCs had been in severe liquidity stress and had, by mid-2019, informed SEBI that they may not be able to service its debt obligations in future.

In January 2019, the investigative news agency *Cobrapost* first accused DHFL of money laundering and misappropriating the debt funds and buying property in the UK, Dubai and Sri Lanka through shell companies in Mauritius and the British Virgin Islands. It alleged that Kapil Wadhawan, Aruna Wadhawan and

Dheeraj Wadhawan, through their proxies and associates, had purchased several properties abroad. It claimed that multiple loans of ₹200 crore and above had been sanctioned to benefit shell companies acquired by the Wadhawans. The Finance Committee of DHFL, chaired by the Wadhawans, had sanctioned these loans, which were in turn routed to overseas destinations to buy property in the names of these acquired shell companies. All these allegations need to be individually investigated now.

Meanwhile, their cousin Sarang Wadhawan of the HDIL group was also accused of money laundering. In August 2019, a complaint was filed by a director of Mack Star Marketing, a private equity firm and a joint venture between an offshore firm, Ocean Deity Investment Holdings, and the HDIL Group, with the ED. The private equity firm alleged that loans of ₹135 crore, given by Yes Bank to the joint venture, were illegally diverted to pay back outstanding loans of HDIL group companies to Yes Bank, without informing the majority shareholder of the joint venture.

Ocean Deity Investment owns 78.09 per cent in the Indian JV with HDIL Group, and complained that it was not informed about the routing of money through the joint venture. According to the Panama Papers disclosures by the International Consortium of Investigative Journalists (ICIJ), where over 2 lakh shell companies participating in money laundering were named, there were three companies owned by the Wadhawans, namely Supremacy Investments Ltd, Sharecorp Ltd and Mystical International Worldwide Ltd. These companies are important because they were said to have links with Rakesh Wadhawan, Sarang Wadhawan and Anu Wadhawan of the HDIL Group, the same group that is at the centre of the ₹6,500 crore PMC Bank fraud case.

Nexus between HDIL and PMC Bank Catches RBI by Surprise

The Wadhawans of the HDIL group, who were on an acquisition spree, had long set their sights on controlling the operations of the 37-year-old PMC Bank. The PMC Bank is one of the 62 banks registered under the Multi-State Cooperative Societies Act, 2002, but accountable not to the state but to the central registrar, as more than one state is involved, and hence it is regulated by the RBI. Like all cooperative banks, it catered to the interests of the powerful farmer cooperatives. Besides, according to some RBI officers, it was one of the most trusted cooperative banks. Incidentally, the RBI officers' Cooperative Credit Society Ltd has a fixed deposit (FD) of ₹105 crore with the Mumbai-based bank. As per its FY 2019 balance sheet, the amount of FDs placed with PMC Bank by the RBI officers' Cooperative Credit Society was higher than the fixed deposits it had in any other cooperative bank.

The PMC Bank has around 1,800 employees, with 137 branches, mostly located in Mumbai, and was a low-profile bank that had a few branches in seven other states. The chairman of the bank, Waryam Singh, was a director on the board of HDIL for 10 years. He was the key connect between the banker and the borrower. Waryam Singh was the chairman of PMC Bank during 1999–2005 and 2015–19. He was a non-executive director on the board of HDIL from 2005 to 2015. There was clearly a conflict of interest between the banker and the borrower, which the regulator was blissfully unaware of. Though DHIL was in dire straits and had defaulted on payments, the PMC Bank sanctioned a loan of ₹2,500 crore to the troubled real estate company, according to its books. This was over 30 per cent of the total advances of ₹8,000 crore given by the bank, which was clearly illegal.

However, the regulator, RBI, did not step in at that stage. This, despite media reports in the financial press about the violation of the RBI borrowing guidelines, which mandated that a bank cannot have more than 15 per cent exposure to a single borrower. Joy Thomas, CEO of PMC Bank, later admitted that he had helped HDIL and hid the fact that the company had been defaulting for three years and that the actual exposure of the bank to the real estate company was ₹6,500 crore and not ₹2,500 crore. This meant that not 30 per cent, but almost 75 per cent of loans of the PMC Bank had actually gone to HDIL. How did that happen? On investigation, it was found that 44 bad loan accounts of the promoters of the real estate company were replaced by 21,049 dummy accounts, as per the police FIR. Fresh loans were issued to these dummy accounts, which in turn fed the funds into the stressed accounts of the builder HDIL, to help them avoid default.

In August 2019, Bank of India approached the NCLT for recovery of dues of ₹522 crore from HDIL. The real estate company pressed the panic button and issued two drafts drawn on PMC Bank. The two payments were through drafts of ₹96.5 crore, drawn on PMC Bank from the sanctioned personal loan to HDIL boss Sarang Wadhawan. The Wadhawans were using an illegally sanctioned PMC Bank loan to pay back Bank of India, which had threatened to drag it to the bankruptcy court.

It was only after Bank of India, in a press release dated 31 August 2019, acknowledged the receipt of two payments from HDIL, drawn on PMC Bank against a one-time settlement of its loan of ₹522 crore, that RBI officers woke up to the scam. Here was an unauthorized loan from a bank where they had deposited over ₹100 crore of the RBI cooperative society funds. Now, if PMC had started servicing the bad debts of a bankrupt real estate company with its depositors' funds, RBI officers would ultimately have to bear the losses themselves.

It is said that RBI officers approached the RBI top bosses in panic, and in a knee-jerk action, the sudden imposition of a ₹1,000 withdrawal limit was announced, causing unnecessary panic amongst PMC depositors. This was a typical mindless response of the regulatory machinery, which was later termed as an overreaction. The limit was revised to ₹10,000 after protests broke out in Mumbai. It only went to show that the RBI was badly prepared to handle such emergencies. Instead of curtailing loan disbursements to large and overborrowed real estate companies like HDIL, it stopped genuine depositors and account holders from withdrawing their own money, with an absurd limit of ₹1,000. The political backlash of the scam and RBI's quixotic decision just before the Maharashtra elections made headlines for a month. Surely, RBI needs to be more prudent and responsible in its quick-fire decision-making.

How Rana Kapoor Turned Yes Bank into His Private Fiefdom

Ashok Kapur, the former country head of the ABN Amro Bank; Harkirat Singh, the former country head of the Deutsche Bank; and a third partner, Rana Kapoor, former corporate finance head of the ANZ Grindlays Bank, got together in 1999 to form an NBFC. While the three professional bankers invested ₹9 crore each, they roped in RaboBank of the Netherlands to invest the remaining capital as a 75 per cent stakeholder. Ashok Kapur's wife Madhu and Rana Kapoor's wife Bindu are sisters, which made Ashok and Rana co-brothers. Ashok and Madhu have two children, daughter Shagun and son Gaurav. Rana and Bindu have three daughters, Radha, Rakhee and Roshni.

The NBFC became Yes Bank in 2003 and acquired a banking licence under the chairmanship of Ashok Kapur when Harkirat Singh quit, citing undue influence exerted by RaboBank in the appointment of the CEO and executive chairman. His stake was bought over by Rana Kapoor. Yes Bank conducted a successful IPO in 2005 and made slow and steady progress in the initial years. In 2008, its CEO Ashok Kapur was killed in the 26/11 terrorist attack on Trident Hotel at Mumbai. Rana Kapoor seized the opportunity and rode roughshod on the rights of his sister-in-law as a shareholder, and started to slowly convert the professionally managed bank into a personal fiefdom.

The loan book of Yes Bank grew rapidly as Rana Kapoor entered into doubtful deals with loss-making real estate financiers DHFL (₹3,700 crore), India Bulls Group (₹27,800 crore), IL&FS (₹2,600 crores), Reliance Entertainment division of the the Reliance Anil

Dhirubhai Ambani Group (ADAG) (₹13,000 crore), Kingfisher Airlines (₹1,080 crores), and Jet Airways (₹869 crores), after he took control of Yes Bank in 2008. In most cases, Yes Bank lent out money to the beleaguered corporates at high interest rates after Kapoor took a considerable kickback against every loan granted. One such kickback currently under investigation by the ED is a ₹600 crore quid pro quo loan by DHFL to Doit Urban Ventures, a firm controlled by Rana's three daughters. As per Rajendra Mirashie, president, Project Finance of DHFL, the loan that was negotiated by Lata Dave, Rana Kapoor's senior executive secretary, was cleverly structured in such a way that the principal was to be repaid only five years later in 2023. Interestingly, Doit Urban offered securities of ₹735 crore against the ₹600 crore loan, which on scrutiny turned out to be property documents worth only ₹40 crore.

Rana Kapoor was arrested by the ED shortly after Yes Bank was placed under moratorium in March 2020, and his daughter Roshni Kapoor was stopped from boarding a flight to London.

Scorched Earth Policy that Emptied Out Yes Bank

The Rana Kapoor family is said to have collected over ₹2,000 crore as kickbacks against loans given by Yes Bank to stressed assets since 2008. Rana Kapoor successfully warded off the entry into the Yes Bank board of the family of his late brother-in-law Ashok Kapur. His sister-in-law Madhu Kapur had to fight a lengthy court battle for a board representation despite having 8.33 per cent stake in Yes Bank. Rana Kapoor knew that he would lose the court battle, so he adopted a scorched earth policy of hollowing out Yes Bank through a fictitious loan book that grew very fast after Madhu Kapur staked her claim in 2011.

Rana Kapoor also bought expensive real estate at a throwaway price from promoters of stressed assets to whom Yes Bank had offered loans. According to the ED, the Kapoor family usurped six plush properties located in Delhi: a 5,005 sq. mt. bungalow on Amrita Shergill Marg worth ₹500 crore, a 1,021 sq. mt. property in Diplomatic Enclave on Sardar Patel Marg worth ₹250 crore, a 1,233 sq. yard property on Kautilya Marg worth ₹350 crore, a residential unit in Jor Bagh worth ₹150 crore and two properties in Hauz Khas worth over ₹100 crore in total at throwaway prices from beleaguered promoters. Gautam Thapar, Vijay Mallya and several others, who were unable to meet the debt obligations to Yes Bank, sold their prime properties to the Kapoor family for a song. Apart from this, the ED has identified seven properties in Mumbai and four properties abroad, including two luxury hotels in New York and London worth millions of pounds, that were bought by the Kapoors.

In 2015, global financial services giant UBS reported that Yes Bank had the highest share of loans, backed by unlisted shares and current assets. It downgraded the target price of the Yes Bank stock from ₹1,000 to ₹720 but the Yes Bank management, instead of taking heed of the warnings, claimed that the UBS report had exaggerated the exposure of the bank to stressed companies. Nonetheless, the stock tanked by 200 points to touch ₹812, and both analysts and the RBI were alerted that all was not well with Yes Bank.

It is not that RBI was not aware of what was happening at Yes Bank. The AQR started in late 2015 by RBI threw up adequate pointers. RBI reported a large divergence of NPA worth ₹4,176 crore in 2015–16 and ₹6,355 crores in 2016–17. The divergence observed by RBI at Yes Bank should have set off the alarm bells. Had RBI insisted on close scrutiny of Yes Bank, the situation could have been controlled with lesser losses.

But RBI did not take action immediately. In fact, Yes Bank's loan book was allowed to grow without check, as the RBI looked for market-driven solutions to stem the tide. Yes Bank also created a quality smog that kept regulators at bay. It developed an integrated comprehensive ERM framework establishing better standards in the industry for identifying, assessing, reporting and monitoring risks, resulting in its IS 31000 certification by the British Standard Institution. As a matter of fact, Yes Bank was able to camouflage the truth by adopting a new way to present its balance sheet. In the year 2017–18, RBI strangely found no divergence in its balance sheet on provisioning and asset classification. The news sent Yes Bank shares soaring by 30 per cent in February 2018, from a low of ₹169 to a high of ₹218 in a single day.

The RBI's monitoring of banks still remains faulty, with great emphasis on tick box checking. They do not have adequate manpower and skill sets and still do not do in-depth analysis, and hence failed to see how Yes Bank had managed to camouflage its NPAs. The auditors of Yes Bank and the rating agencies failed to report non-compliance and structured anomalies in the balance sheet. Rana Kapoor took full opportunity of the auditor lapses and the RBI failure and in the years 2017–18 and 2018–19, the bank's loan book grew by 35 per cent annually. This, when most banks were showing less than 10 per cent credit offtake following demonetization. Rana Kapoor even proposed an out-of-court settlement with Madhu Kapur to ensure that he continued as the CEO of the bank without dispute.

It was only in August 2018 that the RBI detected that Yes Bank was not divulging a true picture of the quality of its assets. But instead of dismissing Rana Kapoor summarily, it asked the promotor-CEO to quit by 31 January 2019 and replaced him with Ravneet Gill, who took over as managing director and CEO subsequently. In September 2018, IL&FS defaulted, shifting the focus from the stressed out banking sector to the deeply troubled NBFC segment.

But the condition of Yes Bank kept on deteriorating. In May 2019, RBI appointed former Deputy Governor R.S. Gandhi as additional director in the Yes Bank board.

Luring Rana Kapoor Back to India

Rana Kapoor, after having stripped Yes Bank bare, was planning to migrate to the UK with his family. In November 2019, his holding company Yes Capital (India) Pvt Ltd sold 2.04 crore shares of Yes Bank, worth ₹142.75 crore, divesting his entire portfolio. Even as he left for the UK along with his family, he still wanted to stall the revival of Yes Bank under the new management. Almost three times after he quit the board in 2019, the new management of Yes Bank engaged investors who entered into negotiations but quit at the last moment. That was when the government suspected that there was some foul play and that Rana Kapoor was behind the sabotaging of the revival deal. Sensing that the government was ready to pump in capital for reviving the bank, Rana Kapoor sent feelers to the RBI that he was ready to bring in new investors and come back and take charge of the bank. The RBI decided to play on and responded positively to his feelers, and as a result Kapoor returned to India for negotiations.

However, as soon as he and his family returned to India, investigative agencies mounted surveillance on him to ensure that he did not leave the country. Besides, investigations into his kickbacks and money-laundering activities were speeded up so that he could be arrested and detained. A day after Yes Bank was placed under moratorium. Kapoor was arrested for graft and money laundering. At the time of his arrest in March 2020, Rana Kapoor was trying to sell off three of his properties in plush South Delhi colonies for ₹1,000 crore. His daughter Roshni Kapoor was stopped from boarding a London-bound flight next morning, as a LOC had been served at all airports for the entire Kapoor family, including the daughters and son-in-law. So for once, the government and the investigative agencies were smart enough to lure back and trap the criminal after the bird had flown the coop.

The Yes Bank story is not a tale of a badly managed bank with badly run operations. It is the story of a corrupt promoter making shady deals with some of the bank's customers who had stressed accounts, and taking kickbacks from them while giving further advances. Everybody knew that the bank needed fresh capital from new investors to continue its journey. But nobody imagined that the effort was being sabotaged by the promoter, who had drawn out his equity, defrauded the bank and was still trying to wrest control of it. I spoke to the country head, risk at Yes Bank Ltd in November 2019 (Chapter 12) and he had no inkling that the bank would find no investor and be put on moratorium just four months later. Nor did a senior officer of the RBI, who was often in touch with the officials of the banking division in the ministry.

To the government's credit, they were able to nab Rana Kapoor and his family before they fled the country. They were also able to ward off a panic-fuelled meltdown. When a few large depositors started pulling out money from Yes Bank, they placed it under moratorium. Further, the government was able to mount a quick rescue operation of Yes Bank where it got SBI and a clutch of private banks to invest ₹11,000 crore within a fortnight and restart its banking operations without restrictions. The stock, bought at par, makes Yes Bank a low-priced acquisition for the banking majors. The bond holders who were offered a higher premium to invest in the high-risk bank lost out, but it was a gamble that high-priced bond holders are always ready to take. Now, after having run the bank for a short period and bringing it out of the woods, the banking majors, led by SBI, can always sell it off to any foreign investor at a premium. So, though one can criticize the slow tightening of the noose by RBI, which allowed Rana Kapoor to expand the loan book and defraud the bank for nearly three years, we must appreciate the fleet-footedness of the government in reviving the bank and the ED in trapping and arresting Rana Kapoor

SECTION 3

THE SOLUTION

EIGHT

BANKRUPTCY LAWS: A SEMINAL REFORM

Over the last four decades, more than a dozen nations have seen their economies crumble due to crony capitalism. Asian markets first saw the influx of crony capitalists during the time of Ferdinand and Imelda Marcos of the Philippines, in the 1980s. In 1997, Thailand, South Korea and Indonesia saw crony capitalism fuel an acute debt crisis. It led to a $40 billion IMF bailout to stabilize the currency volatility, but also pulled half a dozen ASEAN nations into a financial tailspin that came to be known as the Asian financial crisis. Since then, Russia, Greece, Italy, Spain, Argentina, Brazil and Cyprus have periodically suffered from acute debt crisis, largely due to overborrowed businesses, financial frauds and fiscal indiscipline. The much-delayed but determined clean-up of India's bad debt pile-up could just about save India the blushes, but only if it continues uninterrupted for at least a decade.

India has not been immune to this nexus of crony capitalists with politicians and bureaucrats, though its effects have not yet created an acute financial crisis. In my book *Neta, Babu and Subsidy,* I have shared the misappropriation details of several large scams that happened post 2007 in the steel industry, coal sector, oil sector and fertilizer import sector—all these scams were products of crony capitalism. However, the scams did not stop and kept happening post 2015, after the banking reforms were taken up in right earnest by the government. Despite trying, the government and the regulators lacked the skill set to stop these frauds from happening.

Raghuram Rajan's Note to the Parliament on Bad Loans

In 2015, a year after the NDA was voted to power, the then RBI Governor Raghuram Rajan, in a 17-page note to the Parliament Estimates Committee, explained: 'A larger number of bad loans originated in the period 2006-2008, when economic growth was strong, and previous infrastructure projects such as power plants had been completed on time and within budget. It is at such times that banks make mistakes.' The RBI governor explained that the policy of evergreening of loans that refinanced loss-making businesses was the reason of rising NPAs:

> It was in everyone's interest to extend the loan by making additional loans, to enable the promoter to pay interest and pretend it was performing. The promoter had no need to bring in equity, the banker did not have to restructure and recognise losses or declare the loan NPA and spoil his profitability, the government had no need to infuse capital. In reality though, because the loan was actually non-performing, bank profitability was illusory, and the size of losses on its balance sheet were ballooning because no interest was actually coming in.

Raghuram Rajan had been unable to convince the UPA government and the prime minister, Manmohan Singh, that the banks should be forced to declare their stressed assets or NPAs. Banks, during the UPA era, were not following uniform procedures. A loan that was non-performing in one bank was treated as performing in another. Promoters kept shifting their loans and availing more restructuring capital from the banks they moved to. Though Rajan believed that bank loans could not be perennially restructured under what was known as the 'evergreening' policy in banking circles, he was unable to stop the practice despite being at the helm of the RBI.

After the NDA came to power, Rajan was finally able to impress upon the banks as well as the Modi government that the problem of non-performing loans should not be brushed under the carpet. Before his term ended, he was able to issue the notification that would force banks to declare their stressed assets. A team of supervisors was formed by the RBI that ensured that each bank followed the same norms. This team also ensured that the AQR was completed in October 2015 and subsequently shared with all banks, and that it was fair and conducted without favour. The government was kept informed and consulted at every step, after the initial inspections were done. The NPAs came out into the open after the RBI enforced these inspections for the detection of stressed assets regularly from October 2015. The banks were left with no option but to cleanse their books of accounts and implement the decision of the RBI.

This was not the first time that a debt clean-up was being attempted in India.

The Debts Recovery Tribunal (DRT) for overborrowed companies was first framed in 1993 by the Narasimha Rao government. This was supplemented by the SARFAESI Act, which permitted securitization and reconstruction of financial assets in 2002. However, the laws remained largely on paper, with neither the banks, nor the regulator, nor the government seriously pursuing the resolution of stressed assets. So, the DRT became dysfunctional. Instead of resolution, the stressed assets were refinanced repeatedly after 2006, increasing the risk for the PSBs, which were encouraged to lend the money to highly leveraged businesses.

Crony capitalists, forming a nexus with corrupt bankers, bureaucrats and politicians, defrauded PSBs of billions of rupees between 2007 and 2016. The loot continued to grow even after a new government took charge, as nobody had a clue about who was gaming the system and how to stop it. The government's piecemeal approach to reforms in the big banks, leaving the NBFC sector and the politically influenced cooperative banks untouched, further exaggerated the problems.

Insolvency and Bankruptcy Code

If we keep in mind the severe infrastructure constraints in the countrywide legal system, the government's top-down approach to the banking sector reforms could be justified, says a senior legal practitioner. Cutting down losses and pilferage in large banks was the obvious first step to take. That meant speedy resolution of stressed assets. In other words, businesses that had failed to repay debt had to be declared bankrupt and their assets sold to new owners. The starting point of banking reforms was the stopping of evergreening of bad loans and the identification of stressed assets that had been unable to pay interest or repay the principal over a certain time period.

After identification, it was important to resolve or sell off the stressed assets. However, even after 70 years of independence, India had no law to deal with bankruptcy. In May 2016, the IBC was framed and passed in both houses of Parliament in quick time. It was easily the biggest reform since the 1991 economic liberalization. A well-drafted, comprehensive and waterproof act, it emphasized on the 'speed of resolution', keeping in mind the inordinate delays in Indian courts for legal redressal. The law ministry, under Mr Ravishankar Prasad, deserves kudos for not only designing the new law but creating an elaborate legal framework for redressal in quick time. The IBC Act consolidated several existing laws to create a framework for time-bound and comprehensive resolution, and provided a four-tier infrastructure to facilitate it. The first was the identification and resolution of financial distress of all companies, limited liability entities, individual proprietorship and partnership firms. Once banks identified the potential stressed assets, they had to submit them for verification and registration of cases. After the regulator nod, the cases went to the bankruptcy court. Secondly, it led to the setting up of the NCLT to act as the Adjudicating Authority for companies, while individuals and firms were to be dealt with by the DRTs under the DRT Act. These benches now deal independently with the cases related to insolvency, liquidation and the bankruptcy process along with their own appellate bodies, namely NCLAT and DRAT.

The third major initiative was to develop the professional expertise that would be needed for arguing and handling the bankruptcy cases. While thousands of professionals would handle the commercial aspects of the insolvency resolution process, the 'insolvency professional agencies' would develop professional standards and codes of ethics and be the first-level regulators for insolvency professional members, leading to the development of a competitive industry for such professionals. The information utilities would collect, collate, authenticate and disseminate financial information to be used in insolvency, liquidation and bankruptcy proceedings.

The fourth major process was the creation of an Insolvency and Bankruptcy Board of India (IBBI) to exercise regulatory oversight over the insolvency professionals, agencies and information utilities.

Hence, the IBC was not only a new legislation or reform, but an entirely new and comprehensive legal framework that was aimed at early corporate debt resolution and value maximization of the assets of the debtor.

It involved setting up of several special tribunals with professional expertise across the country, finding the manpower which not only included judges but the entire support staff to adequately empower it, and also create a seamless mechanism that would encourage the debtors and creditors to settle their disputes within the framework. Importantly, the IBC provided a time-bound resolution period for the tribunals to settle disputes. The Code clearly states that when a firm defaults on its debt, control shifts from the shareholders/promoters to a Committee of Creditors (CoC), who have 180 days in which to evaluate proposals from various players about resuscitating the company or taking it into liquidation. Even in exceptional cases, where more time is needed, the IBC mandates that an insolvent asset must be resolved in 270 days. But creating the infrastructure for such an ambitious and multilayered legal framework has been daunting.

Creating the NCLT Infrastructure

In June 2016, the NDA government started setting up the NCLT and Appellate Tribunals under the Companies Act, 2013, across the country. It not only created a new infrastructure for resolution of new cases, but ensured that no other criminal court would handle the existing debt resolution cases, which would have to be compulsorily transferred to the NCLTs.

Twenty-four benches were initially planned, which would have a judicial authority (no less than a retired high court judge) and a technical member besides clerks, paralegals, security and administrative staff, stenographers, peons, etc. needed for the functioning of a full-fledged court, along with competent professionals and law officers adept with the provisions of company law. The NCLT judges' roster, as of December 2018, showed that 27 members have been sharing the workload, against the target of 60 judicial and technical members. On 4 July 2019, another lot of 27 new judges took oath to sit on NCLT benches. The government confirmed at the press conference following the oath-taking ceremony that the selection of 60 judicial and technical members had been completed and the final security verification of the remaining members was in process before the final announcement.

The tribunal has benches in over a dozen cities, with more in Indore and Amravathi in the process of being set up. Currently, six benches are operative in New Delhi, five in Mumbai, three in Hyderabad, two each in Kolkata, Chennai and Ahmedabad, and one bench each in Bengaluru, Jaipur, Kochi, Gauhati, Cuttack and Chandigarh.

The NCLT has admitted a total of 2,173 cases till June 2019, as per a filed statement made by Anurag Thakur, MOS, in the Rajya Sabha in December. Out of 2,173 admitted cases, 1,274 cases are ongoing under different stages of the resolution process, 129 cases have resulted in resolution, and 491 cases have been approved for commencement of liquidation process, while 279 cases have been closed.

However, the waiting list of cases that has yet to be admitted in the NCLT courts is 10,860, as of September 2019. So, despite setting up such massive infrastructure rapidly, a much bigger infrastructure will be needed to make the bankruptcy law attend to all cases.

According to the World Bank data, before IBC, the time taken to resolve stressed loans was 4.3 years and the recovery rate was 26 per cent for financial creditors. Two years into IBC, the corporate insolvency resolution process (CIRP) led to 48 per cent recovery, which takes about one to one-and-a-half years through the IBC, one-third of the time taken previously. According to the IBBI, 586 insolvency cases have been closed by December 2018. That makes a resolution rate of over 40 per cent, which is remarkable, considering that the law has been in place for just three years.

Even in the US, the bankruptcy code introduced in the late 1970s had taken a decade to stabilize, while in the UK the stabilization period was five years.

The Challenges for IBC are Multiple

The IBC incorporates wisdom from previous failures, but is still not foolproof. P. Sreejith, managing partner at Indialaw LLP, says this is because the 'delays in judgement, admission of cases and interruptions in the whole process, besides the gaps in infrastructure, have compromised the IBC mechanism.' The law is still in the early stages and the judgements and jurisdictions are still being tested and tried. Every judicial member and bench will proceed at their own pace and according to their own judgement initially, despite the time limits stipulated in the provisions of the law. This is the early stage of IBC implementation and things will take time to settle down, before the processes are cast in stone.

Apart from procedural issues, there are infrastructure issues, too, that are different for each bench. The Kolkata bench of the NCLT has highly stretched infrastructure, with the judges having to juggle with duties of other centres like Cuttack and Guwahati. Besides, there were more adjournments in the cases. 'In order to create a balance between both, the speedy disposal and the delivery of justice so that companies are not liquidated merely due to the expiry of the time frame, we exclude the unutilized period for enabling the CoC to approve a resolution plan', says K.R. Jinan, judicial member of the Kolkata NCLT.

As per the law, all resolutions at the NCLT can be challenged at the Appellate Tribunals or higher courts. Till disposal is done of those cases, the stressed asset cannot be sold to new buyers. Many of the cases that were disposed of by the NCLT in the stipulated time frame have gone through protracted litigation in the Appellate Tribunal or the higher courts. This is the due process of law and cannot be bypassed. In a few years, there will be a library of Supreme Court judgments on IBC cases to ensure faster resolution in future cases. The IBC also bars the promoters of a defaulting company from participting in a bidding process, but keeping them out of divisive litigation has been daunting.

Slowing Down of the IBC Resolution Process

To ensure that global majors show interest in India's bankruptcy sales, the government focused on selling the assets of the 12 biggest defaulters with an outstanding of around ₹2 trillion ($30 billion) first. The banks took these 12 companies to NCLT courts first and got quick success initially, when Bhushan Steel, the company with the largest outstanding debt of ₹44,478 crore, was snapped up quickly by Tata Steel.

The initial euphoria of quick deals was, however, lost when

Essar Steel, with outstandings of ₹37,284 crore (₹372.84 billion), managed to delay its resolution process through protracted litigation to over 600 days, as against the 270-days norm specified in the IBC Act. Several other cases dragged on due to various reasons, as a result of which the early gains made in quick disposal of stressed assets started fading. Lanco Infra with an outstanding of ₹44,364 crore (₹443.64 billion), BPSL with an outstanding of ₹37,284 crore (₹372.84 billion) and Amtek Auto with dues of ₹14,074 crore (₹140.74 billion) were the other big borrowers for whom no recovery was made despite entering their cases in NCLT courts three years ago. Data from the IBBI showed that three years after the IBC came into effect, as much as 34 per cent of the 1,484 cases admitted to the NCLT had exceeded the maximum stipulated resolution period of 270 days, as against 26 per cent a year ago. This meant that banks had been unable to encash a third of the bad loans within the period laid down by the IBC. The legal battle being fought today by the bankers and the defaulters in Indian courts is of epic proportions.

It is not easy to change laws for the better in India, and what is even more difficult is to implement new laws. There are vested interests, political opponents and also genuine cases of wrongly penalized individuals seeking redressal. The courts are not only packed with IBC resolution cases, but also with litigation that stops or slows down the IBC process. The Essar litigation went on for over two years. On 15 November 2019, the Supreme Court allowed ArcelorMittal to pay creditors $5.8 billion and acquire Essar Steel India Ltd. A three-judge bench, headed by Justice Rohinton F. Nariman, scrapped a bankruptcy appellate tribunal order that had given secured and unsecured lenders equal right over the sale proceeds and held up the right of resolution of stressed assets by the bankers. It possibly ended a lengthy litigation process after the promoters of Essar Steel had started to resist a takeover bid. It had stretched to nearly three years as against the 270-days norm stipulated by the apex court.

But reforms in India are not easy. In one such landmark

judgement in April 2019, the Supreme Court reversed the RBI circular dated 12 February 2018 that gave defaulting companies 180 days to agree to a debt resolution plan or be taken to the bankruptcy court to recover a debt of ₹2,000 crore or above. This would slow down the resolution process. The Supreme Court order affected the quick resolution of bad loans worth ₹2 trillion in the power, telecom, sugar and infrastructure sectors. The court's decision restored the discretion of banks on debt resolution, making it extremely difficult for the RBI to force banks to liquidate stressed assets speedily. On the ground, it whittled down the authority of the bank regulator to clear up the NPA mess quickly. The government needs to address this issue and bring in amendments to the law to empower the regulator to direct the banks.

Senior advocate Abhishek Manu Singhvi (a Congress party veteran), who opposed the circular on behalf of the stressed power sector, said that the verdict would possibly have a knock-on effect on the resolution process. 'All action taken up to now, either by banks or creditors, under the circular and not been consummated will stand unravelled. Individual cases pending under IBC, so long as they were entirely under the circular would be withdrawn.' The ruling will, in all probability, be challenged by the RBI, but will provide a lease of life to defaulters to temporarily escape the resolution process and increase the time for resolution.

Proactive Banks Can Mitigate Delaying Tactics

Of the top 12 cases sent to NCLT initially by the banks, only five were resolved within the specified time frame. Some others, like Essar Steel, were repeatedly stalled. Also, the promoters tried a back-door entry to buy the stressed assets, though officially they were barred and could not themselves bid for companies they had run to the ground. Others were trying to escape the legal and prosecution dragnets and ensure that they held up the formal transfers till the bidders for the stressed assets lost interest due to long-winded court battles. Then there were others, like the Kolkata-based Visa Steel, who challenged the right of the banks to take them to the bankruptcy courts, as the amount due was below ₹5,000 crore. In case of Reliance ADA and Essel Group, restrictive agreements had been signed by the borrowers with some lenders, which barred them from selling pledged share in the market, because it would adversely affect the market price.

In October 2019, the PSBs proactively triggered a counter-measure by pushing through the second option they had in the IBC to dispose of bad loans. The waiting period for cash recovery was getting longer and many of the companies with bad debts were playing for time. So, they offered the bad loans for sale to the Asset Reconstruction Companies (ARCs) that buy assets globally at distress values. These companies step in when a stressed asset does not find a buyer willing to revive the unit. The asset is sold at junk value to the ARCs, who have deep pockets. 'So, if banks don't find a regular buyer, they put up the stressed assets for junk sale. Banks are interested in resolution and recovery through NCLT (National Company Law Tribunal), OTS (one-time settlement) or sale to ARCs', said a PSB CEO. 'In some cases, where resolution is delayed for a long time, banks will be opting for sale to ARCs.'

There are over a dozen ARCs in the country, and many of them have been there for a decade. Yet, they are very small in size with insignificant capital employed, amounting to ₹5,757 crore and assets under management of about ₹50,000 crore. None of the Indian ARCs have tie-ups to bring in large doses of foreign capital for acquisition of the stressed assets. With NPAs of over ₹8 trillion due to go under the hammer, the capability of the Indian ARCs to manage these assets is doubtful. India needs global majors with experience and liquidity to own, hold and resell the stressed assets it hopes to put up for sale in the next decade.

The RBI amended the Security Receipt (SR) guidelines in 2018 to ensure that banks could participate in the sale of assets. Whenever a distress sale of a stressed asset takes place, the

ARCs can buy all or part of the stressed assets in cash through security receipts, and the seller banks can buy the remaining part with deferred payments.

From financial year 2019, this guideline will apply even where ARCs hold 10 per cent SRs. This is going to bring more credibility to the SRs and help improve the NAV. This modification will help the smaller Indian ARCs to participate in buying off the stressed assets without investing in the whole of it. At the same time, the overseas distress funds have started showing interest in India, largely due to the sizeable hard assets that could be on sale. The first list of a dozen companies includes many such properties where overseas distress asset buyers—who are long-term players with deep pockets—could pick up bargains.

It is not that global majors are not eyeing the Indian market for stressed assets. Overseas investors including KKR & Co, Blackstone Group LP, Aion Capital, Carlyle Asia Partners V and SSG Capital Management Ltd have either set up their own asset reconstruction units in India or tied up with others. Cerberus Capital, Silverpoint, Varde, Centre Bridge, Davidson Kempner Capital Management and Bain Capital have also started exploring opportunities. Looking at the new and enthusiastic overseas interest from distress funds, the banks have put sticky deals up for sale.

This proactive approach of putting out assets for distress sales was a necessary step to ensure that the process of disinvestment of stressed assets was not derailed by litigation. The move will be contested in the courts and there will be attempts to link the move to the ultra vires RBI circular of 12 February 2018, struck down by the Supreme Court that directed the banks to take action with their own judgement and not as per RBI directives. But these see-saw battles will have to be fought in the courtrooms if the cobwebs of India's deeply fractured banking system are to be cleaned. Rather, this is a unique opportunity for 'taming of the shrew' and the banks should go all guns blazing to clean up their balance sheets and punish the crony capitalists and fraudsters who have compromised the system.

In all, 11 private and state-run banks have put NPAs of ₹40,000 crore up for distress sale. Bank of Baroda has offered assets worth ₹11,000 crore, IDBI Bank is looking to sell ₹9,756 crore of assets, and Andhra Bank, ₹4,887 crore. The banks claim they have every right to put up these assets for distress sale. The IBC mandates that an insolvent asset must be resolved in 270 days. If an insolvent asset does not find resolution through a buyer within that period or if the CoC, the decision-making body for disposal of these assets is not satisfied with the bids, the asset can be liquidated at distress value or the minimum value assessed by the resolution professional managing the asset.

But, though the law permits such a fire sale, selling these sizable assets will not be easy due to the small sizes and operations of domestic ARCs. Secondly, there will be attempts by some of the promoters to buy out their own properties at the minimum value assessed through 'benami' overseas shell companies operating from tax havens. This needs to be stopped and the ED must initiate cases against such promoters and nip such nefarious activities in the bud. 'It is an unique opportunity to clean up the Indian banking system and proactively decimate those who have been gaming the system for decades,' says a banker, under condition of anonymity, who helped us develop this case study.

IBC's Agony: The Promoters Who Will Not Let Go

India's banking system, particularly the PSBs, have long been abused by unusually aggressive borrowers who have exploited the vulnerability of lenders. Lenders have always been vulnerable due to the absence of laws that penalize defaulting borrowers or push them into bankruptcy. Businessmen in India know that if you are a small borrower your bank can harass you, but if you are a big borrower you can harass the bank. Defaulters like Vijay Mallya and Nirav Modi have cocked a snook at Indian banks after they fled the country, and are reported to have repeatedly and publicly displayed wealth and arrogance. They have been found living opulent and luxurious lives in Britain and engaging some of the best lawyers to fight extradition. Though the banks have legally proceeded against them, it is difficult to extradite them from Britain, which has been known to traditionally shelter fugitive billionaires from around the world. The fugitives, in turn, invest their ill-gotten wealth in the pricey London properties and park the money in British tax havens.

There are dozens of others who will have to be arrested and penalized for money-laundering and frauds, apart from debt default. The Wadhawans of HDIL and DHFL, the Singh brothers of Ranbaxy and Religare, the Jiwrajkas of Alok Industries, the Singhals of BPSL, the Ruias of Essar Steel and Essar Power and many others have systematically gamed the banking system. They have not only defaulted in repayment repeatedly, they have continued to maintain opulent lifestyles and have reportedly siphoned off loan funds through benami companies to tax havens outside India. The banks of India have been compromised by crony capitalists, corrupt bank officials, politicians and bureaucrats for decades.

The clean-up needed is massive and the process is extremely tedious and time-consuming. To take the process to its logical conclusion, punishment of offenders is needed. The Vijay Mallyas and the Nirav Modis need to be brought back to India quickly and the Wadhawans and the Singhs need to be prosecuted and tried speedily for the voter to believe that the government means business in cleaning up the banking system. Action needs to be taken against bank bosses, bureaucrats and politicians who helped crony capitalists game the system.

Detecting Money Laundering is Daunting

The art of building businesses with borrowed funds and offshore shell companies had been perfected by the Ruia brothers in the 1970s and the 1980s. At the heart of Essar's operations is the Essar Global Fund, which sources investment for the Essar Group companies through its offices in the tax havens of the

Cayman Islands and Mauritius. This is done through its fund manager, Essar Capital.

As per records obtained from the ICIJ investigation in the Paradise Papers case, Virgo Trust of the Sashi Ruia group and Triton Trust of the Ravi Ruia group, based in the Cayman Islands, were managed by Ishwari Prasad Khaitan, the promoter of Loop Telecom. Loop Telecom and its promoters, Kiran Khaitan and her husband I.P. Khaitan, were early entrants in the telecom industry. They had purchased India's first major mobile network operator, BPL Mobile, in 2005 for ₹700 crore, but were charged by CBI for violation of foreign exchange laws for laundering a sum of ₹384 crore in the 2G telecom spectrum case. Essar Tele Holding, Khaitan's brother-in-law Ravi Ruia and son Anshuman Ruia were co-accuseds in the case.

This laundering was amongst the numerous cases exposed by ICIJ following a leak in the law firm Appleby's database. Records from Appleby, one of the two firms from where the leaked data originated in the Paradise Papers case, show that I.P. Khaitan managed two offshore family trusts for his brothers-in-law Sashi and Ravi Ruia of the Essar Group from 2006 to 2011. According to *The Indian Express*, four Cayman Islands companies owned by the Khaitans, which shared the same address, acted as the enforcers and protectors of the two Ruia trusts—Grand Escalada Investments Ltd and Astra Star Investments Ltd for The Virgo Trust, and Grand Richmond Investments Ltd and Grand Pinnacle Investments Ltd for The Triton Trust. Subsequently, the Ruia trust investments were facilitated by two other trusts managed by Khaitan from the British Virgin Islands, namely, Global Trade and Amber Trade.

According to ICIJ investigations, Appleby operated across 19 tax havens and helped clients open accounts in the countries of their choice without having to visit that tax haven.

The Spike in Borrowings that Led to Essar's Debt Default

One of the companies that took full advantage of the debt restructuring policy of the UPA era was the Essar Group. Its debt was high but not astronomical before 2006–07. Essar's borrowings grew rapidly post 2008–09, with over 50 per cent of its borrowings financed by overseas branches of Indian banks in foreign currency. Initially, the rise in borrowings was fairly stable at less than 5 per cent during 2006–08, amounting to ₹27,676.5 crore. They even sold their towers business to ATS in 2007 to focus on their telecom business. But soon banks left the cautious approach of the Rao–Vajpayee decade and began lending aggressively and even chasing industries with baskets of loans. This was backed by the policy of pushing a credit-fuelled growth and evergreening of bad loans during the UPA II rule. It is important to open investigations into loans granted to Essar and other big borrowers during this five-year period to see how the banks where compromised. It is important to fix accountability of crony capitalists along with bankers, regulators, bureaucrats and politicians.

There was a massive 55 per cent rise of borrowings of the Essar Group in the year 2009–10, to ₹43,008.4 crore, and another 42 per cent jump in the year 2010–11, to ₹60,969.9 crore, following the easy money policy of UPA II, which led to large-scale irregularities. Investigations were initiated to trace round-tripping* of debt funds as equity investments in the telecom business, as Essar partnered Swiss PTT and Hutchison initially and Vodafone later to buy licences and aggressively expand subscriber bases in several telecom circles. As the telecom business was low margin, both its partners, Swiss PTT in 2005 and later Hutchison in 2007, quit. Meanwhile, Essar pumped in

*Round-tripping is an operation wherein money gets circulated amongst a group of companies, each siphoning off a part of the money that helps hide the source of funds and its origin and end use.

credit-fuelled finance to grow the business. In 2011, it realized the futility of growing as a telecom player and sold its telecom stakes to Vodafone for $5.5 billion. Even as it exited telecom, it kept on borrowing hugely to push a $20 billion expansion into oil and gas, steel, power projects and ports. All those expansions created more losses.

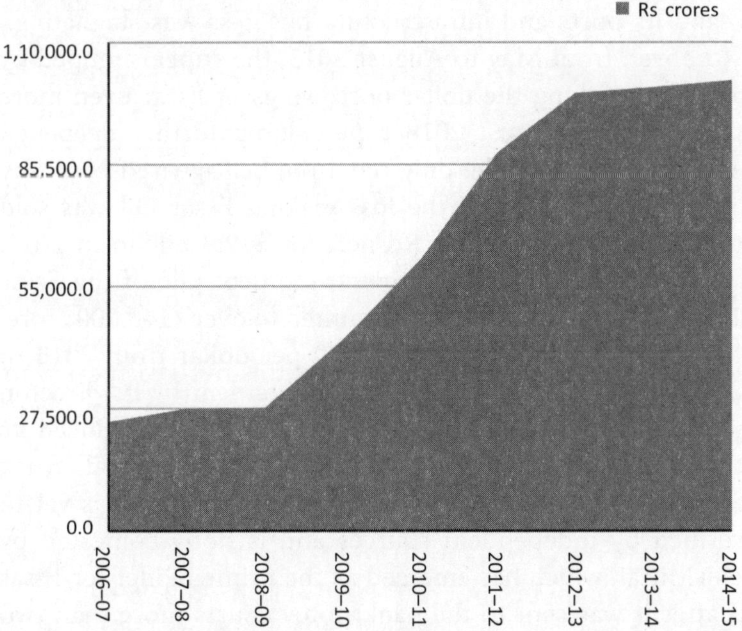

Figure 8.1: Essar Global Debt Spiral
Source: Essar Global and Credit Suisse

Loan funds kept spiralling by a whopping 40 per cent, to ₹85,114.8 crore in 2011–12 and further to ₹98,644.8 crore in the year ending March 2013 (Fig. 8.1). The Credit Suisse 'House of Debt' reports on Asia Pacific/India from August 2013 and October 2015 show that the Essar Group was one of the Indian corporate houses that had become operationally unviable due to such a highly leveraged business strategy. The overall borrowings had risen to nearly a trillion rupees, while the losses had mounted to a massive ₹34, 676 crore (₹346.76 billion) by 2013. Between 2008 and 2013, Essar Group's debt had grown fourfold and it had become a struggling loss-making behemoth. Essar Oil was bleeding, its power and steel business was making heavy losses, its projects division was lacking the needed cash flow, and its ports and infrastructure business was stagnating.

Moreover, from May to August 2013, the rupee slumped by 25 per cent, making the dollar borrowings of Essar even more unattractive; the August 2018 rupee slump further deepened the company's losses. The only relief the beleaguered company got in between was when the loss-making Essar Oil was sold off to the Russian oil major Rosneft for $12.9 billion in 2017. However, despite this disinvestment, the debt pile of the Essar Group has not receded, but has mounted to over ₹140,000 crore, as the rupee moved from ₹45 to ₹70 per dollar from 2013 to 2018. The group, however, in a press statement by its director, Prashant Ruia, in January 2018, claimed that it had reduced its debt by 80 per cent and repaid its Indian lenders, after it struck a deal with VTB Bank of Russia. However, this claim is yet to be verified by independent sources and is hotly contested by ArcelorMittal, which has emerged as the prime bidder for Essar Steel after it was sent to the bankruptcy courts more than two years ago.

Ruias Try to Wrest Back Essar Steel: IBC's Big Fight

The Ruias started making a final effort to stop the sale of Essar Steel after the NCLT and the NCLAT turned down their attempts to buy-back the company, which had gone bankrupt around three years ago. As per IBC, the original promoters of a bankrupt company cannot participate in buying out the entity. So, legally, the Prashant Ruia-led attempts to drive a resolution agreement at Essar Steel was inadmissible. The consortium of lenders had agreed to ArcelorMittal's bid as the potential buyer. They had outbid

Nu Metal, which was alleged to have the support of Prashant Ruia. The ArcelorMittal bid was additionally backed by Japanese heavyweights Nippon Steel and Sumitomo. The Lakshmi Mittal-led ArcelorMittal had offered a ₹42,000 crore (₹420 billion) cash payment to banks as a resolution plan for Essar Steel, along with an offer to invest ₹9,000 crore (₹90 billion) additionally for reviving the ailing unit. It would bring in buyers with adequate cash and technology to revive the unit. Besides, it was an offer that would bring foreign exchange at a time when the rupee was reeling.

The Mittal bid was higher than the Nu Metal bid, backed by VTB Bank of Russia. It was approved by NCLT on 8 March 2019 after two years of protracted court battles. The move was challenged by the Ruia group at the Appellate Tribunal, but the challenge was dismissed by NCLAT in June 2019.

The Ruias, however, did not give up, but furnished a settlement plan of ₹54,389 crore (₹543.89 billion) as a counter offer, which the NCLT rightly rejected. The offer was backed by VTB Bank of Russia but was not considered by the NCLT, and was seen as a time-wasting technique. The Ruias also released press statements saying that they had paid of 80 per cent of their debts worldwide. They then moved the Supreme Court in what was considered another delaying tactic. A group of unsecured creditors filed a plea that their claims be treated at par with secured creditors at the NCLAT. There had been a long delay in the resolution of Essar Steel due to the Ruia group putting up a dogged fight to not let go of the unit. More delay would make the deal more expensive for both the banks and the buyer. The courts need to nip such attempts in the bud so that the IBC Code can be followed in letter and spirit.

'Besides the sabotaging of the deal, a concentrated attempt is being made to hide information about the murky financial deals that were behind this rapid rise and fall of Essar Steel,' claim the Mittals. They have launched a global effort to ensure that the Essar Group is declared bankrupt. This was done after they won a $1.5 billion arbitration award in in the US courts in December 2017, after Essar Steel Minnesota terminated an iron ore pellet supply contract with ArcelorMittal USA LLC (AMUSA). Essar claims that the US company is bankrupt and has assets of less than $2.5 million and is hence unable to pay any compensation to ArcelorMittal. To seek enforcement of the award, ArcelorMittal have now moved the courts in Britain, Mauritius and the Cayman Islands, seeking a 'Garnishee Order Absolute' and a 'Freezing Injunction and Asset Disclosure Award' against Essar Global Fund Ltd ESL. A Garnishee order is an order that would direct a third-party creditor that owes money to the debtor, Essar Steel Ltd ESL, to pay its dues to ArcelorMittal instead. The Cayman island court has, however, taken cognizance of another subordination agreement that EGFL and ESL had inked with VTB Bank, and refused the Garnishee order and the worldwide freezing order on Essar Steel.

Bankers' Feedback: Need to Proactively Build IBC

Meanwhile, Essar Steel's losses keep rising and even proper auditing of its accounts is not taking place. The Secretarial Audit Report of its auditors, DM & Associates Company Secretaries LLP, dated 4 October 2018 for the annual year 2017–18, clearly states: 'We have not verified the correctness and appropriateness of financial records and books of accounts of the company.' This is an alarming situation for banks, says a banker working with SBI as an internal auditor. It shows that ESL is today drifting and rudderless, possibly moving into much deeper losses without the much-needed audit scrutiny. 'The banks, the regulator RBI and the government need to be vigilant during such ownership transfers. The road to take control of Essar Steel is tough but is a test case of India's IBC laws which are in the stage of infancy,' says the banker who has dealt with Essar's debt for the past four years. Essar Steel, according to him, is a doughty customer.

The November 2019 judgement of the Supreme Court, clearing the sale of Essar Steel to ArcelorMittal, was a respite from long-drawn litigation for the bankers. The delay in resolution could perhaps have been avoided if the NCLAT and the courts had been more vigilant.

They need to rigorously implement the IBC in letter and spirit, so that buyers are not handed a scorched earth property. The deal should be one that gives the right incentive to the lenders to resolve outstandings at a fair price within the stipulated time frame, instead of having to go for distress sale of stressed assets.

Moreover, this is not only about Essar Steel alone. It is about the repayment of debts to Indian banks by the Essar Group as a whole. Essar is a group that has been making heavy losses and has a negative net worth in almost all its operations. The group also has opaque cross holdings and is structured with one company holding large stakes in an other. They have been dangerously leveraged, putting the entire banking system at risk. The case of Essar Power and Essar Steel cross-linking can be seen from the 2018 balance sheet of ESL.

Essar Power is independently talking to lenders to restructure its ₹20,000 crore debt. EPHIL runs a 270 MW power plant at Hazira in Gujarat and supplies power to ESL, which owns 26 per cent of stakes in the unit. Its 1,200 MW Mahan project in MP, which is located at the Singrauli coal pit head, has been fully commissioned and has been the battleground for yet another Mittal–Ruia fight for control. In February 2019, bankers led by ICICI Bank took Essar Power Mahan EPM to court for settlement of dues of around ₹7,500 crore. The Ruias offered to pay ₹3,450 crore as debt settlement while ArcelorMittal initially made an offer of ₹4,800 crore. However, the Mittal bid was later lowered to ₹3,000 crore citing large undeclared liabilities of the power producer. EPM reportedly has failed to sign a long-term power supply agreement or secure a long-term coal supply contract and faces an uncertain future.

Need for Vigilance: Rooting Out Corruption

The Supreme Court ruling, upholding ArcelorMittal's bid for Essar Steel on 15 November 2019, came as a big shot in the arm for creditors who were looking towards fair resolution of stressed assets. The Essar Steel saga began in August 2017. Though it has been much delayed, the court has finally ruled that only the CoC of the banks will now be able to decide how the sale proceeds are distributed among the creditors. This marks the exit of the Ruias, the promoters of Essar Steel, who had made several attempts to derail the process and held up the resolution for nearly three years. The court has added that the NCLT cannot interfere with the commercial decisions taken by the CoC and overruled the NCLAT order that had called for splitting of the proceeds amongst secured and unsecured creditors. Essar Steel owes around ₹49,000 crore to the consortium of banks led by SBI and including ICICI Bank, IDBI Bank and Syndicate Bank.

The Essar Steel resolution was a bell weather test for the success of the IBC.

Another area of concern is the entry of brokers in the resolution process, some of whom are crooks. Like in all other areas in India, the DRT or the NCLT is no longer free of corruption. You can visit the DRT office at Patel Chowk and find the negotiations going on in view of all: Hassled bankers offering to take deep haircuts and newly rich resolution professionals, who get decent commissions on every deal made, haggling fiercely to come to an understanding. The chaos is almost like the scenes in the early days of the Bombay Stock Exchange, before trading went online.

The process is vitiated by vested interests, networks of brokers from the legal fraternity that have deep-rooted connections with key officers of lead banks, NCLT technical members, the NCLAT tribunal judges, and the bureaucracy. They are making deals within deals, and now that the Supreme Court has revoked the power of the RBI to order the bankers to close deals, it will be come a greater free-for-all. Here is an example of what is happening, and the government needs to take note and intervene at the ministry level to ensure malpractices do not happen.

According to a senior bank officer, each bank has created its own offer depending on the deals struck with those with vested interests. The Bank of India has reportedly gone to the extent of accepting a 90 per cent haircut on several assets, and the SBI has been offered a similar haircut in the case of Aircel. Banks may be putting up ₹1,30,000 crore for sale to ARCs and accepting haircuts ranging from 50 per cent to 90 per cent, simply to speed up the resolution process. This process also needs oversight to ward off corruption.

In the next chapter, therefore, we will look at the issue of regulatory oversight to suggest measures that streamline the process and root out corruption. Why are the frauds and NPAs ballooning despite the new laws and the regulatory interventions? Are we doing enough? Is the RBI geared up and skilled adequately to regulate the banking industry? Who should be held accountable for the massive frauds, which keep on surprising both the regulator and the government repeatedly? What should be done to check rising frauds and bring down the NPAs to nominal levels?

NINE

RBI AND THE REGULATORY MECHANISM

The role of the bank regulator is key to the story of India's banking reforms. RBI has many direct and indirect responsibilities and has to meet the expectations of the executive, the judiciary, the media, the markets, the banks as well as its customers. The role of the RBI is much more far-reaching than the Federal Reserve or the Bank of England, as it has to also look at funding India's farm sector and its small industries, as well as wealth redistribution to the poor. A look at the operations of the RBI will tell you that it is actively involved in every social banking measure that the government takes up, besides managing the banks, NBFCs, the urban cooperative banks (UCBs), the rural cooperative banks (RCBs), the foreign exchange reserves, its gold and its currency. Be it the Jan Dhan Yojana or the Kisan Credit Card, the PM Lok Nirman scheme or demonetization, it is the RBI that is at the frontline of execution. So, although we would critique the role of the bank regulator for its failure to stop frauds, in this chapter, we would like the readers to understand and appreciate the vast role that the RBI has to play.

Over the years the RBI has evolved and has taken up various challenges and adapted to new roles for the sake of the nation. RBI did an exemplary job in persuading banks to adopt the AQRs and start identifying the NPAs in late 2015. Over the next two years, RBI inspectors repeatedly pointed out incorrect reporting by banks. The Indian Banks' Association (IBA), a national body for the banking industry, lobbied hard for more time to make such provisions as per RBI guidelines, but the RBI did not extend the deadline and was supported by the government. Both private banks and PSBs were guilty of hiding bad loans. ICICI Bank, Yes Bank, Axis Bank, PNB, UBI, Central Bank—all have been repeatedly pulled up for non-compliance and have been forced to declare the correct amount of stressed assets after divergence was reported by RBI. It was not an easy task for the regulator, as there were court cases, too, by the lobby of defaulters to curtail the reach and powers of RBI, some of which succeeded in pulling back reforms.

Bank Frauds: The Elephant in the Room

Once the stressed assets started getting reported in true earnest, the NPA accounts were identified and the scrutiny of those accounts began. There were too many mismatches in the balance sheets. After the exemplary work of enforcing the identification of stressed assets by both the private and PSBs, the RBI hit a roadblock. The forensic audits of NPA accounts showed numerous cases of fraud and money laundering. The ED and the CBI were initially not prepared to handle it, and neither was the bank regulator. 'There has been a tendency in the pronouncements post revelation of the fraud that RBI supervision team should have caught it,' said RBI Governor Urjit Patel, stating that, 'no bank regulator can catch or prevent all frauds.' But if the regulator cannot do it, who will?

There is an urgent need for reforms not only in the banking sector, but also within the RBI. The institution needs to improve accountability. It needs to expand, retrain its workforce, and create a new route map for banking supervision. It has to get its hands dirty to ensure that frauds and NPAs don't happen. It needs to improve its skill sets. It needs to ensure that all other regulators and rating agencies, like CVC, SEBI, ICRA and CRISIL, work together in unison to make the banking industry go through mandatory checks and balances without too much interference.

Surprisingly, with the advent of technology after liberalization, the RBI took a hands-off approach and reduced both its scrutiny and manpower. In 1997, its headcount stood at 33,084. Twenty years later, as the Indian banking industry grew manyfold, the RBI headcount reduced to less than half at 15,461. The last major recruitment happened only in 2016, when it recruited 660 employees. While reducing workforce may be good for improving efficiency and profitability, it has certainly not been good for the RBI, as the regulator's scrutiny has been less than adequate. This needs to improve.

The three dozen commercial banks in the public and private sector, the 11,000 odd NBFCs, as also the 1,500 UCBs and the 96,000 RCBs need better supervision. With a staff count of around 16,000, it is impossible to inspect and supervise records of 1,10,000 financial institutions of the country except by tick box supervision.

It is not enough to regulate the big commercial banks alone, because they account for the largest deposits and advances. It is also important to regulate the NBFCs, because they receive over 50 per cent of their funding from the commercial banks. It is equally important to regulate the UCBs and the RCBs because though they account for just 10 per cent of the business, they cater to 25 per cent of the population, mostly at the bottom of the pyramid. Also because the credit offtake of rural banks doubled to ₹80,000 crore during the year, as the government pushed the MUDRA loans through the RRBs.

Unfortunately, no one other than the government has ever questioned RBI's method of supervision. The venerated regulator, not surprisingly, lost some of its sheen during the political mudslinging between the left and the right after 2014, but the issue is not political but a question of safe banking.

RBI and Government Relationship Pre-Liberalization

It is not that RBI has not been told to step up its act before. After Independence, the Congress party, under Nehru, was extremely unhappy with the functioning of the banks and the RBI. Nehru and his finance minister wanted more social control over banks. They wanted credit to flow from banks to the industry and the agriculture sector. But neither the banks nor the RBI seemed interested. The hardliners within the Congress and the communist parties wanted the banks to be nationalized. But the nationalization proposal was dropped due to opposition by the Finance Minister Morarji Desai, who pitched for greater social control by a high-powered body called the National Credit Council.

At the same time, however, the government kept pressuring the RBI to instruct the banking sector to start lending to industry and agriculture. It knew that without sufficient bank credit, it would not be possible to meet the Planning Commission's Five-Year Plans and their development agenda.

It was during the rule of Indira Gandhi that 14 large commercial banks were nationalized first, in 1969. The other six banks were nationalized in 1980, after she returned to power post-Emergency. While the politics and economics of bank nationalization have been discussed in detail in Chapter 2, here we look at the changing role of RBI during that period.

The banks lost their autonomy post-nationalization, and the RBI was given directions to increase supervision. With Mrs Gandhi in power, the RBI had little choice. Slowly and steadily, it was coaxed into becoming a key player for implementing government policies towards credit disbursal to priority sectors, and started to take up monitoring of various tasks like interests, reserve ratios and visible deposits of banks. So, apart from the department of banking, the RBI, during Indira Gandhi's rule, started to act like a functionary of the government.

We cannot solely blame the government of the day for pressurizing the banks and the RBI to adhere to its lending policies. If the manifesto of the political party had to be met and the development agenda fulfilled in a poor nation, then the banks would have to provide easy credit and the central bank would have to monitor the same. So, if the politician was to be accountable to the people and had to fulfil her election promises, she would have to find ways to provide easy credit for rural and industrial development. Thus began a continuous monitoring by the banking department and the political masters of the day-to-day activities of nationalized banks through the RBI, especially in the context of providing credit. This happened largely during the 1970s and the 1980s, and Mrs Gandhi's socialist leanings ensured that the farm sector and the small and medium industry sector were the priorities, leaving the large industrial houses out in the cold.

Rejuvenation of RBI and Private Banking

The winds of change started to blow during the Narasimha Rao era. The Narsimham Committee Report on Financial Sector Reforms was tabled in the Parliament in December 1991. It suggested far-reaching reforms, out of which only a few could be taken up due to resistance by bank unions and the Left parties. Among the key recommendations were the reduction in the number of banks and creation of a four-tier banking structure, allowing PSBs to open branches and raise capital independently and permitting the entry of private sector banks and foreign banks. The ICICI Bank was incorporated in January 1994 and the HDFC Bank was incorporated later that year. Following this, SBI raised capital from the stock market in November 1994 and several other PSBs followed suit. Many other reforms took place in bits and pieces over the next decade, pushing the concept of liberalization and privatization to the fore.

Following the Narsimham Committee Report and the bank IPOs, the RBI started pushing the PSBs to ensure better capital adequacy norms* and align themselves to the Basel Accord. Employees were given shares during the public issue. They found

*Capital adequacy ratio prescribes the amount of capital a bank must keep as a safety margin.

that the share price was linked to performance and profits. So, if they performed better collectively, the share price rose and they stood to gain both individually and collectively. Even the unions realized that global winds of change were blowing and share price drove the sentiments and recognition of a bank.

At around this time, the Basel I treaty, which had been inked in Switzerland in the early 1990s and set global standards for bank safety and operational benchmarks, was adopted by SBI and the private sector banks.

RBI Governor C. Rangarajan, in a speech in 1997, stated, 'The argument that government banks do not have to follow prescribed capital adequacy ratios, as (the) public are indifferent to the level of capitalization in a PSB, does not recognise the fact that banks are commercial entities and not departments of government.' Rangarajan and Bimal Jalan, the RBI governors from 1992 to 2003, ushered in several reforms. Once banks grew used to following Basel standards, it became easier to ensure their safety. In April 2019, SBI raised ₹3,105 crore via Basel III-complaint bonds.

But several other challenges were faced by the banks and the RBI in the last decade. Autonomy of institutions is highly desirable in any stable democracy. One must not forget that along with autonomy lies accountability, which we rarely question. Is the institution functioning and discharging its role and responsibility adequately? Is it moving with the times to meet the needs of the people of the nation?

The PSBs today are facing a credibility challenge. Frauds and bad loans are haunting both public sector and private banks. The NPAs have risen beyond unimaginable levels, following reforms initiated after 2015. Several NPAs have been due to deep-rooted frauds. The regulators, including the RBI, have failed to check the frauds and were found wanting in not one but several cases. The RBI, revered as a hallowed institution, faces key questions about its role, credibility and autonomy today due to poor vigilance during the last decade. Whereas autonomy of the central bank is needed, introspection and investigation is also needed to detect the many flaws that hamper fraud detection and make systemic changes in the operation and accountability.

Accountability of the Regulatory Circa?

Two issues of accountability and autonomy are often discussed when questions are raised about the independent functioning of the bank regulator. We have seen previously that right from its inception, the central bank had to be nudged by the government, off and on, to take on additional responsibilities. The RBI has a much bigger and more difficult role to play than most other central banks.

Of late, there have been questions raised about the performance and the efficiency of the RBI. Some issues about its functioning have already been raised by its independent directors during the October 2019 board meeting of the RBI. Though this has been raised in lieu of frauds at the PMC Bank, the PNB, and NBFCs like IL&FS and HDIL, it reflects on the overall functioning of the regulator over the last decade. Let us look at the four cases mentioned by the RBI board members and look at accountability issues for regulators in each case. Also, it is important to note that all these frauds had been going on undetected for a decade. The regulators have to be answerable to the taxpayers. However, it is not the sole responsibility of the central bank to stop frauds as auditors, rating agencies, vigilance officers and bank chiefs are also accountable watchdogs. A short account of the types of frauds, why they happened, why they were not stopped, and the possible chinks in the regulatory system, which still remain undetected, unnamed, unprobed and unpunished, is given below.

The first case is the PMC Bank–HDIL nexus (Chapter 7), where the RBI has clearly put itself in the spot. The timing of the PMC Bank scam, just a month before the Maharashtra elections, helped it become a headline story. From 19 September 2019, there were several large withdrawals from the PMC Bank by a few depositors that amounted to 5 per cent of the total deposits. This alerted the RBI, which put unreasonable curbs on cash withdrawals. As per the RBI circular of 23 September 2019, a PMC Bank account holder could not withdraw more than ₹1,500 within a period of six months.

Had it not been for its timing, the PMC Bank episode may have been relegated to the sidelines like the CKP Cooperative Bank case where the RBI put limits on withdrawals by depositors in May 2014. In the CKP Bank case, 12,000 depositors and 1,30,000 account holders lost the right to withdraw their own money above ₹15,000 following the RBI order under section 35(A). There have been similar withdrawal curbs placed on the Mumbai-based Kapol Cooperative Bank, the Rupee Cooperative Bank, the City Cooperative Bank, the Needs of Life Cooperative Bank, the Kolhapur-based Youth Development Cooperative Bank and Shivam Sahakari Bank.

These curbs have been there for five years despite numerous representations by depositors. Clearly, there were serious lapses by the banks and also the regulators in each case. The reason was not because of intermediate servers installed to create a parallel database or the cooking of accounts books by the cooperative banks; those were mere technicalities.

Regulators Must Develop Skill Sets to Stop Frauds

These frauds happened and went on unchecked because of two reasons. First, cooperative banks are political hot potatoes, with politicians or their lackeys managing the banks. These politicians have ensured a dual regulator policy that keeps the responsibility of the management of the UCBs with the state. So, RBI officials really don't want to deal with them. Second, it is simply not possible to regulate the huge number of UCBs and RCBs that exist today. The RBI and the finance minister need to take a stand on compulsory amalgamation of UCBs to less than 100 within a one-year period, much like Morarji Desai took a stand in case of large commercial banks in the early 1960s.

Unlike in the case of large commercial banks, RBI adopts a tick box check of all cooperative banks. There are 1,542 UCBs and 96,606 RCBs today—far too many for any serious audit. Understandably, there is not any detailed scrutiny, but merely a checklist verification to confirm that all procedures have been complied with. So, when loans given by PMC Bank to 44 companies related to the real estate firm HDIL started turning bad, they were easily replaced by a set of fictitious loans. These fictitious loans were given by the PMC Bank to 21,049 dummy accounts related to the HDIL promoters in seven states.

These dummy accounts transferred some of the money from these new loans to the 44 stressed accounts of the HDIL promoters and siphoned the rest of the money to tax havens abroad. This continued unnoticed for 11 years—from 2008 to 2018. RBI had no clue this was happening because its audit format for UCBs did not have provisions for any detailed scrutiny. It is now reported that the PMC Bank even set up intermediate servers, so that the accounts did not reflect directly in the bank's Core Banking Software that could be checked by RBI. 'It appears, there was a parallel or another data base in PMC Bank that was used to fudge information. It's a complex operation, and difficult to believe that a handful of officials could have pulled it off,' says a RBI official on the condition of anonymity. The detailed investigation report of the PMC Bank—expected in a few months—will reveal the modus operandi of the fraud.

The RBI curbs on PMC Bank were followed with inept handling of the depositors' withdrawal rights by the RBI, which led to six deaths in the first month after the discovery of the scam. The PMC Bank was one of the largest amongst a dozen cooperative banks directly under regulatory supervision by the RBI. Most cooperative banks that operate within a single state are under the supervision of state regulators. The PMC Bank had a presence in seven states, though it was overly reliant on a single client, HDIL, which accounted for over 70 per cent of its loans. State regulatory procedures are even more lax than RBI audit procedures, as a result of which thousands of scams could be lying deep within and totally undiscovered. The government knows this, in all probability, but it is intentionally not opening this Pandora's Box as it would disrupt the existing credit lines. Instead, it is taking a piecemeal approach and handling only those patients who are entering the ICU.

In certain cases like the Bank of Rajasthan (now part of ICICI Bank) or the State Bank of Benaras (now part of Bank of Baroda), they have been merged under section 35 (A) after curbs were placed on them. But these were bigger banks. Before the PMC Bank scam unravelled, several other small cooperative banks had collapsed. In 2001, Ahmedabad-based Madhavpura Mercantile Cooperative Bank went bust, landing over 200 UCBs in trouble, many of which had to be subsequently liquidated. Because the patient list is huge, a piecemeal approach could be a problem and disruptions like Madavpura, PMC or CKP could be taking place off and on. So, the government is nudging voluntary consolidation of UCBs like the commercial bank consolidation that took place in the 1950s and the 1960s (Chapter 1). But the need is for a forced consolidation.

In 2004, there were 1,926 UCBs, and as of September 2019, there are 1,524. As per RBI data, in the three years from 2014 to 2017, it has ensured the merger of 129 UCBs. The remaining just folded up. A bigger problem could be tackling the 96,606 RCBs, of which 95,000 are primary agricultural credit societies. These are also politically loaded institutions that have exploited thousands of rural depositors. Fortunately, the UCBs and the RCBs account for less than 10 per cent of the total deposits or advances and hence, are not a huge banking risk. Unfortunately, they involve nearly a quarter of the population, most of who belong to the poor and lower middle class and hence are a huge social and political risk.

Bankers' Feedback: Ambitious Bankers and Complacent Regulators

RBI is extremely sensitive to criticism, like the banks and the Department of Banking. They are not ready to acknowledge that they are accountable and must acquire appropriate skill sets to stop the frauds. They are not ready to acknowledge that their supervision has been wanting, as a result of which taxpayers have lost billions of rupees. They are not ready to accept that there is a very deep-rooted nexus between the corrupt within the regulatory bodies, the banks, the auditors and the borrowers, which has allowed such massive flight of capital since 2015 while the banking laws are being put in place.

The PNB frauds (Chapter 6) also throw up several unique regulatory questions for the RBI. First and foremost is the lack of scrutiny on the need of a bank 'to grow at any cost'. A former director of PNB, who was with the bank during the period when the Nirav Modi and Mehul Choksi fraud took place, says on condition of anonymity that a scam of such a large proportion was possible only because the bank management at PNB was highly ambitious and careless to the point of recklessness. They encouraged the practice of providing LOUs to the jeweller duo, who were treated like VIPs in the bank. According to this former director, K.R. Kamath, the chairman of PNB from 2009 to 2014, when the fraud grew to mammoth proportions, was obsessed with 'growth at any cost'.

> Kamath loved to play to the gallery, was a great networker and behaved like a superstar, instead of a responsible banker. During Kamath's time, the bank lent recklessly not only to the Modi-Choksi jeweller group but to KFA (₹800 crore), to Essar Group (₹2,500 crore) and BPSL (₹3,850 crore), all of which are today under investigation by the Serious Frauds Investigation Office.

Interestingly, Kamath is not under investigation, though his predecessor, Dr K.C. Chakrabarti, has a lookout notice against him and Usha Ananthasubramanian, who followed him as the bank chief, has been arrested and named in the CBI Chargesheet for failing to implement RBI's circular in the Nirav Modi case. Usha Ananthasubramanian was the managing director and CEO of PNB between 2015 and 2017, and also its executive director from 2011 to 2013 when she reported to Kamath.

Bank managers were reportedly asked to court business groups on quid pro quo terms during the Kamath years at PNB. 'You could find a client who borrowed from the bank ₹100 crore at 7 per cent interest and helped improve the bank's loan book, and have the same client subsidiary deposit ₹100 crore to the bank at 8 per cent interest. Similarly, a depositor who would give ₹200 crore deposit at 8 per cent interest could get ₹400 crore advance for one of his companies at 7 per cent interest from the bank.' The Ahmedabad-based jeweller duo was not the only favoured jeweller group at that time who eventually defaulted. On PNB's books, the bad debts are of Winsome Diamonds of the Jatin Mehta group too, whose outstandings exceed ₹1,600 crore. Mehta and family fled to the Balkan state Montenegro in southeast Europe after duping several PSBs with a gross outstanding of ₹6,500 crore.

Then there is the Sandesara group of Vadodara, which has two outstanding amounts that exceed ₹900 crore. One loan of ₹207 crore was given to Sterling Biotech of the Sandesara group, and another of ₹754 crore to Sterling Global Oil Resources, a Mauritius-based investment company that is possibly a shell company for money laundering. Typical of shell companies, this Port Louis company listed in PNB's books is a single-room enterprise whose directors are not listed in PNB's books—surely, an offence that should call for investigation of the top management of PNB during that time.

The Sandesara brothers, Nitin and Chetan, wanted in the ₹5,000 crore Andhra Bank fraud case by CBI, have reportedly fled the country and relocated to Nigeria. The ED has attached assets worth ₹9,774 crore belonging to them in various money-laundering and bank fraud cases. Then there is the Kudos Chemie group from Chandigarh, the Jas Infrastructure group from Kolkata, besides the high-profile Kingfisher Airlines and Jet Airways, who were unduly favoured by the PNB bosses. 'Everyone knew at the bank what was happening, but the management under Kamath was focused on increasing deposits and advances at any cost,' alleged the former banker. So, was the RBI sleeping?

Only a meticulous and thorough investigation of the business practices and the modus operandi of transactions above ₹100 crore during the Kamath period will show the patterns of collusion between businesses and the bank chief, if any. The reader needs to understand that seeking accountability in India is still considered as witch-hunting, especially in the Government and PSB's and that is why the corrupt and well-networked still stay in the system without being purged on a regular basis. Kamath was not given an extension at PNB by the government, but heads the powerful lobby of bankers, the IBA. Governments may change, but despite accountability issues, nobody will touch some of these powerful bankers despite a questionable track record.

A former banker says,

> As a matter of fact, PNB's rapidly growing loan book made Kamath one of the most high-profile bankers of India. The bank won the SCOPE Trophy for 'Best Managed Bank for the year 2009-10,' won the 'Best Bank Award 2011' from *Business India*, 'Overall Most Productive PSB' from FICCI and IBA, 'Best PSB' from *CNBC TV 18* India, within two years of his arrival. All this when the frauds happened.

We also found from his profile that PNB under Kamath indeed collected a dozen more awards from the IBA, *The Sunday Standard*, Dun and Bradstreet, Ministry of MSME, IDRBT, BANCON 2013, *Business World* PWC, *Economic Times*, *Dainik*

Bhaskar and several others.

While the allegations levelled by the former director are yet to be proven by any investigation, and it is not an offence to be ambitious, it is also true that the maximum frauds that occurred in PNB, happened during the hectic growth phase post 2009, when Kamath was at the helm. Also, Kamath has not been investigated till date. Instead, he was re-elected as the Chairman of IBA in 2013. He holds the influential position of the chairman of the governing board of Institute of Banking Personnel Selection (IBPS) and is heading several other organizations. This makes him a key person in bank appointments, despite a past that brought huge frauds to the bank.

Failure of the Regulators: The Case of IL&FS Silos

The IL&FS fraud of ₹90,000 crore (Chapter 3) is a classic case of regulatory and audit failure. There were multiple layers of regulatory failures that occurred. As per insider reports, the company is uniquely structured to work in opaque silos that are difficult to supervise. This is a case where the RBI or the government should have ordered a total restructuring of the company.

In 2006, C. Sivasankaran, better known as Sterling Siva (of Sterling Computer fame), a street-smart global dealmaker and ambitious telecom entrepreneur, shifted base from Chennai to Delhi. Siva was a close friend of IL&FS founding directors Ravi Parthasarathy and Hari Sankaran, and started getting funded by IL&FS illegally. IL&FS disbursed several loans without due diligence to Sivasankaran's shell companies, which were laundered back as investment for his telecom ventures.

Siva had sold his Tamil Nadu circle telecom licence to Shashi Ruia of Hutchison Essar for ₹1,200 crore in 2005. Sterling Siva was close to the DMK and was looking for an all-India telecom rollout. However, he fell out with DMK's Dayanidhi Maran, who became the telecom minister in UPA I and troubled him endlessly. It is rumoured that Siva managed to develop links with

P. Chidambaram during the Aircel Maxis deal in March 2006, and this finally led to the appointment of the Shivraj Patil Committee on the appropriateness of telecom licences issued during 2004–09 which opined: 'The clarifications sought, (by DOT during the Maran period), besides being vague, were also irrelevant for consideration of application for grant of the universal licence.'

The criminal complaint filed before the additional special judge in Mumbai by SFIO in the IL&FS case has charged 30 respondents including the entire board of IFIN, led by Ravi Parthasarathy, and all the audit firms and their key partners along with telecom entrepreneur C. Sivasankaran. The chargesheet alleges that, 'C. Sivasankaran was given loans without adequate collateral and, when they went bad, [the] senior management connived with him to cause a wrongful loss to the company.'

It is believed that Parthasarthy developed links with the powers that be in the UPA through Siva, and a new journey began to drain out IL&FS funds through special projects, many of which were fictitious. The RBI turned a blind eye to complaints against IL&FS during the UPA rule.

On 6 June 2011, Sivasankaran complained to the CBI that he was forced by the Maran brothers, Dayanidhi and Kalanithi, to sell Aircel to Maxis. He provided CBI with a list of ten witnesses, including overseas bankers, venture capitalists and lawyers, to prove his charges. Subsequently, a case was lodged against Maran, who was eventually replaced by Raja as the telecom minister during UPA II. However, in February 2012, the Supreme Court cancelled all the 122 licences allotted by Raja to Siva's telecom venture STel, which had about 3.6 million subscribers in five circles. The funds lent by IL&FS to Siva's telecom ventures through fictitious entries and shell companies all became a cropper.

The RBI chose to ignore the irregularities at IL&FS. The number of loans given to such fictitious companies is still being investigated; the estimated losses to IL&FS as per unconfirmed sources could exceed ₹5,000 crore. Siva has an English court order to freeze his assets worldwide and has been declared bankrupt in Seychelles, the offshore headquarters of his $3 billion empire. Despite the loans being in the limelight and the clients under the CBI scanner for a decade, the RBI did not launch any investigation into the IL&FS funding of the Sivasankaran group. Governor Urjit Patel rightly said that no regulator has the hindsight to detect frauds. But the truth is that frauds of such large proportions take years to develop and leave many red herrings on the road to track and trace. The regulator needs to be alert and stop the frauds before they balloon and lead to defaults, and before the fugitives escape. In the case of IL&FS and other HFCs, the investigations and arrests only happened after they went bust.

After arresting Parthasarathy and Sankaran, the Mumbai Police arrested Arun Saha and K. Ramachandra, former directors of IL&FS, along with former CEO R.C. Bawa in misappropriation and money-laundering cases. Bawa was involved in several property acquisition cases with money diverted from IL&FS to the Silverglades group and the Ansal group at various points, during his tenure as the managing director of IL&FS Financial Services. It was during his tenure at the top that IFIN lent money fraudulently to real estate companies owned by his wife and daughter. The SFIO also accused the auditors, BSR & Co LLP, Deloitte Haskins & Sells LLP, and others, of helping to conceal information and falsify IL&FS accounts. It cited the modus operandi exposed by the Grant Thornton forensic audit, of repeated round-tripping funds through a host of other companies to pretend repayment and show the accounts as being standard.

The regulatory failures in case of IL&FS happened at five levels, as watchdogs failed to red-flag its fraudulent operations for over a decade. At the primary level, the auditors, who were primarily the associates of the big four audit majors, failed in their duty to raise concerns about the dubious accounting practices and money-laundering activities at IL&FS.

Secondly, the bankers who financed IL&FS projects failed to see that their funds were not put to good use and the RBI failed to detect and monitor the frauds.

Thirdly, the rating agencies, namely CRISIL, CARE, ICRA, India Ratings (a Fitch subsidiary) and Brickwork Ratings, awarded false ratings over the years and failed to inform the investors about the perils in investing in IL&FS.

Fourthly, the market regulator SEBI permitted repeated public issues by IL&FS and its subsidiary companies and did not check their attempts to raise funds from the market despite poor fundamentals.

Fifth and finally, the failure was of the Income Tax department and the ED, which failed to check money laundering to offshore shell companies, on a massive scale, from IL&FS accounts.

It is wrong to assume that such frauds could happen only during the UPA era and everything would be fine now that the banking reforms have started.

We must remember that the IL&FS borrowings grew rapidly from ₹48,671 crore (₹486.71 billion) in 2014 to ₹91,091 crore (₹910.91 billion) in 2018, and the interest payout nearly doubled to ₹7,922 crore (₹79.22 billion) before it finally defaulted. This shows that unless the corrupt and complacent individuals are weeded out from the banks and the regulatory agencies are made more accountable, the frauds in the NBFCs and banking sector will keep on occurring, irrespective of who is in power.

Restructuring of IL&FS a Must in Order to Avoid Future Frauds

The government acted quickly to take over IL&FS, thereby avoiding a cascading effect of loan defaults that could lead to a contagion crisis in the financial markets. A default of ₹90,000 crore (ten times bigger than Kingfisher Airlines) would have devastated the market. It superseded the board of directors and appointed a new six-member board, headed by Uday Kotak, the managing director of the Kotak Mahindra group. Prima facie,

IL&FS has enough assets in its books to raise capital to meet its financial commitments. But do the books of account reflect the true picture? Probably not. Now that the government has taken over the company, it would have to take a call on recasting its books. This will help to understand where hidden losses have been stage managed. On preliminary inspection, Kotak has stated that IL&FS actually had 348 subsidiaries and not just 169 as reported in its books of account. The books are cooked and the amount of losses IL&FS carries in reality is anybody's guess.

The government appointed Grant Thornton for forensic auditing of IL&FS and its subsidiaries. It was found that the maze of subsidiaries was actually created for round-tripping and money laundering. These expenses were routed to IL&FS employees and their associates. The money also flowed from one subsidiary to another to repay interests, so that they could borrow more. Operational cash flow was negligible and the capital and reserves were siphoned off, so interest payments became more difficult by the day.

As many as 35 auditors were involved in the audits, each validating omissions referring to the reports of the auditors of other associate companies or subsidiaries. For example, the principal auditors of a key subsidiary, IFIN, were Deloitte Haskins & Sells and BSR, the E&Y associate. IFIN raised and spent over ₹17,000 crore illegally through bonds and debentures from the public and has been charged with fraudulent practices by the Serious Fraud Investigation Office (SFIO).

After the default, the regulator ICAI reported that the auditors did not highlight the RBI's inspection report, which had labelled IFIN as over-leveraged, besides failing to report negative cash flows and adverse key financial ratios. Instead of looking deeply at the ₹17,000 crore money-laundering and round-tripping fraud, they relied on the reports of eight other auditors, such as MP Chitale and Co., Sharp and Tannan, Manubhai and Shah LLP, among others, to ratify the transactions. The SFIO probe alleged that Deloitte, which audited IL&FS for over a decade, was hand in glove with IL&FS. The Deloitte top management was well aware of the frauds but kept ratifying the accounts in exchange for several advisory contracts awarded to them. But aside from the auditors, the regulator ICAI also missed the elephant in the room, till IL&FS defaulted.

The next step the government shall possibly take, after the forensic audit, is to fix accountability of all executives who were privy to this illegal money raising and laundering. Another round of forensic auditing cannot be ruled out. It is not a few men at the top but dozens of executives within the company who were involved in the cooking of books and siphoning off of money. Along with them were auditors, regulators, bankers, bureaucrats and ministers who were beneficiaries of this decade-long fraud on the Indian banking system. The government will also have to conduct a thorough probe to fix executive accountability within the organization and, according to insiders, the numbers may run into a hundred-plus. Many heads may roll. Though such a surgical strike could affect the morale of the company, fixing accountability is much needed. It is also the only way to avoid future frauds. The Ministry of Corporate Affairs sought the permission of NCLT to freeze the bank accounts and lockers of the auditors, Deloitte and KPMG associate BSR, in August 2019. Unless exemplary punishment is given to both the guilty employees and the auditors, such frauds will keep happening.

The third important step is to sell some of the assets of the beleaguered company to meet its liabilities. There are several toll roads completed by NHAI that have the collection rights bestowed to IL&FS, the lender. Operating those roads would bring revenue in the long term, but selling the rights would bring cash immediately. It is critical that such liquid assets are immediately sold to meet the short-term debts of the company. Raising fresh capital may take longer in the currently depressed market conditions, so the company needs to raise cash by asset sale. An AQR may also need to be done, says Uday Kotak, witness to the large number of assets shown on the books. However, leaving no stone unturned, the government has turned to LIC, SBI and foreign funds like Abu Dhabi Investment Authority to pitch in. Maintaining liquidity of IL&FS is crucial to completing the infrastructure projects at NHAI and elsewhere, and is the cornerstone of the development agenda being pushed by the Modi government.

Finally, IL&FS and its subsidiaries need to be restructured. The subsidiaries are one too many. Besides, the concept of each contract being treated as a special purpose vehicle is faulty and needs to be revisited. But this can happen only if the banking regulator maps out the auditing failures, conducts its own enquiry into the money laundering, and recommends structural simplification.

Now that the government has taken over the unit, it needs to simplify the accounting procedure of the company and drastically cut down the subsidiaries by amalgamation. Once that processing is done, the fictitious companies owned by employees to siphon out money will be found and dissolved. Restructuring IL&FS is not going to be easy, but it needs to be done in order to make it transparent. A maze of subsidiary companies with cross-linked transaction makes the operations of a company opaque, and reducing the number of IL&FS subsidiaries is the key to avoid future frauds.

The Vexing issue of RBI and Bank Autonomy

Apart from accountability, there is the issue of autonomy of the central bank, which has been in the limelight. Autonomy of institutions is a hotly contested issue in India. There are two types of autonomy that we need to discuss here. Should the Central Bank be truly independent of the government and allowed to chart its independent path as a regulator? In that case, who will it be accountable to? The question gains relevance today in light of the frauds in banks and the failure of the regulator in the last decade.

There is also a second question that has come into contention after the Supreme Court verdict of 2019 on an RBI directive. Should the banks that it supervises have their own autonomy to chart independent paths in relation to their creditors? This question is in light of the judgement by the Supreme Court recently, wherein it declared the 12 February 2018 circular issued by the RBI directing banks to act against creditors as 'null and void'.

The government has been targeted by the Opposition for interfering in the banking industry and the autonomy of the RBI. The first salvo was launched when Raghuram Rajan was not offered a second term. Rajan, who came to India as economic advisor to Prime Minister Manmohan Singh, went on to become the RBI governor from 2013 to 2016. His not being given an extension did not go down well with the Opposition.

The demonetization and its after-effects, and the lack of a role for the RBI in the decision-making process also was a matter of discussion in the newsrooms. Rajan's deputy, Urjit Patel, who replaced him as the next RBI governor, quit office voluntarily before he completed his full term, leading to intense speculation of government interference in RBI functioning.

While the government has pushed its agenda and pushed the RBI into improving regulation, the Opposition tried to say that its action was undemocratic. Shaktikanta Das, a career bureaucrat, has replaced Urjit Patel, leading to more protests by the Opposition parties. There have been four ICS officers and three IAS officers, all career bureaucrats, who have held the RBI governor's office previously. Still, the Opposition was able to run headline news stories for two days, criticizing his appointment 'as an undesirable and disastrous move by the government' bent on usurping the central bank's autonomy.

When Das proactively reduced the interest rates sensing an economic slowdown, there was further insinuation that he was forced by the government to do so and that the RBI's independence was being compromised. But Das, who took over at a difficult time from Urjit Patel, has performed reasonably well in very difficult circumstances. Still, there were more protests when the RBI was asked to share some of its excess reserves with the government. Over the years, the RBI had amassed more reserves than what was recommended by the IMF. To meet the high recapitalization needs of banks, the government in March 2019 had asked for a much larger payment of ₹1.76 lakh crore from RBI as dividend, a move that was criticized as diluting the autonomy of the regulator. So, the autonomy of the central bank, which had been a vexing issue in the 1960s has come back into the headlines with a bang.

The IMF Guidelines on Forex Reserves

At this point, we need to know that the IMF proposes a forex reserve for every nation, with a higher and lower band limit. Since the BOP crisis of 1990s, the RBI and the government ensured that India's reserves each year were comfortably more than the higher band limit proposed by IMF. This steadily rose and crossed the $100 billion mark by December 2003. For the first time in three decades, India had two successive years of current account surplus in 2002–03 and 2003–04, when exports exceeded imports, leaving a forex surplus. Even the PSBs were in good health, with NPAs well below 2 per cent of gross debt. This meant only 2 per cent of bank borrowings were bad loans.

The Central Bank earns steady interests from bonds, both international and domestic, and from short-term lending to banks. Besides, it generates a healthy surplus, managing the currency by buying and selling dollars at opportune moments for macroeconomic stabilization. The higher the volatility in the financial markets, the more the intervention by either selling dollars or by lending to banks. So, a lot of credit for managing and building up the currency reserve that India boasts of today, actually goes to the RBI. The RBI also generates a very healthy profitability while managing the currency, and it is widely believed that the larger the global volatility, the greater the central bank's annual profits.

This profit is now under scrutiny, as the government feels that the RBI surplus is way above the safety limit. But we will come to a detailed discussion about the RBI's reserves and their adequacy later. A paper titled 'Assessing Reserve Adequacy in India' was released by the Department of Economic and Policy Research of the RBI in 2015, with a detailed optimization model and risk analysis, which suggested that India's foreign exchange (forex) reserves are more than adequate to cover potential stress scenarios. Despite the fact that we have moved from a moderate to a severe scenario in the post-Covid era, the RBI reserves are still adequate.

TEN

REVIVING CREDIT FLOW

Bank lending in India grew rapidly between 2006 and 2011 despite the global banking crisis. The Rao–Vajpayee era had brought about economic stability and created a strong foundation for growth. This created a high credit demand and the Manmohan Singh government pushed up overall credit. The only problem was the exorbitant interest rate, which kept borrowers away.

The big challenge was to ensure credit flow to the MSME sector. This was a difficult sector to tap, especially because recovery was difficult and risk of failure was assumed to be comparatively higher for small loans. Besides, it needed much more manpower and resources than handling loans to large industries. For the bank manager of a PSB, a ₹100 crore loan to a big industry was less likely to fail and would be easier to recover than 400 loans of less than ₹25 lakh, which was the priority-sector limit for individual medium- and small-scale enterprises. Meeting the priority sector target of 40 per cent loans was pretty difficult, to say the least, with limited resources available to the branch managers.

Aggressive Lending Practices through NBFCs

Meanwhile, the private sector banks grew aggressively in the retail banking space with a lot of marketing support, which included partner agencies for direct marketing, call centre support for telemarketing and recovery agents for loan recoveries. Still, targets had to be met, and the priority sector target of 40 per cent was daunting.

To achieve the priority sector targets, the branch managers of PSBs started sanctioning bulk loans to NBFCs, UCBs and RCBs that operated in those sectors. Ambitious targets for priority sectors were thus easily met and a large number of NBFCs started getting funding from the banking sector during UPA II.

However, a lot of the funds that the NBFCs got for slum development, small businesses and low-cost housing projects were misdirected and misappropriated. Infrastructure sector NBFCs like IL&FS, HDIL and DHFL, all of which have emerged as defaulters, had grown at a reckless pace during that period, using loans targeted at the priority sector. Similar were the cases with UCBs and RCBs.

The RBI realized what was happening when industrial growth started slipping despite credit expansion. So, they began choking bank funding to NBFCs in May 2011. Banks could no longer lend to all NBFCs, the low-cost funds earmarked for the priority sector. Banks could only lend to NBFCs in the microfinance segment. This substantially raised the cost of funds for most NBFCs. So, the NBFCs started to tap the non-convertible debenture (NCD) market to raise funds at a lower cost. This made default recoveries even more complex, which we will discuss later.

The rupee crashed by more than 20 per cent during the summer of 2013. It disturbed the economy, with prices of imports shooting up. RBI issued several stipulations to curb import trade.

However, the evergreening of loans to large industries with high stressed assets continued unabated. Soon, there was a new crisis in the offing. The advances of PSBs increased from ₹18,19,074 crore (₹18.19 trillion) as on 31 March 2008 to ₹52,15,920 crore (₹52.15 trillion) on 31 March 2014. But over 10 per cent of those loans were to industries that had very poor repayment records. They were being sanctioned just to service their debt and help them escape default status. It was a crisis situation for the industries as well as the banks that serviced them.

The UPA government was voted out in 2014, largely due to voter perception about economic mismanagement and corruption. The crisis, however, did not end, but continued to balloon. This was partly because the incoming Modi government started declaring 'Achhe Din' before attending to the teething problems that plagued the industry and the banks. They introduced too many new initiatives before plugging the old leaks of the banking industry. It was like revving up the engine of a leaky boat before attending to its repairs.

New Priorities: Taking Focus Away from Lending

PSBs have several strengths and are indispensable to politicians who would want to initiate pro-poor schemes in India. They have a wide footprint and a banking infrastructure that is good but not world class. They have been in business since much before their nationalization in 1969, and have had a headstart over the private sector banks that began operations in the 1990s. Still, they did not develop their loan disbursal and loan recovery arms independently. Instead, they relied heavily on the branch manager for both activities.

The year 2014 saw a new aspirational government come in, with a new set of objectives. Three months after taking office, the Modi government launched the Pradhan Mantri Jan Dhan Yojna (PMJDY), with ambitious targets for the lower middle class and the poor, who did not have bank accounts. The move was a game changer for the unbanked poor population, but this created a recurring cost for the banking sector, who had to service these unprofitable 30 crore zero balance accounts that were opened in the next six months. This put added pressure on the already stretched banking services. So, opening new accounts became critical and restoring the banking infrastructure and the badly managed loan books became low priority for the Branch Managers of PSBs. Even lesser priority was to push for credit growth.

There is an interesting anecdote that shows how some people benefitted from the workload increase of PSBs due to the PMJDY.

A manager of a PSB was so short-staffed with the increased workload that he asked the bank's security guard to assist in the work and even gave him a regular allowance for the work through a voucher payment. His request for increase of staff did not get a positive response from the zonal office. Soon, the guard Ramesh was seen assisting the cashier at the bank in counting of notes, as endless bundles poured in during demonetization. In 2018, Ramesh appeared for the banking exam and cleared it. He now functions as a clerk and not a security guard in the same bank.

Meanwhile, the RBI had been trying to get the AQR of the banks implemented ever since 2013. But despite the best efforts of the then RBI governor, Raghuram Rajan, the banks and the Manmohan Singh government had been loath to introduce the AQR. There was an apprehension about its introduction amongst bankers and bureaucrats. Everyone felt that it could open a Pandora's Box, exposing deep-rooted corruption and that would hurt both the bankers and the borrowers. But the rot had set in deep and needed cleansing.

It took more than a year after the NDA came to power for Raghuram Rajan to convince the Modi government and get this cleansing implemented. Once it was done, IBC and a spate of other reforms were unleashed. This was a complicated and elaborate process to remove the stress in the banking industry. The discovery of stressed assets threw up new challenges. And as NPAs rose, the banks struggled to cope with the frauds. The resolution of stressed assets and its fallout created an environment of risk aversion in the branch managers of the PSBs, irrespective of their outcomes. So, instead of increasing the risk appetite for growing credit, there was risk aversion after the AQR got invoked.

Demonetization: Disrupted Cash Flow and Credit Lines

Only 1.7 per cent of the citizens paid taxes, but nearly 5 per cent of Indians could be called rich and another 20 per cent could be termed as upper middle class. India Ratings and Research, a Fitch Group company, in its report of December 2016 had estimated that black money in the form of unaccounted cash at that point of time was 12 per cent of the circulated currency or ₹4 lakh crore (₹4 trillion). The economic cost of demonetization was estimated to be ₹1.5 lakh crore (₹1.5 trillion), indicating that it would be a profitable exercise even if half the black money was tracked and denotified. Unfortunately, due to planning and execution lapses, nearly 99.3 per cent of the currency returned to the banks and just ₹11,000 crore was kept out of the banking system. So, even without the cascading effects of cash flow, which severely disrupted the economy, demonetization was a loss-making exercise. Clearly, it was an exercise that was weak in math. More importantly, it created a separate set of disruptions in the banking sector, tying up the entire workforce in the banks in an exercise that was not related to its core banking activity of advances or deposits.

The entire exercise of demonetization revolved around banks. It was aimed at eliminating black money that had been salted away and hoarded at homes, clearly outside the banking system. A four-hour notice was given before the high-value ₹500 and ₹1,000 currency notes, constituting 86 per cent of the currency in circulation, were made obsolete on 16 November 2016. A 45-day window was allocated for the monetary sanitization process, wherein old notes could be exchanged for new ones. This meant 150 million high-value currency notes had to be replaced every day, which was a tall task for bankers. This was a time-consuming exercise, as it needed a five-fold rise in the daily normal cash flow through the banks. There was no manpower nor technology to handle this kind of operation.

Additionally, the ATMs could not dispense the new currency notes, as they were smaller in size than the older notes. The cassettes holding the currency notes needed to be physically replaced, which took two weeks, and were then re-calibrated, which took another two weeks. This further slowed down the regular currency distribution process in the banks, which had to be manual while the ATM machines were modified to distribute the new currency notes. All this disrupted the cash flow of the banks and their customers, and the last quarter of the year 2016 was devoted to restoring liquidity and the processes in the banking system.

There was little time or intent to restore credit flow into the industry or look at the slipping targets for priority sector lending. The demonetization exercise also failed, from the corruption test point of view. Rather, it deepened the fault lines of the banking system and showed the nexus of the bankers with the tax deceivers across the country. Bank managers were induced and were active partners, helping to recirculate the black money into white and bring back the illegitimate cash into the system. Over 99.3 per cent of the cash in circulation flowed back into the banking system, most of it duly legitimized.

The money saw the arrival of cash mules, wherein the poor Jan Dhan account holder served as surrogates for the rich. The rich, with unaccounted black money, bribed the bank staff to facilitate the transfer of illegitimate cash funds through the accounts of poor people who had opened Jan Dhan accounts only a few months ago.

At times, the rich—with bank accounts in the metropolitan cities—saw their money being transferred through various banks in small towns, all facilitated through the managers and staff of the banks. This exposed the problem of deep-rooted corruption across the banking sector, which was beyond control. They outwitted every move that the government and the RBI made to stop the illegitimate cash making its way back into the system. They also co-opted the poor into the corruption process.

One such case is that of a branch manager at a bank in Delhi and his cousin in Uttarakhand, who earned over ₹1 crore each by charging 30 per cent commission for regularizing demonetized currency. The Delhi manager provided the clients while his Uttarakhand cousin provided the cash mules. So, bundles of notes in steel trunks were sent by Kotdwara Express to Kashirampur every week. A steady trickle of villagers, who had just opened Jan Dhan accounts a year ago, collected ₹10,000 each for converting ₹2 lakh through their PMJDY accounts. The small town branch, which had never seen cash deposits of ₹1 crore in any month before, saw deposits and withdrawals of ₹8 crore in December 2016.

For nearly one year, from November 2016 to September 2017, bank credit did not grow as businesses tried desperately to come out of the cash crunch.

Meanwhile, the effect of the AQR was taking its toll as banks were asking overborrowed clients to cut down their debt. As per RBI data, no fresh credit was given to the industrial sector during the financial year 2016–17. The emphasis during this period was to downsize and survive the cash crunch without trying to grow or expand credit.

Private Banks Race Ahead of PSBs in Credit Disbursement

Credit flow slowed down after 2014 because there were too many disruptions. From the era of corruption, the banks were suddenly ushered into an age of transparency. They were also asked to expand the banking service to nearly 300 million citizens and then execute the time-consuming demonetization, which was not a core business activity. These changes may have been much needed, but were too much to handle for an already overloaded banking system.

The change management of the Modi government has been overambitious and, as a result, the core function of credit flow from the banks, particularly in the public sector, has been deeply affected. The reason the private sector has been less affected is because of its profit orientation and accountability to the shareholder. But before we analyse the reason of the vastly different performances of the private and PSBs, let us see what the data over the past five years says about credit disbursement through both the PSBs and the private banks.

The RBI data shows that industry credit growth has declined in the past five years from—12 per cent growth year-on-year to a net annual decline of 5 per cent for PSBs, while for private sector banks, the increase has been modest but is still is over 20 per cent year-on-year growth. In spite of the government's push towards the farm sector, agricultural credit growth has fallen to 12 per cent as against 16 per cent five years ago. The private sector banks have doubled the farm sector credit growth to 20 per cent per annum.

Similarly, in personal loans and in the housing sector, the annual credit growth of the private sector banks has been higher than that of PSBs. And it is not only credit growth but also deposit growth that has fallen from 15 per cent to around 5 per cent in the PSBs during the last five years. The rise has been marginal in the case of private banks, but is still around 20 per cent year-on-year. So, there are two questions we put to the bankers in the public sectors. Why is this happening? How can this trend be reversed?

Bankers' feedback: PSBs Struggle to Revive Credit

According to Rajesh Gupta, AGM at Bank of Maharashtra,

> This is happening largely because of various reasons. Firstly, because the incentive to push credit has been lost in lieu of the losses that each of the PSBs incurred due to write-offs from bad debts. Every branch of the PSBs that had been giving out large advances in the past have been part of the write-offs process. The banks have been incurring heavy losses due to quarterly write-offs. So, it was a case of once bitten twice shy for the bank staff. Also, if one loan goes bad today, there could be an departmental enquiry or even a chargesheet. So, nobody wants to sign on the dotted line unless there is no option.

The position is getting worse because the government is forcing PSBs to give loans without adequate time to do proper due diligence. First, there was the pressure to release the MUDRA loans en masse before the 2019 elections, and now there is pressure to give loans of ₹1 crore, under the outreach programme, to the MSMEs. As long as all the signs were positive, loans were given without reservation. But now that the entire 'advance system' has been under a cloud and bank liquidity under stress due to high write-offs, the environment has turned cautious and risk averse. Nobody likes to lend aggressively on a weak balance sheet. There is pressure on the branch managers to find less risky streams of revenue that add to the banks' profitability without increasing risk.

'Secondly, this was also because the spectre of investigation of frauds looms large when a borrower goes into default mode,' he explains further. 'Nobody wants to take a risk during bad times. Importantly, nobody wants to take the blame. This is because there is nobody to make the difference between bonafide and male-fide intentions.' Our investigation shows that this is true, but perhaps unavoidable. This is because it is also highly desirable to drive in a sense of accountability. The government has already ordered the SFIO to investigate the top 50 NCLT cases for frauds. This has resulted in the SFIO giving notices to the directors and executive directors of the lender banks to clarify their roles in giving loans to the defaulting companies.

Third is the structural deficiencies of the PSBs that have become a bottleneck for the accountability-driven banking system that is being introduced. PSBs are understaffed and are not structured to derive maximum efficiency and accountability. Some banks, like the SBI, the Bank of Baroda and the PNB, have made some changes in their organizational structure, but most of the others are lacking. For example, the PNB has branch offices, as of 31 March 2019, which are at the core of its banking operations. The branch reports to the circle office or zonal office, which in turn reports to the head office. But the prime executing officer is still the branch manager. PNB generated an annual revenue of ₹11.34 lakh crore (₹11.34 trillion) and incurred a net loss of ₹9,975 crore (₹99.75 billion) in 2018–19. It is the 6,989 branch managers who are responsible for the functioning of the massive ₹11 trillion business, including core banking operations. Every other officer, including most senior officers, are just supervisory. We will take a look at the operations of the PNB and compare them to those of a large private sector bank, the ICICI bank.

A cursory look at the range of activities of a branch manager shows why re-structuring matters. A branch manager of a PSB is not only responsible for the daily operations and administrative affairs of the bank, including all advances and deposits, but also for all other branch activities. Though Credit Processing Cells have been created for PSBs of late, they have no specialist manpower. For example, the Credit Processing Cell of Bank of Maharashtra was set up in 2016, but it is manned by senior branch managers and not by credit professionals, analysts and verification experts. They do not function independently, assuming all functions of loans and advances. The branch manager is still responsible and involved in advances and recoveries, along with other products like general and life insurance, mortgage, investments and equity, and IPOs, besides documents and records, and legal validation, audit and vigilance checks, talent acquisition, strategy framing, online trading and IT incorporation, accounts, finance, communication with customers clients, and head office and infrastructure management. It is just not possible for one person do justice to all these functions as well as grow the advances of the bank under adverse industrial growth conditions.

Another reason is the complexity of having one person be responsible for advances and recoveries, which makes the PSB bank manager risk averse. For example, in case of advances, the branch manager of a PSB handles the marketing, sales, assessment, risk analysis, repayment capability evaluation, borrower credit record evaluation, documentation, legal aspects, loan execution and disbursement before a loan is granted.

Once a loan is granted, the financial health of the borrower and the industry have to be monitored continuously, which again is the function of the branch manager. For example, banks have formats for stock or inventory statements that have to be filled up on a monthly basis by the borrower taking a working capital loan. These statements must be inspected every month to ensure that the stocks are moving and not dead. If the inventory has not been sold for three to six months, it will need to be written off by the borrower.

Also, verification of the stock statements by annual physical visits to the party premises is the responsibility of every branch manager and legally mandatory. This is an important field function that most banks don't have sufficient manpower, and at times even the expertise, to assess. For example, in the Nirav Modi case, the assessment and pricing of the quality of diamonds on inlaid gold jewellery re-exported by the jewellers was a black box for the bank. The Brady House branch of PNB simply did not have the capability to assess the stocks exported by Nirav Modi or check the valuation against which the LOUs were issued. It goes to show that the challenges of monitoring every loan account can be complex and need domain expertise.

The recovery function for advances is even more complex. Borrowers, both the successful ones and those on default mode, try to tap banks for more funds, either for expansion or to ward off closure. At times it is not apparent from the outside if the business is on the rise or on the wane. Promoters use ingenious techniques at times to fake their financial health. The bank manager must be able to look through the deceptions and identify stressed assets, and then hand them over those to the recovery cells to force timely closure of stressed accounts.

For many PSBs, the recovery function, especially for the smaller accounts, still remains with the branch. This is especially true because a large part of their advances are to the priority sector, with loans lower than ₹25 lakh. These small loans have to be settled at the branch level in many PSBs. So, that again becomes a field activity dependent on regular site visits, assessment of losses, pressurizing borrowers to liquidate assets, sale of stressed assets, and finally the recovery of bank debts. All these need the active participation of branch managers, who are responsible for both the disbursal of credit as well as its recovery in the public sector banking structure. It is, therefore, not unnatural that the branch managers today at PSBs have all turned risk-averse and credit disbursements have dried up.

Bankers' Feedback: How Private Banks Are Growing Credit

'The business of advances grows both during a downturn and a market boom,' explains Rajat Kothari, a senior manager of ICICI Bank. He adds,

> Most clients are going through a liquidity crisis during this period. To run their businesses, they must find cash. This is applicable for both our old clients as well as new clients who were previously banking with others and also the first-time borrower. The demand is good and since the PSBs have cut down on lending temporarily, there is lesser competition. There is lot of credit demand across sectors and we have been giving personal loans at the rate of over 11 per cent interest and industry loans at 9 per cent interest, which will help improve our profitability.

It is not at all paradoxical that private sector banks are quickly growing their loan books despite the industrial slowdown. Rather, this is an opportunity to exploit and grow in the hour of a countrywide liquidity crisis. The private sector banks are using this opportunity, and most of them have shown double digit growth rates in advances.

As a matter of fact, industry data shows that credit growth of ICICI bank improved by 12 per cent during the first two quarters of 2019–20, and may even touch 15 per cent at the end of the third quarter. This is completely opposite to the trend witnessed in the second largest PSB, PNB, with revenues of ₹13,290 crore. Both banks have been hit by NPAs and have the SFIO investigating fraud cases against their former management.

However, there are two major differences between the two banks. ICICI is a profitable bank with a modest earning per share of ₹5.22 and a net profit margin of 5.3 per cent. Despite its current problems, it has given a 1:10 bonus in 2017 and a 50 per cent dividend in 2019. PNB, on the other hand, is knee-deep in losses. It last give dividend in May 2015 and loses ₹1 for every ₹5 revenue it generates. While the PNB share price hovered round a modest ₹60 in November 2019, the ICICI shares kept touching the ₹500 mark, giving the latter ten-times the market capitalization of PNB despite a similar equity base. This difference in profitability gives the bankers confidence to lend.

Secondly, giving a loan, monitoring and ensuring repayment and recovering a loan are three separate functions, handled by specialists in a private sector bank like ICICI. The marketing is done by third-party telemarketers, along with marketing partners of the bank, largely on commission basis. This is an independent and aggressive task force, whose work is to get the borrower to the assessment team. The loan assessment is done independently, strictly by assessing the income statement, repayment capacity, the regularity of cash flow in the account of the borrower and the credit score. This team is different and not connected to the marketing team. The monitoring of repayment is done by the IT department and is system-fed, and automatic. Penal interests for delayed repayment are high, and the legal department, which is an independent entity, steps in quickly without information or permission from the branch. Marketing, loan assessment and loan recovery are three entirely different activities under different heads and are not controlled by the branch manager. The branch manager is the facilitator and not the key person responsible for the marketing, assessment, disbursement, execution and recovery of these advances. Unlike in PSBs, he is not burdened with the role of credit allocation or recovery.

Restructuring of Post-Merger Business Model

The government has proposed the merger of several PSBs under four lead banks: PNB, Union Bank of India, Canara Bank and Bank of India, from April 2020. This is the fourth round of bank mergers, after the merger of SBI with other state banks was first announced in August 2017. After this, merger PSBs will be reduced from 27 to just a dozen in a three-year time frame. We will discuss the proposed merger of PSBs in Chapter 11. Here, however, we would like to discuss the restructuring of the PSBs to make them more customer-oriented, like the private banks.

After the merger of the aforementioned three, the combined entity amalgamated into PNB will become the second largest bank in India, with 11,437 branches and a combined revenue of ₹18 lakh crore (₹18 trillion). However, a restructuring of the banks will be needed before the merger, and the exact structure is yet to be formalized. The UBI Chief, Ashok Kumar Pradhan, says, '[W]hile PNB's and UBI's respective administrative structures are more compliance oriented, OBC follows a vertical structure which is more business focussed. The merged entity may follow a mix of both—with every circle acting as "bank within a bank" with higher business focus like in SBI.' The SBI has 24,000 branches, but does a significantly larger business of ₹51 lakh crore (₹51 trillion).

The SBI is clearly the benchmark for other PSBs in the country that have struggled to live up to expectations. It is much more business-oriented than other PSBs and more technologically updated and profitable than any of its peers in the public sector, says a former PNB general manager. The structures are not similar in every PSB, and neither is the technology. SBI has a different business-like organizational structure, OBC has a similar structure to SBI in parts, while PNB and Union Bank of

India have compliance-based organization structures. Similarly, the CBS softwares for the banks are different. While SBI and PNB use FINACLE 10, both UBI and OBC use FINACLE 7. So, arriving at a homogenous structure or having a homogenous technology will not be easy and may take months to evolve. Bank mergers are going to be an additional distraction for PSBs, which will further take their focus away from their core business of increasing deposits and advances.

However, since the mergers have been announced, the government must focus on restructuring of the banks as efficient and fleet-footed business- and growth-oriented entities. For this, there should be ease of business, like in the private sector banks and not the public sector behemoth SBI. The SBI has been historically getting a very large amount of its business from the central government, the state governments, and their institutions, hence its size and revenue. There is no doubt that it is the largest bank, with the widest footprint, but it is hardly the best or the fastest growing bank of the country.

Several bankers I talked to opined that the ICICI bank structure may be a better model to follow for the merged banks than the SBI model. The ICICI bank is a function-oriented bank with different specialist classifications, and not one based on compliance or hierarchies. Its organizational structure provides a clear understanding of roles and responsibilities, giving each executive a small but focused target instead of all operations being conducted simultaneously. The ICICI Bank is more prone to taking risks, and also lends in the infrastructure sector like PSBs. It is more business-like, but it is also trying to enter small towns and rural India. Under the current circumstances, it would be ideal to structure the merged identities in the manner of ICICI Bank to unleash its risk-taking capabilities and boost credit growth at an early date.

ELEVEN

BANK MERGERS: WILL 2 + 2 BE 5 OR 3?

Soon after the Modi government came to power, it started considering reducing the number of PSBs through mergers and consolidations. However, mergers and acquisitions require a tremendous amount of effort that could be disruptive and chaotic, if not properly managed. For the merger to be successful, compatibility issues and the synergy need to be looked at. Thereafter, the comparable IT systems need to be merged, and the spread and overlapping of branches need to be looked at. What is also required is to merge the cultures and finally the human resource systems of banks, some of which have a large regional but small national presence. All this involves more disruption within the already overloaded banking industry.

The big question is whether bank mergers will be beneficial or detrimental to credit growth, governance issues and the overall health of the banks. Will 2+2 lead to 5 or be significantly less?

Twitterati burst into hyperactivity on 30 August 2019 when Finance Minister Nirmala Sitharaman announced the merger of 27 PSBs into 12 large PSBs.

'Is there a Tinder for banks that I don't know about,' tweeted one Twitter user, creating a Tinder page for the merged banks, garnering likes, dislikes and comments. Others were not so charitable. One went on to say 'So we merge all small problems into one big problem, that no one knows how to solve.'

The rising NPAs, after the massive banking reforms post 2015, left the government with little or no choice. Bank consolidation became essential to protect the weaker banks. Like many of its other actions, the government's decision of bank mergers will be under scrutiny for decades. The former RBI Governor Raghuram Rajan and the former Finance Minister P. Chidambaram have already criticized the move as hasty. India Ratings has warned that it could lead to the deterioration of Asset Liability Management (ALM) of the lead banks. But looking at the spate of NPAs that are likely in the next few years, the government had no option but to merge and reduce the number of banks for easier control and governance.

After the AQR was rigorously enforced from late 2015, it was found that the stressed assets were growing well beyond the capability of the smaller banks to cope with. Several weak banks would not be able to meet the capital adequacy ratio (CAR) of 12 per cent imposed by the government. So, one way to ensure better capital adequacy was to consolidate and merge the weak banks with the strong banks.

Keeping this in mind, a long-term plan was drawn up by the finance ministry to merge banks that were having similar business and technology synergies. Mergers also meant several other things, such as fair assessment of shareholder value, increase and streamlining of operational jurisdiction of the bank, the reduction of the number of branches after mergers for optimization, the negotiation with bank unions to ensure smooth functioning, technology integration and the use of similar technology for the core banking software by the merged banks, and so on. We look at each aspect in the six mergers that have been taking place since 2017 to discover their strengths and weaknesses.

SBI Acquires Five Subsidiary Banks: Losses Post-amalgamation

The first consolidation was led by SBI. It started after an announcement by the then Finance Minister Arun Jaitley in March 2017 that the State Bank of Bikaner and Jaipur, State

Bank of Mysore, State Bank of Patiala, State Bank of Hyderabad and State Bank of Travancore would be merged into the SBI. Thereafter, the Bhartiya Mahila Bank was merged with the SBI. Subsequently, the State Bank (Repeal and Amendment) Bill was passed in parliament in August 2017, amending the SBI Act of 1955 and removing reference to all SBI subsidiaries. Each of these subsidiary banks were niche players with strong footholds in their respective territories and have been in operation since the days before independence. They served the erstwhile princely states, which were outside the direct supervision of the British, and became subsidiary banks of SBI after the Imperial Bank was nationalized and renamed as the SBI in 1955.

Over the years, they played second fiddle to the bigger commercial banks, which spread their wings faster. The SBI subsidiaries lost their niche as key players after the bank nationalization of 1969 and should have been consolidated long ago. However, previous governments adopted a hands-off policy of wait-and-watch. They went for mergers only as a last-minute resort to avoid defaults. The State Bank of Saurashtra and the State Bank of Indore were merged with the SBI in 2008 and 2010, but others were left to operate as subsidiaries, despite poor health.

After the government decided on this merger in 2017, SBI chairman Rajnish Kumar asked for a three-month time frame to implement it. The integration is being done in three phases. The first phase was data integration, where the data systems were integrated and new passbooks were issued to all account holders. Now, each bank has its own core banking software and its SWIFT technology for international transactions. Most of these PSBs use the CBS of FINACLE from Infosys, but there are some who use Oracle Financial Services and BaNCS from Tata Consultancy Services. Even banks using FINACLE have different versions of CBS. For example, while the larger banks like SBI, Bank of Baroda and PNB use the updated FINACLE 10 version, most of the smaller banks use version 7.

The integration was easier for SBI and its associate banks, as they were governed by a common platform. Yet, there are many fin-tech companies, and phone and digital payment systems that are linked differently with different banks through the CBSs. They had to be individually checked and integrated into the system. 'However, technical integration is a time-consuming process and will take perhaps more than a year to complete. It will require the system of record and the system of engagement at every level to be compatible. Though the integration will be challenging, in the long run, the combined system will prove to be very efficient,' explains Dr Rajendra Sinha, a veteran of SBI who is today the chairperson, Centre of Excellence in Banking IFIM, Business School, Bengaluru.

The second phase was branch integration, after which 1,500 to 1,600 branches were closed down because of duplication. This was a huge exercise. It wasn't that only SBI branches replaced the branches of subsidiary banks. There was a huge overlap of branches in Rajasthan, Karnataka, Andhra Pradesh, Punjab and Kerala. Here, some of the regional players were stronger and catered to larger businesses. In such places, some of the SBI branches had to be closed down. Besides, the Regional Rural Bank Act of 1976 had created dozens of RRBs that had been sponsored by these subsidiary banks. Some of them had been amalgamated previously, while some remained to be consolidated. Every state in the country had RRBs. They were also to be consolidated into a single entity. Their branches had to be closed and all accounts reassigned to the local operating branches after consolidation. Thereafter, there was an integration of ATMs in the merger, which was not an issue for SBI and its subsidiaries, who had shared a common platform at all times.

With the merger of all the five associates, SBI is expected to become a lender of global proportions, with an asset base of ₹37 lakh crore. According to the annual report ended March 2019, SBI post-merger has combined deposits of ₹5.41 lakh crore and total advances of ₹2.98 lakh crore. Due to higher provisions, SBI reported a net loss of ₹6,547 crore for the year against a net profit of ₹10,484 crore in the previous year. The combined entity will operate from 22,500 branches and 58,000 ATMs and have over 50 crore customers.

But, as the provisions for bad loans will go up after the merger, with the bad loan basket of subsidiary banks added, the losses may continue for another year or two. The associate banks had staggering bad loans of ₹35,396 crore. This amount is almost half of SBI's ₹66,117 crore stressed loans in 2015-16.

Besides, there is the prickly issue of integrating the culturally different employees of SBI, who are better trained and more professional than their poorer cousins arriving from the subsidiary banks. Bank unions have not been very vocal, but a strike was called in January 2020 to oppose the mergers. They too have to be managed. Getting the bank operations rolling with the same rhythm as before will be daunting.

However, due to the sheer size and sophistication of the anchor bank, SBI, this is a case where two plus two may become five.

Bank of Baroda Takes Over Vijaya and Dena Bank

The next major merger took place when the Bank of Baroda took over the operations of Vijaya Bank and Dena Bank with effect from April 2019. This, again, was a merger forced by performance issues, following the problems that surfaced with Dena Bank. Along with 10 other PSBs, Dena Bank was put under the Prompt Corrective Action (PCA) framework by RBI. Lending and other restrictions had been specified for banks under PCA by the RBI way back in 2017. While most other banks were improving after being put on the PCA framework, Dena Bank continued to have solvency issues due to high-contagion losses.

Dena Bank had a gross bad loan pile of ₹16,140 crore, for which the lender had made provisions for less than 60 per cent. When things did not improve despite red-flagging, it was a trigger for takeover. Dena Bank was in a precarious condition and would have defaulted had the government delayed the decision. Its gross NPA level had touched 22 per cent in 2019, as against 12.4

per cent for Bank of Baroda and 6.9 per cent for Vijaya Bank.

Vijaya Bank not only added strength to the balance sheet, but also helped the business of the acquiring bank, Bank of Baroda (BoB), grow by 20 per cent. To ensure that the integration process was smooth and problem free, the government decided to infuse ₹5,042 crore into BoB by issuing preferential equity shares.

There were not many issues in the technical integration, because all the three banks used the FINACLE software for CBS. But the real challenge would be the manpower integration of human resources, especially those of the better performing BoB and Vijaya Bank employees with the workforce of Dena Bank.

BoB has highly skilled manpower, with a lot of influx from the private sector over the last three years. Since its CEO and Managing Director P.S. Jayakumar's term ended in October 2019, it has now been without top leadership for over six months.

Dena Bank was not only financially weak, it had a network of 1,874 branches and 2,354 ATMs and an employee workforce of 13,440 employees with no great performance record. Vijaya Bank had 2,031 branches and 2,001 ATMs, with a workforce of 16,079 employees who were better skilled and had high output. So, not much was quantitatively different. But the training and culture of the employees of both banks were starkly different, says a Vijaya Bank employee, at least qualitatively. 'We were one of the best managed banks and they were one of the worst managed banks. We have hardworking employees with no fraud cases, but their record is poor. So, while the share swapping and valuation of the bank has been done in proportionate to the performance, the employee valuation has not been done properly, and that is a problem.

'So, donkeys (gadhe) and horses (ghode) have been bunched together,' he complains, confirming that there would be some exodus of high-quality employees to the private sector. 'Then there is the regional divide that cannot be easily bridged. We are primarily a South Indian bank and the staff of Dena Bank and BoB employees are mostly Gujaratis and North Indians. So, the culture is different and we have to adjust to them, because they are a much larger group. Merger will be more difficult than being now perceived,' he adds.

However, with two strong banks—the BoB and Vijaya Bank—coming together, the chances are that two plus two may well become five in this case.

PNB Takes Over OBC and United Bank of India

This is one of the most challenging consolidations, because the NPAs of the acquiring bank, PNB, were extremely high at 15.5 per cent before the scheduled merger. In comparison, the NPAs of the other acquiring banks before their mergers were lower (SBI's at 10.35 per cent Bank of Baroda's at 12.23 per cent), which made it easier for them to take up the liabilities of the smaller banks acquired by them.

Not only were PNB's own stressed assets massive, the frauds surrounding the bank were just about erupting. While the extent of the fraud in the Nirav Modi–Mehul Choksi case has been quantified, that in the cases of BPSL, Electrosteel Steel, DHFL and several others are still to be fully quantified. The CAR of PNB at 9.73 per cent is also well below the Basel III norms.

The PNB frauds have been largely more sophisticated than the other loan frauds committed in the PSBs across India. They were all foreign currency loans that were siphoned off easily, as they were disbursed outside India but on documents, like LOUs/LCs, generated within India. In July 2019, PNB reported another massive fraud of ₹3,800 crore (₹38 billion) involving loans and advances granted to the bankrupt BPSL, with total outstanding liabilities of ₹37,248 crore awaiting liquidation and sale at the NCLT courts. The bank is the lead bank and has the largest exposure to BPSL. Incidentally, PNB also had the second largest exposures in Bhushan Steel Ltd and Electrosteel Steel Ltd, acquired by the Tatas and the Vedanta Group respectively in 2018 from the NCLT courts. The fraudulent advances of ₹3,800 crore were granted to BPSL (different from Bhushan Steel) largely from the PNB Chandigarh branch, and involved LOUs financed by the Hong Kong and Dubai offices of PNB. The NBFC frauds, however, are just starting to open up, with big infrastructure financiers like IL&FS and DHFL being pushed to the NCLT courts. These exposures will bring about a second wave of large NPAs and further weaken PNB's balance sheet.

Another weak link in the three-way merger is the United Bank of India. The United Bank of India was a created out of a cluster of weak banks operating in Eastern India in the 1950s. After nationalization in 1969, several other small private banks on the verge of collapse have been merged with it. In December 2013, the bank reported a net loss of ₹1,683 crore in nine months of financial year 2013–14, leading to the resignation of its Chairperson and Managing Director Archana Bhargava, barely 10 months into the job. By March 2018, the CBI had booked Bhargava for amassing assets worth over ₹3.6 crore, allegedly disproportionate to her known sources of income. In February 2014, an RBI-appointed forensic audit of its accounts by Deloitte discovered serious lapses in the detection and reporting of NPAs by United Bank of India. The bank has now reported losses of ₹2,316 crore in the year ending March 2019 and outstanding NPAs of 10.82 per cent, amounting to ₹8,546 crore, which is a mammoth 188 per cent jump over the previous year.

The third bank in the three-way merger, OBC, is slightly better, with a paper-thin net profit of ₹55 crore and gross NPAs of 5.93 per cent, amounting to ₹9,440 crore. With all three banks using the FINACLE software, there may not be many compatibility issues in technology integration. United Bank of India and OBC use FINACLE 7 and need only to upgrade their software to FINACLE 10 used by PNB.

The human resources integration of the three banks will be more complex, primarily because the integration of the banks has been done largely keeping in mind the technology compatibility and not the locations. The three banks have set up two dozen committees to look into the HR, IT and product offering issues to ensure a smooth merger, and are likely to follow the Bank of Baroda template for mergers. However, challenges persist post merger, say bank insiders, as there always exists a regional and cultural divide.

Given the high NPA exposure of both PNB and United Bank of India, the case of this merger may be complex and two plus two may add to just three.

Merger of Canara Bank and Syndicate Bank

If the PNB merger is considered the most challenging, Canara Bank's merger with Syndicate Bank can be termed as the easiest of consolidation exercises. Both the banks have been promoted by the Pais, an influential and dominant Konkani business community that originated nearly a century ago. They have a similar work culture and use similar technology. Importantly, both the banks have well-managed operations despite the NPAs, and have moderate amounts of stressed assets. Nonetheless, Syndicate Bank has not performed very well in the current year and could require more bailout money to stay liquid.

Though they have not been amongst the headline stories, they have been part of the PSB consortiums that took large NPA hits. Apart from these losses, the 2019 operation has been lacklustre. Even the interest income of Syndicate Bank declined marginally from ₹21,775 crore to ₹21,725 crore. Its NPAs rose from ₹24,610 crore to ₹25,758 crores. At 12.03 per cent, the gross NPAs are much higher than most other banks.

The operations of Canara Bank, however, improved during the year ending March 2019, with interest income showing double digit growth at ₹46,810 crore. This year, it posted a small net profit of ₹347 crore. Its gross NPAs reduced to a moderate 8.82 per cent from a high 11.84 per cent the previous year. The government has promised to infuse ₹6,500 crore into the merged bank. After the merger, this bank will be the third largest in terms of branches with 10,342 branches mainly in South India. It will also have an option to shut down around 2,000 branches due to location overlap. It will also be the fourth largest bank in India in terms of revenues, which are expected to be 1.5 times that of the Canara Bank. Since both banks work with the iFlex core banking software technology of Oracle Corporation, integration will not be an issue.

This is a merger where two plus two could easily make five.

Merger of Union Bank, Andhra and Corporation Bank

This is another tough merger because there are three troubled banks merging, with high NPAs and large losses. The operational areas of the three banks are largely south of the Vindhyas, so, though cultural integration may not be too problematic, branch rationalization may be needed. The total number of branches after merger will be 9,609, while the number of ATMs will be 13,438. There is, however, an asymmetric balance in the number of branches in the states, which needs to be corrected. For example, Andhra Bank has 1,591 branches in AP, which is more than half its total branches. Adding the branches of Union Bank and Corporation Bank, the total number of branches in Andhra Pradesh after consolidation will exceed 2,100, which amounts to 22 per cent of the total branches after merger. Besides, the consolidated bank will have over 1,200 branches in UP, 1,000 in Maharashtra, and over 800 in Karnataka, but very few branches in the prosperous states of Punjab and Telangana. So, the consolidated big bank will have to balance out its footprint to get more pan-Indian business.

The technology problems are not many because they use the same basic FINACLE software developed by Infosys. But, when we see the financial performance of the three banks pre-merger, we find the challenges within. Firstly, their financial statements are pretty opaque, with NPAs not adequately provisioned. The three banks have been found wanting on many accounts, but unconfirmed reports say that the regulators at RBI have been treating them with kid gloves. Andhra Bank was able to increase its interest incomes during the year to ₹18,932 crore and reduce its losses significantly to ₹2,786 crore, as per its annual report of 2018–19. The bank has had two big loss-making years and could face rough weather even in future. Importantly, its NPAs remain high at 16.2 per cent.

The Corporation Bank is a smaller bank, but in deeper trouble. The bank's interest income dipped over the year from ₹3,817 crore to ₹3,643 crore. Its operating profit, at ₹693 crore, is also lower than what it was last year. What is surprising, however, is the very high provisioning of NPAs for the bank this year, which, at ₹8,505 crore, is around 10 times the provisioning done over the last year. This has adversely affected the numbers and pushed up the net losses to ₹6,587 crore, which is nearly two times the revenue generated by the bank. The situation at Corporation Bank is fairly grim and even after the merger, it will require a lot of help to set its books in order. It may be also told to write off the losses from its reserve and surplus accounts and have its share swapped at a lower rate. Since 93.5 per cent of the stakes are held by the government, that should not matter much.

The key issue with this merger is that three big-time losers are merging, who have not still done their homework. They have not written off their NPAs from their balance sheets, as most other banks have. Union Bank of India, the biggest of the three banks in this merger, is still carrying over last year's losses of over ₹5,000 crore in the 2018–19 balance sheet. How this has been permitted by the regulators at the RBI is anybody's guess, but this makes the balance sheet of Union Bank look very weak, as last year's losses at ₹5,406 crore were nearly twice this year's losses at ₹2,947 crore, and the cumulative effect that has to be now written off is well over ₹8,000 crore. Additionally, the losses declared by Union Bank of India initially for the current fiscal was ₹2,947 crore, while the loss with RBI provisioning stood higher at ₹3,978 crores.

There is a huge difference in the way banks present their financials to the shareholders, some camouflaging the truth and some misinterpreting it. Many of them are opaque, and some are at best translucent. In most cases there is no transparency because it is considered a creative freedom and is permitted by law and encouraged by CAs. By disguising the numbers or creative presentations, they help their clients fool investors and also save taxes through suppression or illusory presentation of facts.

This happens despite the existence of an RBI format and despite the fact that they are all PSBs with majority holdings by the government as representative of the taxpayer. The Union Bank of India reported a NPA of ₹48,729 crore this year, which has once again pushed the gross NPAs of the bank to well above 15 per cent. So, here we have three banks each with large carry forward losses and with a history of unreported NPAs coming together.

This is surely a deadly combination where two plus two could only become three.

Indian Bank Takes Over Allahabad Bank

This is a merger of near equals, where there is not much difference between the size of the anchor bank and the merged bank. The big difference is the net worth, where Indian Bank is much better placed. Other than the number of client service points (branch plus ATMs) and financial performance, there is very little to place Indian Bank in position as the anchor bank. As a matter of fact, the staff association of Allahabad Bank claims that the amalgamation is unjustified because on several counts, it is the bigger bank. So, they are opposing the merger, as Allahabad Bank has higher levels of current account and savings account (CASA), more staff strength and a bigger volume of business compared to Indian Bank. Also, being the first Indian commercial bank to be set up in the country (1865), decades ahead of Indian Bank and three decades ahead of PNB, it has a strong sense of identity that its employees do not want to lose, says a bank insider. However, performance does matter in today's world and the Chennai-based bank is financially much stronger and better managed than Allahabad Bank. As a result, 115 shares of Indian

Bank are being swapped with 1,000 shares of Allahabad Bank.

Indian Bank has a strong footprint in South India and the Calcutta-headquartered Allahabad Bank is predominant in the North and East regions. It is true that Allahabad Bank has 3,245 branches, which are more than Indian Bank with 2,900 branches, but Indian Bank, which has almost twice the customer service points, with 3,956 ATMs as against 864 ATM machines of Allahabad Bank. So, despite a smaller employee base of 20,924 as against 23,210 of Allahabad Bank, it does more and better business and has more customer service points than Allahabad Bank.

Allahabad Bank's Gross NPAs were extremely high at 17.55 per cent, as against a moderate 7.12 per cent for Indian Bank. The CAR of both banks met the revised RBI Guidelines and the Basel III norms easily. While Indian Bank had a CAR of 13.46 per cent, Allahabad Bank also met the standards with a CAR of 12.59 per cent. Both the banks work with the BaNCS software developed by TCS and face no issues of technological integration. The finance ministry must have had performance in mind when deciding the anchor bank in this merger of the two.

This could be an integration where two plus two makes five.

Six Banks Merge, Six Banks Left Alone

The mergers have been planned to make six strong and big banks, each with a balance sheet size that exceeds ₹10 lakh crore. SBI will be the biggest of the lot, followed by Bank of Baroda, PNB, Canara Bank, Union Bank and Indian Bank in that order. That leaves out six more banks, including four regional banks with major presence in one single region each. The largest of them is the Chennai-based Indian Overseas Bank with a network of 3,400 branches, 2,955 ATMs and employee strength of 31,000 plus. It has revenues exceeding ₹23,000 crore and has a large footprint in South India.

Next in line is UCO Bank, headquartered in Kolkata, with 1,700 branches 2,300 ATMs and an employee strength exceeding 24,000. This is one of the financially weakest banks in the link. The bank has revenues exceeding ₹18,000 crore and is largely based in East India. Bank of Maharashtra, the third largest regional bank, has revenues of over ₹13,000 crore and an employee strength in excess of 12,000. It has 1,897 branches and 1,000 odd ATMs, half of which are in Maharashtra. Punjab and Sind Bank has 1,559 branches and 623 ATMs, a third of which are in Punjab. It has an employee strength exceeding 9,000 and revenues exceeding ₹8,000 crore. Whether these banks have been left alone outside the ambit of mergers to operate as regional banks or for disinvestment, only time will tell.

Apart from these four, there is the Bank of India and the Central Bank, which will not be merged. While Indian Overseas Bank will receive a capital infusion of ₹4,360 crore, Central Bank will get assistance of ₹3,300 crore. The UCO Bank will receive capital infusion of ₹2,100 crore and Punjab and Sind Bank will get ₹750 crore. The Centre has allocated ₹55,250 crore towards bank recapitalization in 2019. This, however, is just the beginning of what could turn out to be a long journey ahead. For the next two to three years, the government has to keep up the pace of bank reforms.

The finance minister Nirmala Sitharaman has said that the banks not merged would be sold. However, it is unlikely to be done in the near future.

We must realize that the proceedings from the NCLT courts have yielded less than 20 per cent of the bank loans advanced to the defaulting companies. This is inadequate and much lower than previously planned. So, banks need regular cash infusions to make up for the massive haircuts that they are going to take from the NCLT courts. Bank mergers can at best be a mixed bag of success and disappointments, but the process will be time-consuming and long-drawn and is likely to be streamlined only in the next five years.

TWELVE

MASS BANKING VERSUS CLASS BANKING

Though modern-day banking in India has been prevalent since the 18th century, it had a limited footprint outside the metros and larger cities till the late 1960s. Credit was available to well-established traders, but was totally absent for industry and agriculture. There were just around 8,000 bank branches in urban India and 1,400 bank branches in rural India in the first two decades after Independence. The privately owned banks were more interested in profits than increasing customers. Not everybody went to a bank.

As per Babu Jagjivan Ram, the common man was too scared to enter the shuttered gates. In the early 1950s, some banks in the towns of Bihar used to be called 'sahukaro ka sandook' or the rich men's vault. The only people who went to banks were rich traders or zamindars. There used to be two gunmen in full uniform, often sporting majestic moustaches and high leather boots, sitting at the front of the bank—one with a fully loaded 303 rifle and the other sporting a rifle with a bayonet. But even if you walked past the daunting sentries, the collapsible steel gates of the bank used to be half opened and chained at the top, so that you would have to bend twice to enter and exit the bank. Opening an account was equally difficult, as you would have to have a permanent residence address and at least three account holders to introduce you. The banks took added precautions as a security measure in those days to reduce the chance of bank robberies, which were not infrequent those days in Bihar, where

Babu Jagjivan Ram lived, but the message it sent out to the larger public was that it was the rich men's preserve.

Mass Banking: The First and Second Experiments

It was only after the nationalization of banks in 1969 that the number of urban banks quadrupled and the number of rural banks grew ten-fold over the next two decades. This mass banking experiment was needed then and changed the lives of billions. During the 1970s and the 1980s, there was a concentrated effort to provide banking facilities to the masses and to the industry and agriculture across rural India. The push was primarily from Prime Minister Indira Gandhi, who had three intermittent terms spanning a period of two decades. Slowly, banking became available to the masses.

The emphasis shifted again after the liberalization of the economy in 1991. Class banking entered the fray with the arrival of private banks. These retail banks were modern and progressive. They were focused on the urban elite and provided high-quality services at par with global banks. They met the rising demands of the aspirational salaried class and provided the facilities and conveniences of personal banking. They also had high service charges and a minimum balance requirement of ₹10,000. Clearly, class banking had arrived. This was a phase when PSB-led mass banking took a backseat and private sector-led class banking forged ahead. HDFC Bank and ICICI Bank raced ahead of the competition and became the second and the third largest banks of the country. The PSBs grew slowly by comparison, and once again a part of the population was left out from low-cost banking.

Soon after assuming office in 2014, PM Modi recharged mass banking activities through the PMJDY. The scheme put the PSBs back in focus, as they were set targets to spearhead the initiative where any individual could open a bank account with zero balance on the basis of their Aadhaar card. This benefitted around 30 crore people or a quarter of the Indian population. They were primarily those who did not have permanent residential addresses or two account holders to introduce them to the bank.

According to PwC, India's unbanked population reduced from 557 million people (44 per cent of population) to 233 million people (18 per cent of the population) in the year 2015 due to PMJDY. The government started transferring subsidies to these accounts through the DBT, as a result of which these accounts had a balance of over ₹1 lakh crore (₹1 trillion) by March 2020. But though there were 245 million active accounts, there were also 80 million inactive accounts that would come to haunt the system. So, though the NDA government revived mass banking through PMJDY accounts, which was the first step in creating a social equity matrix, we find that the journey has not been easy.

Can Mass Banking Raise the 'Bottom of the Pyramid'?

Opening the Jan Dhan accounts was just the first step towards mass banking. The second step was to ensure that the zero balance accounts become active with some cash infusion from the subsidies that the poor were entitled to. The most important step, however, was to ensure credit facilities, including issuance of unsecured loans, to these less-privileged account holders. The MUDRA loan initiatives were devised so that those loans and advances for the poor and underprivileged could be distributed. That would ensure wealth redistribution and increase the popularity of the political party that took such initiatives. But it was risk-prone for the banks, because it could lead to large write-offs periodically. This is only because the poor often cannot pay back their loans. This is a statistical reality, despite exceptions like Grameen Bank. Despite the good intentions of the borrower, the means for payback are not often available, largely due to circumstances beyond their control.

Since the PSBs cannot recover loans from the underprivileged easily and it becomes politically inappropriate to use force for recovery, the only way for the PSBs and the government is to write off these loans. Thus, it is ultimately the taxpayer who foots the bill of this largesse. But since it helps the poor and earns goodwill and votes, the politicians want to continue with this experiment despite the risks involved.

After 2014, a unique attempt was made to push the envelope once again towards mass banking. The MUDRA loan effort was primarily pushed by the PSBs after the Modi government's incessant prodding. The effort in both cases was primarily to expand credit to the masses. Prime Minister Modi tried to achieve mass banking through an effort that surpassed even Indira Gandhi's efforts in the 1970s and the 1980s.

Not only Indira Gandhi, but many thinkers and management gurus during the Nehruvian era and later realized that mass banking was needed for making a difference to India's development and growth. C.K. Prahalad, the renowned management guru, author and the proponent of the theory of 'fortune at the bottom of the pyramid', was clear in pointing out that moneylenders who charged astronomically high interest rates were bleeding the rural poor and the unorganized sector only because of the lack of banks to service them. In the introductory chapter of *Next Generation Business Strategies for the Base of the Pyramid*, Prahalad wrote, 'The total market for credit in rural India is ₹15,000 billion (now mostly done by moneylenders at 100 per cent interest rate maybe). The banks have just scratched the surface with ₹40 billion. If only the organised sector got only ₹10,000 billion and reduced the interest rate from 100 per cent to 20 per cent, you can calculate the income generated for the poor.'

Taking a leaf from the thinkers and the politicians before him, Prime Minister Narendra Modi set an ambitious target of loan disbursement of ₹3 lakh crore (₹3,000 billion) annually where banks would give loans under three categories of the Pradhan Mantri MUDRA Yojana, popularly known as the MUDRA loan scheme—the 'Sishu' loans for borrowers who wanted credit below ₹50,000, 'Kishore' loans for those who wanted credit above ₹50,000 but below ₹5 lakh, and 'Tarun' loans for those who wanted credit between ₹5 lakh and ₹10 lakh. He believed that like the Grameen Bank experiment in Bangladesh, mass banking would succeed and the delinquency rate would be low. He also thought that the poor in cities and villages would be turned into an entrepreneur class and bring prosperity for themselves and their neighbourhoods. So, while the UPA attempted to redistribute wealth through MGNREGA, the NDA tried to do the same through MUDRA loans.

Consolidation of All Priority Sector Loans as MUDRA

Instead of starting new loan schemes, PMMY loans consolidated all existing priority sector lendings under MUDRA loans and re-organized the same into a single category, with no new loan categories created. It was just that the diverse instruments were consolidated and targets set for an ambitious goal. The entire loan sanction process was made easier, and it was all digital. The plan was simple and looked achievable. Since the loan amount was to be transferred directly to the bank accounts of the people, it was believed to be largely corruption free. The target of ₹3 lakh crore per annum (₹3,000 billion) would be double of what was achieved in the previous years. In five years' time, the banks would be able to disburse advances of ₹15,000 billion to the needy, a dream that Prahalad had outlined years ago. Would that help them get out of the clutches of moneylenders and high interest borrowings, and thus create enormous savings for the rural poor? The idea was marvellous, but only if it ensured a smooth and stable credit flow and repayment between the banker and the borrower. For that, the PSBs had to be structured to deliver as well as recover such large loans. Completing the credit and recovery cycle with a moderate delinquency rate was the key to the success of the ambitious MUDRA loans for the lower income groups.

In July 2019, RBI Governor Shaktikanta Das told chief executives of PSBs to be cautious of disbursing loans to MUDRA beneficiaries and to monitor repayment of loans disbursed to avoid a pile up of bad loans. Months later, in November, Deputy Governor M.K. Jain raised a red flag over the sharply rising NPAs in MUDRA loan accounts.

As per the MUDRA loan website, 21 crore (210 million) people have been disbursed loans worth ₹10 lakh crore (₹10,000 billion) between 2015 and 2019. These loans were issued to the economically weaker section (EWS). Of this, 40 per cent were disbursed to women entrepreneurs and 33 per cent to socially backward categories. They came in handy to sway the electorate during the 2019 elections, without having to resort to illegal cash distribution.

During 2019–20, the average loan size dropped to ₹48,000 and the total disbursement was made to 3 crore people, as of November 2019.

The government released two sets of data when queried about the NPAs in the MUDRA loan scheme. In January 2019, the RBI cautioned that the PMMY, dubbed as the biggest employment creator and having generated ₹11,000 crore NPAs, could upset the credit market severely. However, Financial Services Secretary Rajiv Kumar, in a statement to the press, said that since PMMY loans were mostly under ₹1 lakh, they were all securitized and the government was not unduly worried about the NPAs in PMMY, whose average ticket size was small. However, the securitization deals have been done with small, private NBFCs like Janalakshmi Financial Services and SK Financial Services, and not with global bankers that have sufficient muscle to stand up against any major loan default in the sub-prime segment. This could lead to complacency and the misplaced confidence that the MUDRA loan NPAs are adequately hedged.

MUDRA Loan NPAs and Frauds in PSBs

Finance Minister Nirmala Sitharaman informed the parliament in a written reply that as of 21 June 2019, over 19 crore MUDRA loans had been extended under the PMMY. She stated that the total amount of NPAs under PMMY in all categories has shown a nominal rise from 2.52 per cent in 2017–18 to 2.68 per cent in 2019.

There is very little information about the performance of MUDRA loans. A bank loan becomes an NPA if it has not been serviced for more than 90 days. But bank loans under MUDRA are mostly below ₹1 lakh. Being small loans, these have all been distributed at the branch level. There is no mandatory reporting on the health of small loans on a regular basis at most banks. In some banks, a branch gives to its zonal office the total value of bad loans on a yearly basis, while in some banks, if the limit of NPAs for small loans is not breached, the branch manager has to merely give a statement certifying the same.

There is no RBI notification for reporting any stress for special mention accounts (SMAs) below ₹5 crore (₹50 million). So, it is not sure how foolproof would be the bank's reporting of small loan NPAs under the present circumstances. This is not, however, to say that there are many more NPAs in the MUDRA loans segment, but merely that the detection and reporting of defaults of small loans is still not as robust as that of large loans.

In February 2019, the CBI filed a case against Inder Chand Chundawa, a senior branch manager at PNB's Barmer branch in Rajasthan. The CBI alleged that he dishonestly and fraudulently sanctioned and disbursed 26 MUDRA loans between September 2016 and March 2017, causing a loss of ₹62 lakh (₹6.2 million) to the PSB. The field verification done appeared to be fake and prepared on the table at the office. Some borrowers were found to be residing 100 km away from Barmer, whereas the bank could only sanction loans to people residing within a 25 km radius of the branch. Several other fraud cases were reported and reports of large NPAs surfaced in the media.

Considering that 21 crore loans have been given in the last four years, the number of frauds and delinquencies reported by the finance minister are few. This could be because of a lag in the reporting system, as frauds usually get reported three years after they are committed. The RBI annual report of 2018–19, released in August, stated, 'The average lag for large frauds, i.e. ₹100 crore and above, amounting to ₹52,200 crore reported during 2018-19, was 55 months.' So, would small loans be reported any faster?

Bankers' Feedback on MUDRA Frauds

This made us talk to several bankers to get a better assessment of the ground situation for small loans under MUDRA. The report we got was that frauds are happening as before; no more, no less. Any claim that frauds have gone away due to better digitization was incorrect. So, we spoke to a few bankers in the PSBs to understand why and how these frauds are still happening. Some of the allegations made by the bankers were eye-openers. We are, however, not sure whether these are true or false allegations and have no means of checking the same.

According to unconfirmed reports, some of the inactive Jan Dhan accounts were revived by some corrupt bank managers during demonetization to regularize unaccounted cash into the banking system. The bank managers used agents and field officers of the bank to locate poor clients with dormant Jan Dhan accounts, who were ready to work as cash mules. They got them to give their bank passbooks and Aadhaar numbers, along with fingerprints, on blank deposit and withdrawal slips at a small price. These dormant Jan Dhan accounts were used to hold unaccounted cash and functioned as benami accounts for the rich.

The branch managers who operated these accounts charged anywhere between 10 per cent and 30 per cent of the cash being laundered through these accounts, depending on the need and the urgency of the customer, while the account holder got a lumpsum payment. The amounts regularized through these benami accounts were very large and helped regularize more than 10 per cent of the cash in circulation into the system. Demonetization made some branch managers of PSBs and private sector banks very rich. It also put them in control of the operation of lakhs of benami accounts, where the sim numbers of phones linked to Aadhaar cards were bought at a price, thus transferring all identifiable legal rights to the benami operators. These regularized benami accounts were then given MUDRA loans without verification. If these allegations are true, the scam could be a major setback for free and fair distribution of MUDRA loans.

Why is Class Banking so Different from Mass Banking?

Class banking in India provides banking facilities, loans and advances primarily for the rich and the upper middle class. They create a barrier for the masses with a minimum balance criterion of ₹10,000 for the ordinary customer and a further barrier of ₹1,00,000 balance for the privileged customer. Class banking is primarily provided by the private sector banks. It is not that class banking majors do not attempt to be mass banking players. HDFC Bank has recently shown that it is able to quickly disburse unsecured loans en masse without looking at large-scale NPAs. Its growth in advances to the MSME and retail sectors has been phenomenal during the past three years, when most PSBs (the mass banking players) started slowing down advances.

So, how did HDFC Bank grow so fast in the unsecured loan business without large NPAs where most others have failed? Many competing private banks feel that HDFC is a late entrant in this segment and has indeed grown very fast. But it is too early to talk about low delinquency, and the real figures could be much higher in the next three years.

We were curious about the claims and counter-claims. This is especially because the numbers put forward by HDFC Bank were in stark contrast with the PSBs, where there was a slowdown in the credit offtake. Also, we wanted to check the process of loan disbursement at HDFC Bank to see whether it would succeed or fail and if it was vastly different from the PSBs. We found huge differences between PSBs and HDFC Bank, not only in the organization structure of the banks but also in the approach to its operations and credit disbursal.

The branch manager at HDFC Bank was merely a facilitator with limited responsibility and powers. The job of the branch was to open accounts for customers, verify KYCs and forward all requests for loans without sanctioning any at the branch level. The branch manager and the officers at the branch were merely lead generators for loans to customers. They were the first point of contact with customers, and while they ensured a smooth banking experience, they also ensured that the prospective client had the credentials to get a loan even before accepting a loan application.

For example, if he was a businessman, he would have to submit income tax and GST returns of the past three years along with his bank statement. Only if all these three items showed a steady business return without hiccups, would his loan application be accepted. For a salaried employee, the firm where he worked would have to be registered with HDFC Bank. The bank maintained the financial data of registered companies and also rated organizations on its approved list and varied the interest rates given to its employees based on the organization's credit ratings. Also, the income tax returns for the borrower and his bank statement for three years would be checked prior to accepting the loan application. After this entire due process, the application for loan would be accepted by the branch office. This would be the start point of a very long and elaborate verification and qualification process. Before we go through this process, let us understand the roles and responsibilities given to the officers of the HDFC Bank at various levels of credit appraisal.

The branch is merely the customer interface point in HDFC Bank. The manager is responsible for the business the branch generates, and like ICICI Bank and Axis Bank managers, takes care of both customer relationship and sales. But he neither sanctions the loan nor disburses it. While the organization's set-up does not permit him from being the power centre, it also isolates him from professional risks he takes as a banker. So, once he gets the loan application from the customer, he has to pass it on to the credit department for processing. Thereafter, it goes to the relevant department for approval.

There are dozens of retail products that the branch manager processes, but he does not handle the credit appraisal, the documentation, the legal or the monitoring of the loan, which are handled by separate verticals. These verticals are essentially back offices with expertise that have little or no customer interface.

There are no power centres in the entire operation. Every loan is process-driven, with checks and balances and analytics for monitoring. The appraisal and disbursal of credit is only the first point of engagement and is thus of limited importance to the bank. Its health, however, depends on the use of funds and the repayment of interest and principal, which are of prime interest to the bank. So, the bank monitors the use of funds closely after disbursement, and that ensures timely repayment of credit. The HDFC Bank has also started sanctioning loans on basis of software and analytics that assess the credit score and the cash flow of the borrower and sanction loans on application automatically, with a processing time of 10 seconds.

Tech Banking through Artificial Intelligence

Several private banks, like ICICI Bank, HDFC, Axis Bank and Yes Bank, have all developed artificial intelligence (AI)-based assessment modules that can give instant credit approval on data and documents submitted by the borrower online. Asheesh Maroo, the Country Head, Risk at Yes Bank Ltd, says that banks are gearing up for automatically assessing credit applications through AI. Technology is leaving its impact on banking and will go a long way to make banking risk free. This could happen quickly if the Supreme Court permits banks to assess Aadhaar information of account holders, which is currently barred on account of concerns of privacy. Already, credit bureaus like Trans Union or Experian provide the credit score of businesses, just like the CIBIL, which provides the credit score of individual borrowers.

These credit bureaus have been in existence since 2006 and provide relevant credit information to several banks, NBFCs, and insurance majors. They not only provide balance sheet data of borrowers but also provide credit reporting solutions that use predictive data spanning the entire consumer lifecycle. The CIBIL score effectively predicts whether a potential borrower is likely to default on one or more trade lines after 90 days in the next 12 months. The information is updated quarterly and helps the lender assess the possibility of fund recovery throughout the business cycle.

Scorecard-based assessment is the next step in tech banking. 'The PSBs are mostly lacking in the use of technology and third-party services that provide quality analytics at a cost. They need to set up their inhouse scorecard-based system for risk assessment and credit appraisal. Most private banks have developed their scorecard-based system', says Maroo. This should integrate the IT data, the GST data, the Balance Sheet data, the bank account data and the credit bureau data. The software integrates all the above data and gives a score for a particular borrower. This score is updated every quarter and gives sufficient notice to banks to jettison clients who are becoming overleveraged over time. The idea of this move, to develop a scorecard at the bank level, is to stop getting into a follow-the-leader loan trap. But while the private sector banks are all working with fintech majors to create their in-house scorecard-based softwares, the same cannot be said of the PSBs we spoke to.

THIRTEEN

BANKING IN THE POST-COVID-19 ERA

On 31 December 2019, health officials from China's Hubei province first reported to the World Health Organisation (WHO) that 41 patients who had contracted a mysterious type of pneumonia were not responding to any conventional treatment. Since most patients were from the Huanan Seafood Wholesale Market area of Wuhan, the market was shut on 1 January 2020. At that point, nobody thought that this mysterious respiratory disorder that had surfaced just as we entered the year 2020 would torment the world for months, killing hundreds of thousands and rendering millions jobless.

The Huanan wet market sells seafood and meat that are very cheap. You can find meat of all sorts of animals here—pangolin, bats, lizards, snakes, baby crocodiles, koala bears, baby turtles and shellfish—which are largely consumed by the poor. The animals are caged in unhygienic conditions. They are often sick and injured, and when under severe duress, the viral pathogens they carry intermingle and swap parts of their genetic code to mutate in ways that can make them jump across species. It is widely believed that such pathogens jumped from the animals to the meat merchants who slaughtered and sold those animals, through spilled blood or other body fluids. Such spread of virus has affected humans previously as well, like during the SARS, Ebola and HIV outbreaks.

China Locks Down Hubei Province But Pushes Foreign Travel

The Wuhan Institute of Virology, which had been working with the SARS-Cov 2002, quickly started studying this new virus. On 7 January 2020, China identified the virus as a novel Coronavirus or 2019-nCov, and it was later termed as COVID-19. By 11 January, the virus had claimed its first life, and two days later it had spread to Thailand. On 20 January, China's lead scientist in the Corona resistance, Zong Nanshan, confirmed that the virus can be transmitted human to human. On 22 January, at a meeting to decide the measures to be taken, the WHO was, however, not able to warn the world of the severity of the 2019-nCoV, as China objected to creating 'unnecessary panic'. WHO referred to it as 'locally controllable'. It noted that a 'severe warning' was not issued to the rest of the world due to 'divergent views'. By that time, though, COVID-19 had started to hurt Korea, Iran and Italy seriously, and had spread to nearly 30 nations.

On 23 January, Wuhan city was put under 'quarantine', and within the next two days lockdown was enforced across the entire Hubei province. This province has an area of 186,000 sq. km and a population below 6 crore (smaller than the Indian state of Karnataka on both counts). Its GDP is $540 billion, which makes it the seventh biggest in revenues among 23 Chinese provinces. Authorities, in the next few days, quarantined an unprecedented 50 million people and completely locked down 15 cities in the province. In the last week of January, when China started to celebrate the year of the rat—a period when the Chinese close down businesses for their new year and travel—all plane and train traffic from Hubei province to other Chinese cities ground to a halt. Even buses and cars were stopped, but surprisingly, all international traffic was permitted.

The influx of Chinese tourists to Italy and the sudden rise of COVID-19 cases alerted the European nation, which closed down international traffic to and from China on 31 January. Qin Gang, China's vice minister of foreign affairs, told Italy's ambassador to China, Luca Ferrari, in Beijing following the flight ban: 'Italy's decision to stop flights without contacting China in advance caused great inconvenience to citizens of both countries. Many Chinese are still stranded in Italy.' Following the US travel advisory issued against travel to China on 2 February, the Civil Aviation Administration of China stated, 'In order to meet the needs of passengers in and out of the country and the international transport of supplies during this special period... airlines [are required to]...continue transport to nations that have not imposed travel restrictions.'

Surprisingly, WHO chief Tedros Adhanom Ghebreyesus seemed to support the Chinese contention that all was well and truly under control. He stated at the opening of the agency's Executive Board meet on the 3 February, 'There is no reason for measures that unnecessarily interfere with international travel and trade. We call on all countries to implement decisions that are evidence-based and consistent. WHO stands ready to provide advice to any country that is considering which measures to take.' The Chinese Foreign Ministry spokesperson Hua Chunying, criticizing the US advisories, said, 'The US government hasn't provided any substantial assistance to us, but it was the first to evacuate personnel from its consulate in Wuhan, the first to suggest partial withdrawal of its embassy staff, and the first to impose a comprehensive travel ban on Chinese travellers.'

WHO Belatedly Declares a Global Pandemic

Forty days after China started its lockdown, on 11 March, WHO belatedly declared COVID-19 a global pandemic. By that time the number of COVID-19 cases globally had grown thirteen-fold. As per the WHO website, more than 118,000 cases had been reported in 114 countries, and 4,291 people had already lost their lives before a global pandemic was declared. By the time countries scrambled up a response strategy, it was end-March.

So, the world started its lockdown a clear two months after China. Data from Tom Tom traffic index, a location-based traffic site headquartered in the Netherlands that collates traffic data from 416 cities in 57 countries, tells a unique tale of how the global lockdown affected international traffic in major cities of the world. Figure 13.1 shows normal traffic congestion in all major cities of the world in January 2020. In February, average traffic density in Wuhan and Shanghai dropped to 10 per cent of the normal while in Beijing the traffic density was just 5 per cent. Paris, Rome and New Delhi had 80 per cent traffic density in February, London had 70 per cent and New York had 60 per cent traffic density, which is normal for these cities. In March 2020, after successfully locking down Hubei province, China relaxed traffic for Beijing and Shanghai, where traffic density rose to 30 per cent and 40 per cent respectively, while Wuhan traffic density was still pegged below 10 per cent. Other major cities of the world showed no signs of lockdown, with the same traffic density levels as the month of February.

Traffic Density	January	February	March	April
100 per cent	Paris			
90 per cent	Beijing			
80 per cent	Shanghai, Rome, New Delhi	Rome, Paris, New Delhi	Rome, Paris, New Delhi	
70 per cent	London	London	London	
60 per cent	Wuhan, New York	New York	New York	Beijing, Shanghai
50 per cent				
40 per cent			Shanghai	
30 per cent			Beijing	
20 per cent				Rome, London,
10 per cent		Wuhan, Shanghai	Wuhan	Wuhan, New York, Paris, New Delhi
5 per cent		Beijing		

Data Source: Tom Tom Traffic Index

Figure 13.1 China locks down in February, two months prior to the global lockdown

Only after WHO declared a pandemic in mid-March did other countries start to prepare for lockdowns. In April, traffic density in Paris, New York and New Delhi dropped to below 10 per cent, and in Rome and London, to a little below 20 per cent. But in April, the lockdown had been lifted in Beijing and Shanghai, where traffic density rose to 60 per cent. In reality, the industrial and commercial activity resumed in full force across China, barring the Hubei province, by April. Wuhan and the other cities of the Hubei province remained locked down, with traffic density well below 10 per cent.

Though Kenya Airways, Rwanda Airways, Air Mauritius and Royal Air Maroc suspended flights to China in February, Chinese airlines continued to fly all routes across Africa, except where they were barred. China has major mining and construction projects across several African nations and an estimated two million Chinese workers in that continent. In the last week of March, after a telecon with US President Donald Trump, the Chinese President Xi Jinping agreed to curb international flights from China. The Civil Aviation Administration of China, after the discussion, stated 'that 90 per cent of international flights would be temporarily suspended. The number of incoming passengers would be cut to 5,000 a day, from 25,000. China has also ordered local airlines to maintain only one route per country, once a week, as of 29th March.'

Was COVID-19 Used as an Economic Warfare Tool?

The COVID-19 pandemic caused death and devastation in China as well as in the rest of the world. However, China, which locked down the earliest, was able to escape with minimum losses. By end-May, it had restricted its deaths to below 5,000 and its economic losses to less than $100 billion. By end-March the Chinese economy was back on its feet, and by May had made fresh gains in the global medical equipment market as the world struggled to cope with the COVID crisis. Things were grim across the rest of the world, with deaths exceeding 350,000 and economic losses expected to be worth almost $10 trillion.

By end-May, the US death toll crossed the 100,000 mark, accounting for nearly around 30 per cent of the global casualties. UK and Italy with around 35,000 deaths each and France and Spain with around 30,000 deaths each were the other major nations that were hard hit. India, with one of the most severe lockdown programmes, applied diligently from 25 March, was able to contain the impact of the virus despite its large population, high population density and relatively poor medical infrastructure. By the end of May, India had over 150,000 infections and 4,000 deaths, which was considered very nominal given its population and related parameters. But the country may pay a huge price for the extended lockdown and consequent economic disruption causing joblessness and poverty.

The COVID crisis caught governments and administrations across the world in total panic. Nearly 1 per cent of the global population was affected and five people out of 10,000 died. Besides, it hit the powerful Western economies the hardest. It locked down major business centres across the world, like New York, London, Paris, Rome, Madrid and Mumbai, for months. It also disrupted industries and services worldwide, rendering more than 500 million people jobless across the globe. The last disaster with such severe consequences had occurred a hundred years ago during the advent of the Spanish Flu, when 500 million people were reportedly affected and an estimated 20 million to 40 million people were killed.

It was inevitable that the blame game would soon start on the COVID crisis. There were many conspiracy theories that started doing the rounds, suggesting that this was an accidental leak from the Wuhan Virology Lab. A few others suggested that this was bio-terrorism, and some suggested that it was just an instrument of economic warfare, unleashed by China to counter American trade sanctions. Some suggested that China's expansionist policy across Africa, Asia and Latin America was faltering due to its sharp rise of debt, and it needed a new tool to grow its markets as a dominant supplier of goods and services to the world. It, therefore, used the pandemic to create a global uncertainty, so that the world would lock down in panic and businesses across the world would come to a standstill.

We investigated each of these theories and found that though there is no evidence to point at bio-terrorism, there is sufficient proof that China used the COVID crisis to gain undue economic advantage by suppressing critical information about its severity and suspiciously pushing foreign travel at the height of the pandemic. We have, hence, presented the authentic traffic data and recorded statements of Chinese leaders and administrators to show beyond doubt that China locked up internally but pushed international traffic till the end of March. Why? China's rising economic debt and its need to bridge the gap with the US could be the motive for this unprecedented economic warfare. So, how much did China actually gain intentionally or unintentionally due to COVID-19?

Australia Asks for Independent Probe into China's Intent

Conservative estimates today suggest that the economic losses of the Western economies could exceed $4 trillion, which would be easily a hundred times more than the losses incurred by China. This would not only narrow the gap with the US, but help China dominate the world economy when serious supply-side disruptions occur. Also, China would sweep in on several global companies, which would be available at near distress prices due to the Corona crisis. This low-priced asset acquisition would help it justify its mammoth debt, which just keeps growing.

Even prior to the COVID crisis, the global debt burden in the first quarter of 2020 had crossed precarious levels of $250 trillion and was three times higher than the global GDP. The biggest borrowers were the US and China. According to the Washington-based Institute of International Finance, China's corporate, household and government debt rose to 303 per cent of its GDP in the first quarter of 2019. This is much higher than the grossly overborrowed US economy, where the debt equals its GDP.

China has long been influencing the global index and debt funds to corner an increasingly larger share of the emerging market pie. Unknown to most American and global investors, $400 billion of investment went to Chinese companies in 2019 due to subtle changes in allocations within benchmark indexes. This happened because of technical changes made by the three major index providers—MSCI, FTSE Russell and S&P Dow Jones. The MSCI Emerging Markets Index, which guides more than $1.7 trillion in investments in 26 developing nations, included Chinese companies listed locally in November 2019, as a result of which China's total weight in the index rose to 34 per cent. Previously, only companies listed in the US bourses were included. The FTSE Russell and the S&P Dow Jones increased China's weightage to 37 per cent, which not only hurt the interests of other emerging economies but put all the eggs in one basket called China, increasing investor risk. Normally no single country has a quarter of its investments allocated, so that in case of default by one nation, the entire index fund does not go under. India, which remains blissfully unaware of how global investment moves, lost heavily due to this index shift.

Apart from this, China has been liberally using zero interest credit from international investors and pension funds to finance its bond markets and business interests in Asia, Africa and Latin America. Since China has access to these zero interest borrowings that other emerging nations don't, it undercuts global competition and offers long credit periods to win orders. Over the last decade, China has managed to fully decimate competition offered by emerging markets and virtually monopolize equipment exports, international project contracts and mining leases in most overseas markets. This has not only been due to cheaper prices, but the attractive debt packaging it offers with its supplies. So, while China borrows from global investors at 0 per cent interest, it captures global markets as it offers liberal credit terms to the rest of the world at a nominal interest rate.

China's urge to dominate the global economy, ride roughshod over global best practices and manipulate and corner investments had long been under watch. So, connecting the dots, analysts assessed that there was a very high probability that the suppression of information about the severity of the Coronavirus and the push to 'export the virus' was an active economic warfare tool. Though only President Trump has been openly critical of China's role and intention in suppressing information during the COVID crisis, others have now started to speak out.

China is Australia's largest trading partner. Yet, Scott Morrison, the Australian prime minister, in the last week of April, called for an independent international investigation into the Coronavirus pandemic in phone calls with US President Donald Trump and the German and French leaders. He also called for a probe into the role and effectiveness of WHO in handling the COVID crisis. Chinese Ambassador Cheng Jingye reacted to Morrison's statement and warned that pursuing an inquiry could spark a Chinese consumer boycott of students and tourists visiting Australia as well as of sales of major exports, including beef and wine.

Nonetheless, a probe is justified and may be conducted, in all probability, once the immediate urgency of handling the pandemic is attended to. President Trump, who has been unable to carry his EU colleagues on most issues regarding sanctions, would be more than happy if such an initiative gathers speed. This is an election year for him, and he would not stop at stalling China's global influence with all the weapons at his disposal. The US senate has already passed a bill with the support of both Republicans and Democrats to delist 800 Chinese companies from US exchanges to ensure that pension funds do not invest heavily in Chinese companies in search of higher profits. The key to any joint international investigation will, however, be the consent of Chancellor Angela Merkel of Germany, as the Bavarian nation has been China's largest trading partner and has not been greatly affected by the pandemic. She and Emmanuel Macron, the French President, are the prime decision-makers at the EU, and their support will be crucial to any meaningful international initiative.

Indian Response to the COVID Crisis: Quick and Defensive

India quickly reacted to the global pandemic. It took the necessary measures to curb the proliferation by imposing social distancing, monitoring of foreign travellers, and quarantine. It was slow to start testing due to infrastructure constraints, but the ICMR managed the segregation of the infected through a well-thought-out optimum testing methodology. Two weeks after WHO declared COVID-19 a global pandemic, India was one of the first off the block to impose a total countrywide lockdown for three weeks. The effort was mammoth and well-coordinated, despite some inherent flaws in supply chain management that were subsequently corrected.

The first lockdown was followed by a second lockdown of two weeks, which was logical, since more time was needed to set up the medical and hospital infrastructure and the response mechanism to the pandemic. By that time, it was fairly clear that though the effect of COVID-19 could be delayed by lockdown or social distancing, it would eventually spread, with millions contracting the virus. All businesses and industries were closed and over 5 million migrant workers were rendered jobless in cities, without any livelihood or income. The state governments as well as NGOs opened relief camps for jobless people needing food and shelter. Most people, including migrant workers at the camps, expected the lockdowns to be lifted in May, and there was little to no attempt at going home during the first month of lockdown.

On 27 April, days before lockdown 2.0 was due to end, the states of Delhi (AAP), Odisha (Biju Janta Dal), Maharashtra (Shiv Sena, NCP, Congress), Madhya Pradesh (BJP), West Bengal (TMC) and Punjab (Congress) batted for an extended lockdown of two more weeks. Political parties across the spectrum, usually at loggerheads, were all on the same page. The Modi government, instead of allowing just those six states to implement lockdown, promptly extended the nationwide lockdown by another two weeks, which would keep most of the economic activity across 36 states and union territories closed till the third week of May. The reason could have been the fear of COVID-19 that China had successfully implanted throughout the world, or just a play safe attitude, but it resulted in extended loss of livelihood and total business uncertainty.

The decision of lockdown 3.0 created panic among the millions of jobless workers stranded in India's large cities, who were now totally dependent on doles and food and shelter provided by camps run by state governments and NGOs. They realized that as migrant labourers, they would not be part of the consultative process of any state or central government about opening the lockdown. That they would be subject to whatever decisions the financially secure elite took—decision-makers who would keep getting salaries from state or central governments, namely the politicians, bureaucrats and administrators. That since elections were far away, they would not be prioritized. Instead, politicians would not take any healthcare risks and play safe, so that they would be seen to contain the rapidly growing pandemic of COVID-19.

It was out of this insecure helplessness that thousands of migrant workers started moving back to their home states. They knew that the journey back home would not be easy, but also knew that they would be able to survive an extended lockdown once they were back. But since bus and train services in all states remained shut, the only way to return was to walk back home. The exodus first started from Mumbai and Delhi, two of the largest cities, reputed to be insensitive and brutally heartless, which, between them, employed over half a million migrant workers. As thousands of workers moved out of the camps and trudged back home, news channels focused on their misery and migrant displacement. But while the migrant movement crisis took the spotlight, a new crisis had started, unnoticed, as India went in for an extremely defensive strategy of lockdowns, one that was not restricted to migrant labourers—a crisis that would devastate industries across the board and take years to recover from.

What Extended Lockdowns Meant for the Economy

FICCI President Sangita Reddy, at the end of the first lockdown, said, 'Estimates show that India may be losing close to ₹40,000 crore daily due to the nationwide lockdown with an estimated loss amounting to ₹7-8 lakh crore during the past 21 days.' As per data released by the industry department on 30 April, the crude oil sector had contracted by 5.5 per cent, natural gas 15.2 per cent, refinery products 0.5 per cent, fertilizers 11.9 per cent, steel 13 per cent, cement 24.7 per cent and electricity 7.2 per cent during the month. Retail, Construction, Hospitality, Tourism, Airlines and Education had been totally shut, and hence had 100 per cent output drop. Unemployment had risen from 8 per cent to over 24 per cent after the first month of lockdown, as per CMIE. It was pretty obvious from the industry data that another month of lockdown would be disastrous for the economy. But people who look at data and analyse the consequences unfortunately do not take decisions in India.

The bureaucracy and political class taking decisions at the state and the central governments have no time for such economic data. So, ignoring the writing on the wall, India went in for Lockdown 3.0, Lockdown 4.0, and beyond. Indian administrators played into the Chinese strategy of creating more business uncertainty than the virus could physically cause. India has always been a bureaucrats' paradise and never a business-friendly nation, irrespective of the political party at the helm; so, the attitude of its political leadership was not unexpected. The socialist mindset of control economics was evident in its actions.

India was quick to lock down everything, but laboured to open up the economy ever so slowly, a bureaucratic exercise that could go on for months. Circular after circular was issued by the Ministry of Home Affairs (MHA) and the secretaries of the state governments, which read like an ode to its socialist past of the licence permit raj. It reminded me of the Indira Gandhi regime, when manufacturers were told by the excise department what and how much they could produce through circulars issued each month. Since the bureaucrats issuing those circulars have no idea how businesses function, they created endless confusion in the industry. I spoke to a few of my PAN IIT alumni who are part of the industry, and they had harrowing stories to tell. One machinery manufacturer, who had a total of 132 suppliers of bought-out parts, did not start manufacturing despite permission because 19 of his suppliers where in containment zones and expressed inability to supply, and 24 were in different states and could not guarantee that part truck load of material would be transported or even permitted to cross state borders.

Across industry and business, there was chaos and uncertainty and people were unsure whether they would lose less money if they remained closed or if they opened up 33 per cent, as per the extremely theoretical plans developed by the bureaucrats of India. Each business had its own problems, and after ringing half a dozen businesses, I realized that I would eventually gather enough material for another book on 'Lockdown India' that I had no intention of writing. However, to sum it up, there were three distinct problems that could be envisaged. Twenty per cent of the establishments that had closed would never open at all. Fifty per cent of the establishments that would open would be lacking cash for normal business activities and struggle through the financial year. The remaining 30 per cent of the industries, who had the financial muscle to survive the lockdowns, would still make losses due to the loss in production of nearly a whole quarter and weak consumer demand thereafter.

At the end of Lockdown 3.0, India had incurred losses of well over ₹20 trillion or 10 per cent of its GDP on a conservative estimate. Opening the economy was nowhere in sight and it was apparent that the bureaucrats of the states and centre would not permit free trade till the state treasuries creaked and their own salaries were at stake. The writing was on the wall. The good work of banking reforms done by the Modi government would all evaporate, as economic chaos would prevail due to the extended lockdowns. The rupee could come under intense pressure in the future, especially as the government needs to borrow close to ₹25 lakh crore in 2020 due to rising deficits of the state and central government. Goods and services would become expensive to produce, and despite fall in consumption, may have higher prices, negating all the rate cuts by the RBI.

Bankers' Response: Can Finance Minister Nirmala Sitharaman's Liquidity Measures Cross Lockdown 4.0?

As the extended lockdown devastated the economy, Finance Minister Nirmala Sitharaman unveiled an elaborate stimulus package to boost the economy in the second week of May. The ₹20 lakh crore stimulus package was largely a liquidity package cleverly designed so that the depleted coffers of the state would not be unduly hurt. The package, which was declared in five tranches and touched a dozen sectors, could be broadly divided in three segments. The first was liquidity measures, the second was fiscal measures or tax rebates with direct budgetary impact, and the third was intent. Though the gross impact of these three measures, including RBI's liquidity measure of ₹8 lakh crore, would cross ₹20 lakh crore (10 per cent of GDP), the direct impact on the treasury would be less than 1.5 lakh crore or 0.75 per cent of the GDP as per Barclay's Bank, and 0.8 per cent of the GDP as per Edelweiss economist Madhavi Arora.

This additional allocation would raise the fiscal deficit for the year to around 6 per cent, a safe limit for the government in these turbulent times. Whereas critics were vocal that it meant doing too little for the industry and the people in distress, I seriously doubt if any political party would have done more, considering that the next general elections are four years away as of writing. The stimulus included measures declared previously by the government and the RBI, as well as those declared by the finance minister in May 2020. The liquidity measure was carefully packaged in the first tranche of ₹5.95 lakh crore, which included ₹3 lakh crore additional credit facility to be provided to existing MSMEs, other liquidity schemes for NBFCs, power companies, etc. of around ₹2 lakh crore, and the balance to support EPF, TDS/TCS, etc. The second tranche of ₹3.1 lakh crore was largely directed towards supporting the PDS scheme and the migrant workers, who were neither beneficiaries of the National Food Security Act (NFSA), nor of the state-level ration cards.

The third tranche of ₹1.5 lakh crore was a mixture of policy announcements of intent and project funds and talked of setting up an agriculture infrastructure fund, beekeeping fund, animal husbandry fund and other initiatives including changes in the Essential Commodities Act (ECA), 1955, which has been a work in progress for the last five years. The fourth and fifth tranches were new pushes to old reforms with an allocation of ₹48, 000 crore and together with the earlier announced Pradhan Mantri Garib Kalyan Package (PMGKP) of ₹1.92 lakh crore, the total 'Atmanirbhar Bharat' package amounted to nearly ₹13 lakh crore. The RBI liquidity measure, if added, pushed up the package past the ₹20 lakh crore announcement made by the prime minister. The pros and cons of this package were being deliberated upon extensively in the media, so I decided to instead check the effectiveness of the package and write a piece for my ET blog on why Finance Minister Nirmala Sitharaman's MSME loans can't be disbursed.

I started looking at the first major announcement of automatic credit facility provided to the MSME sector by Finance Minister Sitharaman, of ₹3 lakh crore, which had been announced a fortnight back on 13 May. I asked some of my PAN IIT associates who had MSME units whether they had benefited from the scheme. Only one person with an account at a PSB said that he had received an email from the bank about the scheme. When I asked him if he had availed the facility, he said the bank would disburse the same only after the lockdowns were lifted. So I rang up a few bank managers to ask what would be the disbursement procedure and time frame. One of them said that the bank was working with a skeleton crew and the only commercial activity that was both viable and visible currently was the withdrawal of ₹500 by the Jan Dhan Account holders. The second bank manager told me that the printed instructions had arrived from the head office a day ago and permitted the enhancement of 20 per cent working capital to those MSME holders who had cash credit limits. But no action could be taken, as the bank was not giving any loans during the lockdown because of two reasons:

> Firstly there is no staff to deal with loan documentation in view of limited staff working during the lockdown. Banks were only undertaking essential services which meant cash withdrawal and deposit, clearing of cheques, inter-banking operations and government transactions etc. Giving loans were not part of essential services. Secondly there are no bank guarantee papers. Stamp papers that are needed for the loan documentation prior to disbursement of the loan are not available as courts are closed. The BG (Bank Guarantee) documents are usually typed out on the stamp papers and attested by the notary before release of any bank loan. A Delhi Bank usually has half its MSME account holders from the neighbouring states of UP, Haryana and Rajasthan, so opening of courts in Delhi alone would not solve the problem.

Since the government has not given any circular waiving the requirement of the BG in view of its own credit guarantee, no action could be taken by the banks to process the loans notified by the finance ministry recently under the MSME scheme. The truth is that unless the lockdowns are totally lifted, businesses cannot run, and even loans cannot be disbursed. The bureaucracy do not understand how the operations at the ground level are conducted and still want to do micromanagement, leading to part lifting of lockdowns, which is slowly leading to a crisis point.

Extended Lockdowns Will Hurt Bank Reforms

Extended lockdowns are going to be extremely problematic for the banking sector, which will ultimately have to bear all the losses. Both industry and trade run on money from the banks, and if they close down for long periods and become sick, the problem will automatically shift to the banks. The banks are aware of the problems, but cannot stop the inevitable from happening. Banks earn money by giving credit. But now they have nobody to lend to. Industries are closed down, and so is trade. When they get back to working after a prolonged shut down, they will no longer be healthy. Banks have been taking some measures in curtailing fresh credit, which in the long run could even prove counterproductive.

What started as an excessive credit problem during 2007–09 has turned into an acute credit squeeze situation. In the year ending March 2017, there was no fresh industrial credit given by the banks, while in the year 2017–18 credit growth was just 3 per cent. Compare this to ten years ago, when the industrial credit growth grew by over 25 per cent in both financial years ending March 2007 and March 2008. But a large number of industries misused the credit facilities, leading to massive frauds and NPAs due to what was known as the evergreening of loans. We have seen in Chapter 5 that after the banks were compelled to declare stressed assets, the high number of NPAs, especially in the PSBs, made them risk averse. So banks, despite prodding from the government, stopped lending to the industries, leading to an acute credit squeeze. The industries, instead, were advised to reduce the high leveraging and bring in more equity for the debt they carried, to meet the asset quality norms as per the RBI guidelines. The excess liquidity that the banks had was funneled towards retail business, where credit offtake was strong and banks were willing to lend. Between 2015 and 2018, retail loans grew by 20 per cent to 25 per cent annually on an average, as industrial credit plummeted.

But that was all before the disruption, which has been extended now to over two months under lockdown 4.0. Both the retail and the industry sectors will come out of the lockdown, whenever it is lifted completely, battered and bruised. They will take many months, and perhaps years, to recover. Some may not recover at all, and simply go belly up. So, what happens to bank credit that has been tied up with businesses for so long? The industry sector accounts for 35 per cent of the non-food credit, and the retail sector accounts for 25 per cent. If even half of these accounts default, several banks will also collapse.

After the extended lockdown, many of these bank loans will turn into NPAs despite the best efforts of the entrepreneurs, and extending the moratorium period of term loans alone may not help. What will the RBI do to stop the domino effect of debt default? The IBA has suggested setting up a bad bank, which is a really bad idea. This is because Indian ARCs are very small and would not have the financial muscle to buy off the large number of stressed assets on sale. So, a bad bank would be a veritable junkyard with no buyers. Foreign ARCs have not shown any interest, till date, in Indian assets, and are unlikely to bite, looking at the industrial climate and difficult business conditions of today.

It is not that the situation is totally hopeless. But the recovery process will be slow and will have to be carefully nurtured. While the dead wood or the stressed assets identified before COVID-19 should be disposed of without any leniency, fresh norms should be formulated for all others that have got into financial trouble due to the extended lockdown. The entire process of revival and reconstruction has to be well thought out, process-driven, and totally different for the pre-COVID and post-COVID default cases. This book provides some solutions to the pre-COVID problems, given by bankers themselves. Solutions for the post Covid period can be found only once the lockdowns end and the amount of collateral damage quantified.

FOURTEEN

SEVEN MEASURES THAT CAN RESHAPE INDIAN BANKING

Speaking to bankers, both in the private and public sectors, gave the deep insights needed to write this book. In the search for solutions, I am listing below a few suggestions that were simple and made sense, and some that were extremely insightful and innovative.

1. Crime and punishment
2. Lending is a knowledge business
3. Relieve branch managers in PSBs: overburdened and risk-averse
4. Multiple banking arrangements increased risks, says the CVC
5. Introducing the scorecard system for AI evaluation
6. Pruning and regulating NBFCs and cooperative banks
7. Introducing a proactive Whistle-blowers Act

Crime and Punishment

Whatever be the justification, punishment should follow any crime, to establish the rule of law. Today there is no punishment for the wilful criminals and no protection for those who may have taken a wrong business decision, say several bankers.

Many bankers feel that criminals will eventually get away. Ensuring the return of Vijay Mallya and Nirav Modi to India is needed well before the 2024 elections to establish the rule of law. Mallya cheated not only the bankers but also his employees by not depositing the money collected from PF and gratuity funds into the government accounts. He laundered money, evaded taxes and submitted false affidavits to repeatedly extract money from the banks, because he was well-connected with the powers that be. These are all unpardonable crimes that need redressal. True, there was a buzz created about the return of Mallya and Modi before the 2019 elections, but after the landslide victory of the BJP, that buzz has practically subsided. It will require more serious effort than a buzz to bring them back to India, and definitely a better strategy to get the money back.

Bringing Mallya and Modi back to India is a big challenge. This is because the UK is known to be friendly to fugitive billionaires. It has a history of supporting such billionaires who have parked their ill-gotten wealth in the UK and other British tax havens. According to a Deutsch Bank report, the UK received $129 billion in laundered money in its offshore tax havens—the British Virgin Islands, the Cayman Islands, Gibraltar, Jersey and Guernsey—from fugitive asylum seekers between 2006 and 2015. Most of these asylum-seekers have bought expensive property in London and have been living lavishly with the British elite, as extradition cases against fugitive billionaires never lead to favourable results. There is indirect political support received from the law firms that support the fugitive billionaires. *The Independent,* a reputed British daily, says that Britain is known as the 'Switzerland on the Thames' due to its opaque financial laws. It says that 'more than 200 foreign law firms now have offices in the UK, while more cash is said to be managed out of a couple of square miles of Mayfair than in the whole of Germany.'

Vijay Mallya, and later Nirav Modi, engaged Boutique Law, a firm run by Anand Doobay and Christina Russell, which shields clients from 'Corruption and Bribery, Money Laundering and Sanctions, Extradition and Interpol.' Doobay has good links with the Conservative Party and was appointed by ex-British Prime Minister Theresa May to a panel to review the UK's extradition arrangements when she was the home secretary not so long ago.

The British are known to have devised opaque laws against financial crimes despite the pressure from the US, the EU and many other nations. 'The Financial Control Authority (FCA)—which is the regulator for the financial sector—has brought zero prosecutions for breaches in UK's Money Laundering Regulations since 2007', claims Corruption Watch. The NGO estimates that, 'UK's wealth management industry manages $800 billion of global wealth at particular risk of laundering'. According to Tulip Financial Research, Britain has some 135,000 'high networth' individuals, with liquid assets averaging £6.4m. Among those sheltered are fugitive Arab sheikhs, African despots, Russian oligarchs and East European criminals, apart from Mallya and Modi.

Nonetheless, bringing Vijay Mallya and Nirav Modi to justice in India is a must, to establish that the government really means business. It is the first step in the process to restore the order of law in a corrupt system. Getting convictions quickly in Indian courts will be another challenge. Then there is the investigation and conviction of the bankers, bureaucrats and politicians who helped Mallya and Modi amass such wealth and launder it in tax havens.

There are 75 more fugitive billionaires who have escaped India since 2015. They need to be brought back too and tried in Indian courts. Thereafter comes the investigation of other frauds that have happened in the banks and NBFCs. The criminals who were behind the financial frauds of IL&FS, PMC Bank, HDIL, DHFL, Religare, Essar, BPSL, ICICI Bank, Yes Bank, Winsome Diamonds, Gitanjali Gems, Sandesara Brothers and many others will need to be proceeded against. It must be remembered that they will all fight back both individually and collectively to beat or bribe the system, so the path to eliminate corruption will never be easy.

Just like setting up the extensive NCLT infrastructure was crucial in the resolution of stressed assets, setting up of a speedy and streamlined route map is needed to punish financial fraudsters speedily in a corrupt system. Benchmarks provided for resolution times of 180 days and 270 days in the IBC have helped the resolution process immensely. Similarly, there should be a benchmark time limit of three to four years adopted for the sentencing of financial fraudsters. The entire executive and judicial machineries need to function efficiently to create a firm belief in the minds of people that every financial crime will be investigated and punished in a reasonable period of not more than four years.

Lending is a Knowledge Business

In today's world, lending is a knowledge business. Technology is quickly changing the economic viability of most industries. Mobile phones disrupted the fixed line business; Google disrupted the publishing business, the media business and the trade directories business; Ola and Uber are disrupting the taxi services and car ownership business; and Airbnb and OYO rooms are disrupting the hotel business. Several disruptive changes are happening and will continue to happen in the coming decades.

Most of these changes are linked to the increased use of data to disrupt conventional business. As data prices fall and speeds increase, data storage and applications grow. This helps businesses to use data to usher in disruptive changes that create the economic viability of a new business with unmatched scalability and low costs. The old businesses simply collapse in the face of these disruptive changes and banks that fund businesses are left high and dry.

These banks need to be aware of the disruptive changes that are happening in the industry. Similarly, alternate processes are being adopted today to meet business needs. We have studied in Chapter 3 the use of the BF/BOF route and the sponge iron/ DRI route to produce steel. Similarly, in the textile industry, we find the PTA route and the DMT route being used by Reliance and Bombay Dyeing to achieve similar goals. In printing technology, we have the offset printing and digital printing technologies competing, and in the renewable energy industry, we have the CSP and PV technologies to choose from. Banks must know what technology to back and when to ensure success, and that needs a lot of learning.

The PSBs have been falling behind in the technology assessment business. This is needed, because technology disruptions will increase manyfold in the future. With renewable energy becoming affordable, there will soon be energy industry disruptions due to the sharp fall of energy prices. Fall in energy prices will lead to better energy storage and increased use, and usher in new applications that are unknown today. Businesses that are stable today could become entirely unviable and loss-making tomorrow. Start-ups can quickly replace these businesses with huge profitability but shorter life cycles. So, those lending to businesses today must be aware of the changing technologies and life cycles of industries that are quickly transforming. They must know when to go ahead and invest in and support a business, and when to pull out of it.

Fraud detection is another business that banks need to learn. They have to hire specialists who can sniff out opaque balance sheets and financial statements, track and stop money laundering, and quickly act before the crook has fled with the loan funds of the bank. The detection time of large frauds is too high, and must be brought down to around two years for any actionable result.

Banks need to build their own knowledge banks or have institutions that give them reliable advice on the state and life cycle of every business they finance. Before the 1990s, institutions like the IDBI, ICICI and IFCI used to provide such knowhow. All major banks in those days were in the public sector. They used to wait for the appraisal reports from these financial institutions before committing funds to any client or project. That could be a reason why there were very few NPAs during the pre-liberalization period, despite a weak industrial climate.

Relieve Branch Manager in PSBs: Overburdened and Risk-averse

In the last four years, more than 200 branch managers of PSBs have committed suicide. In my discussion with bankers, I found that it is the hot seat that everyone wants to avoid today. Most PSBs have an operating model where the branch manager is responsible and accountable for every action taken by the branch. Whereas there are several advantages in having a single power centre for each branch within a geographical territory, there are severe handicaps too. This is only because banking today is a diversified operation, with several dozen identifiable product groups and functions.

Each product group has multiple segments that need a lot of domain expertise, study and analysis. For example, the credit and advances product group has cash credit and overdraft loans; there are LCs and LOUs against exports; export credit against Letters of Intent, against purchase orders, against shipments; import credit against exports; unsecured personal loans; secured personal loans; home loan; loan against mortgages; loans against properties; loans against security; loans for two-wheelers, there is loans for four-wheelers; loans against consumer durables; and many others. Apart from this, there are half a dozen loans in the priority sector for the MSMEs, another dozen for the agriculture sector, and many more for corporates and the big industries. All of these loans and advances need specialized handling, but are dealt by the branch managers of the PSBs. Unfortunately, these managers also do not have trained people in their teams to assess the risk factor in each of these loans.

Besides, most branches of PSBs are not adequately manned. Agriculture loans and industry loans usually turn bad because of faulty assessment of risk as well as the inability of the banks to monitor end use. Monitoring the deployment of funds cannot be done by these banks simply because of manpower shortage.

But without monitoring the use of funds, the banks are missing a very important function that plays a key role in their recovery.

Giving loans and monitoring them is just around a tenth of a branch manager's responsibility in a PSB. He is responsible for day-to-day operations, including account opening and KYC verification. He is also responsible for bringing in deposits to the banks, which incidentally come in more than a dozen types. You can often see that the branch manager is usually the most harassed individual at the branch, desperately trying to deputize manpower at the customer services desks. The role of keeping the customer happy lies solely with the branch manager. But the branch manager is also responsible for the loan recoveries, which pits him/her directly against the customer.

Besides, banks are today selling several other instruments, like life insurance policies, vehicle insurance policies, health insurance policies, debentures, fixed deposits, pension schemes, and many others, to reduce the risk of credit-based business. It becomes the branch manager's responsibility to conduct the miscellaneous businesses too. Needless to say, the branch managers of the PSBs are an overburdened species. It is not only the workload, but the fact that the branch manager is made accountable for loans gone bad, makes them risk-averse with respect to giving credit to customers. The only way to galvanize credit is to revamp the organizational structure of PSBs and distribute the workload amongst a wider base of officers.

The bankers' feedback that we have received says that the branch managers of most PSBs want this role change to happen. The finance ministry needs to conduct an independent survey to get their individual feedback and push reforms in the organizational structure of the PSB. While writing this book, we have seen that the branch managers of the PSBs themselves are aware of the problems, but nobody wants to listen to their solutions. There is no communication system in a PSB that processes the feedback of the key middle-level executives and brings reforms.

Consulting branch managers for reforms is also a good way to manage the change, because they will appreciate that the solutions have come from within. If the feedback is for change, the banks should introduce a system that adopts the vertical organization structure that splits the responsibilities and makes different people accountable in their own fields.

While it is true that the high number of NPAs is the trigger for reforms, it must not be forgotten that operational efficiency and profitability are also key factors that separate the private sector banks from the PSBs. To achieve better efficiencies, it is important to adopt an organizational structure that is successful, accountable and proven. Over the last three decades, many private banks have shown that despite providing world-class services and having conservative lending practices, they could remain the fastest growing banks with nationwide footprints. They have successfully grown into the MSME sector as well as provided unsecured loans to the bottom of the pyramid without reporting large delinquencies. HDFC Bank's loan book has been expanding at ₹8,000 crore per month, while its delinquencies are low at below 0.5 per cent, claims Arvind Kapil, the bank's head of credit.

Private sector banks that had just a 19.9 per cent market share of advances in 2014 have increased their loan book by nearly 40 per cent year to year in the last five years. They are growing credit quickly and safely, as discussed in Chapter 12. Despite India's worst banking crisis and the shadow of NBFCs, the market value of HDFC Bank has soared by over $21 billion, as per an ICRA report from October 2019. The report, which claims to have surveyed 54 global analysts, says that HDFC stock commands the highest price, relative to earnings or net assets amongst the 25 biggest global lenders. Under these circumstances, adopting the vertical organization structure adopted by HDFC Bank could be worth emulating for the PSBs that are currently undergoing consolidation.

Multiple Banking Arrangements Increase Risk: CVC

A consortium of banks lending to big borrowers has been a standard industry practice for decades. But the CVC did a detailed analysis of the top 100 bank frauds in India (Chapter 6) and came up with certain observations that are worth taking note of.

The CVC report says, 'Multiple banking arrangements in large value financing have done more harm than good to banks. This type of arrangement enabled corporates to secure multiple finances from various banks, far in excess of their requirements. Funds raised were easily diverted through [the] company's accounts with various banks in the absence of effective exchange of information between the banks.'

The fact that every bank wanted a share of the profits in the growth plans of an industry made the funding easier and the loan size grow bigger. Banks thought that since risks were distributed because of the consortium approach, it was a less risky bet to take. But the comfort of the distributed risks approach actually made banks casual towards an assessment of the project risks.

The CVC also points out that 'Banks currently do not have a foolproof system of checking and confirming whether the company has actually been working on the contracts and whether the contracts were genuinely business based.'

It was found that the monitoring of the use of the loan funds after disbursement was nobody's baby in the consortium approach. The excess funds were laundered. Every loan that became a bad debt happened because the lenders failed to monitor the end use. Loan funds were laundered into offshore tax havens, some of which were recycled back to be shown as equity funds. A large part of these loan funds were invested in properties abroad by the promoters and their associates. Whether it was Essar Steel or Firestar Diamonds, Kingfisher Airlines or IL&FS, Jet Airways or DHFL, BPSL or Amrapali Constructions, there was a serious diversion of funds that banks failed to monitor. This book has looked at just about a dozen cases in depth, but there are hundreds of other frauds that would take many volumes of writings to describe.

Money-laundering became a key instrument that provided promoters equity to Indian businesses over the past decade. Rigorous monitoring of the use of loan funds was clearly absent in the consortium funding approach. Once the loans were sanctioned, the lender was free to go from one bank to another, issuing cheques favouring third parties both locally or globally. You could never know whether the funds were paid to suppliers for a legitimate business or simply to profit the benami associates who fronted for them. Banks paid a heavy price for not monitoring the end use of funds. The Mauritius Treaty, which legalized routing of investor funds into India through tax havens, further accelerated the process. There was massive money laundering that happened due to the poor monitoring of funds by banks, and that was one of the principle reasons for both frauds as well as delayed reporting.

Scorecard System for AI Evaluation

Many private banks are developing an AI-driven lending model for advances. They have devised a scorecard-based system where every client's risk profile is assessed and monitored through a scorecard. The CIBIL credit rating has been an important first step in risk profiling a customer.

Credit bureaus like Trans Union, Equifax and Experian had arrived in India a decade ago, somewhat streamlining the risk profiling business. The CIBIL score can even predict if the potential borrower is likely to default on one or more trade lines after 90 days, in the next 12 months. Private sector banks are risk profiling consumers independently, not only taking into consideration CIBIL score but also data from GST returns, IT returns, sales data, balance sheet data and bank statements to create a scorecard for each consumer.

The interest rates vary as per the credit score and work as

incentives for the customer to pay his dues to the banker and meet the benchmark financials for good business practices. This also speeds up the time for assessment of customer credentials for any mass lending exercise. According to a top banker with a multinational lender,

> While developing a scorecard-based system speeds up credit disbursement for small unsecured personal loans, it does wonders while assessing large loans to corporate clients. Today, many triple AAA-rated industrial houses in India have become dangerously leveraged. Though the market value of the company is high, a stock market crash could do endless harm to the bankers who have lent them huge amounts of money during the last five years.

'The Credit Suisse report of August 2019 red flags Reliance, whose debt has jumped from $19 billion in March 2015 to $65 billion in March 2019,' says a senior banker with a multinational bank that has reduced its exposure to India's largest conglomerate. As a result of increased debt scrutiny by international lenders, the company's foreign debt mix has reduced from 60 per cent to 40 per cent in the year 2017. It is now reportedly working on a plan to be a zero-debt company in the next couple of years, and the disinvestment deals with Aramco, Facebook and several others are part of the ongoing effort. While Reliance successfully managed to bring in both foreign investors following its Facebook deal and hold a mega rights issue to reduce its exposure, others like Adani, Biyani, Vodafone and Airtel have not been so lucky.

A few PSBs like the Bank of Baroda, Syndicate Bank and Union Bank of India have also taken baby steps to risk profile customers. They have recently started transparently segregating retail loans into their own versions of prime and sub-prime risk exposures. However, this is not based on their own scorecards but on third-party credit scores of potential borrowers, in order to offer them different home-financing rates. A senior manager with Bank of Baroda says that the bank will offer a lower interest rate of 8.1 per cent to customers having a high credit score—above 760 out of a maximum of 900. For customers with a credit score between 725 and 759, the interest rate will be 8.35 per cent, while those with a CIBIL score between 675 and 724 will pay a higher interest rate of 9.1 per cent. Consumers with CIBIL scores lower than 675 will not be offered any credit. If PSBs start adhering to credit benchmarking, it will help lower risks to their loan books.

Tightening the norms of credit and adhering to benchmarks is needed to reduce the risk of loan defaults. Interest rate variation gives incentive to the borrower to improve credit ratings. 'If, after one year, the borrower improves his/her credit score, the risk premium will go down. Conversely, it could go up if a borrower's credit score drops below 760,' says Virendra Sethi, head, Mortgages and Other Retail Assets, Bank of Baroda.

While that is the first step in the process of reducing delinquencies, the ultimate goal should be for banks to develop their own credit rating systems. Both for small borrowers as well as large conglomerates, banks need to adopt a scorecard-based system to lend. This will address the issue of both corruption and the urge to grow the loan book at any cost, which has been the bane of the industry during the last decade.

Consolidating NBFCs and Cooperative Banks

We have already discussed in detail various aspects of the NBFC and the Cooperative Bank crisis in Chapters 2, 3, 4, 6 and 9. The primary faultlines appeared decades ago, largely due to the lack of supervision and regulatory control. But the blame cannot be put on the regulator's doorstep either. There are more than 11,000 officially recognized NBFCs and over 1 lakh urban and rural cooperatives in India. They are far too many to regulate. It is simply not possible to do effective supervision of hundreds and thousands of loosely knit organizations that are collecting and distributing funds to millions of citizens at the bottom of the pyramid in a disorganized environment. Even in 2020, there is still no mechanism laid down to regulate them. The crisis is similar to the banking crisis after Independence, when 1,284 banks were present and the RBI expressed its inability to regulate them.

After the bank failures of 1960, during the Nehru era, the then Finance Minister Morarji Desai issued orders for forced amalgamation of the weaker banks. By 1964, the number of banks had been reduced to just 92. Of these, 20 banks were called unscheduled banks and were eventually merged or liquidated. Once this was done, the RBI started the supervision of the 72 scheduled banks on a regular basis. The Banking Companies (Second Amendment) Act was one of the first significant reforms that came into force in September 1960 to expeditiously facilitate the payments to depositors of banks that went into liquidation. But no such law exists for NBFCs or cooperative banks.

A large part of the credit and advances are managed by NBFCs, UCBs, RCBs and RRBs. They account for nearly half the credit distributed today but have little or no regulation or oversight. The RBI does issue guidelines and circulars for these sectors, but does not have the manpower to ensure that they are monitored. While the total number of registered NBFCs came down from 52,000 in 1997 to around 11,800 in 2015, their asset share grew from around ₹76,000 crore to over ₹16 trillion. Their asset share in the credit system more than doubled from 7 per cent to 14.8 per cent in 2015, according to RBI Deputy Governor R. Gandhi. He has also stated that, 'the business model of NBFCs is inherently risk-prone due to weaker underwriting standards, enhanced risk-taking capabilities and increased complexities of their activities.'

The weakness of the NBFC sector was well-known by the government as well as the regulators ever since the 1990s. But nobody did anything about it. Even the banks that were financing the NBFCs were not too happy lending to them. One senior manager of a PSB says, 'We all knew that it was like pouring money down the drain. Still we kept doing it just because it had been done before.' The bank used to lend nearly 30 per cent of its annual advances through the NBFC sector.

'Some years, we did not find enough NBFC projects worth lending to but the managers at the head office still insisted that we do not deviate from the norm,' he says, confiding that nearly two-thirds of the NBFC loans given by his bank will turn into NPAs. So, though the NBFC problem was well-known, matters came to a head only with the collapse of IL&FS. The government, the regulator and the banks that provided credit to IL&FS were all caught napping.

The IL&FS default (Chapter 3) was just the starting point of the NBFC crisis. Apart from the cascading effect of the loan default of over ₹90,000 crore, it created an atmosphere of suspicion and mistrust and banks slowed down credits offered to the NBFC sector almost immediately. The massive frauds at DHFL and HDIL (Chapter 7), managed by the Wadhawan cousins, showed that the NBFC sector had more skeletons in the cupboard than the banking sector. The bank NPAs and frauds are smaller and more manageable in comparison. Besides, NBFCs have few hard assets to show that can be recovered.

The PMC Bank (Chapter 7) nexus with the HDIL showed how the shadow banking sector operated and how easy it was for unscrupulous promoters to empty out cooperative bank deposits. It also showed how unprepared the RBI was to handle the PMC Bank fraud. Like in the NBFCs, the problems in the cooperative banks are many, but the primary problem is that there are far too many of them to regulate. The RBI and the government need to put their heads together to chart out a three-year road map to consolidate and revitalize the twin sectors. Not more than a hundred NBFCs and a hundred cooperative banks should remain after consolidation for effective supervision. The consolidation and cleaning efforts need to be simultaneous over the next three years of this fiscal. For without cleaning up the shadow banking sector and the cooperative banks, the core banking sector that funds the smaller financial institutions can never be healthy.

Strengthening the Whistle-blowers Act

This is the last but not the least of all the measures that need to be introduced to clean up the banking sector.

At least four senior managers of banks have suggested this as a remedy to make banking practices more transparent. Bank operations are so interlinked that it is 'virtually impossible for any one individual to conduct a fraud today,' they say. Although a fraudulent transaction could be done by a borrower siphoning money out of a sanctioned loan to a benami beneficiary at a tax haven, there would be more than one bank staff who would know about it. It is, therefore, important to encourage the employee whistle-blower to give advance and critical information on the corrupt practices that are hurting the interests of the bank. If whistle-blowers get due incentive, protection and opportunity to report on the omissions and commissions committed by businesses and fellow bankers working in league to defraud the bank, they will make a huge difference to operational transparency.

The Whistle Blowers Protection Act, 2011 was amended by Parliament in February 2014 and approved by the president, but not made operational. The Act provides a mechanism for receiving and investigating disclosures, made in public interest, about acts of corruption, or wilful misuse of public property or machinery and services, or criminal offences by public servants. But the amendment bill prohibits a corruption-related disclosure if it falls under any of 10 categories of information, which is a key bone of contention. These include information related to economic, scientific interests and the security of India, cabinet proceedings, intellectual property and inputs received in a fiduciary capacity.

While there was pressure from the activists to operationalize the bill passed during the UPA rule, the NDA government has had reservations about operationalizing it. So, the NDA has brought in the Whistle Blowers Protection (Amendment) Bill, 2015, which was passed by Lok Sabha in May 2015. But it failed to the clear the Rajya Sabha. In January 2016, the Supreme Court directed the Government of India to make the bill operational in three months' time. But due to lack of majority in the Upper House, the bill lapsed, as it could not be passed in both Houses of Parliament before the 2019 elections.

Meanwhile, whistle-blowers played a key role in highlighting several irregularities that happened in many large corporates. The investigations in ICICI Bank, Yes Bank, Sun Pharma and Infosys started due to whistle-blower revelations about irregular business practices in those organizations. Adding provisions to the Act to protect whistle-blowers and process feedback can go a long way in detecting bank frauds and eliminate financial crimes. It should be used as business intelligence by the CVC and the vigilance departments of banks.

Also, several other banking and NBFC frauds have erupted in recent times, some based on inside information and others based on specific complaints by employees. The bank employees we spoke to felt that it is important to enact and operationalize a modified bill that allows for the reporting of all irregularities and unfair banking practices and frauds. 'If banks are to be protected from frauds from within, the policing must start from within. Additionally, incentives could be added during the investigations for employees who help unravel the scams,' says a senior vigilance officer at a PSB. Any protection given to bank employees that maintains the secrecy and anonymity under the Whistle Blowers Act will help. It will ensure no action against employees while reporting a malpractice. That alone will ensure employee activism against the corrupt and make sure that the bank is safe from unethical practices.

CONCLUSION

One book is never enough to write the inside story of Indian banking. I am sure a host of books from different authors will soon arrive to give the widest possible perspective to India's most ambitious reforms. While the IBC reforms can be the starting point of change, they are just the first step in a thousand-mile journey. The banking sector will see endless frauds erupting in the next few years. The RBI and the government must act quickly to stop them from severely rupturing the banking industry.

Else, every year, there will be new stories to tell. But that should not be worrying. Bank frauds have happened in almost every other nation. Each nation handled its banking crises differently. The handling of the US banking crisis shows that not every nation has been able to clean up its act. The US, where the frauds were much larger in 2008, has simply buried them. But while economies like the US or China can muscle past large-scale financial irregularities, other nations cannot.

We have seen the Asian financial crisis, when smaller nations that ignored financial reforms collapsed just before the turn of the century. It took the IMF and the Organisation for Economic Co-operation and Development (OECD) nations to pump in over $100 billion to revive the economies of South Korea, Thailand, Indonesia and the Philippines. Fortunately, the banking reforms in India started before the situation reached a crisis point. It will slow down the economy for the next few years, but will not lead to a precipitous fall. International investors will arrive to help the process, but only once they see that the reforms are sustained and are making real headway. Reforms in India have often been one step forward and two steps back, as a result of which there is some apprehension in the international investor community. Global investors want well-thought-out reforms, and policy stability thereafter. That does not, unfortunately, happen easily in India.

The identification and resolution of big bank defaults is the first baby step in the right direction. The legal processes and the convictions of the fraudsters will be another lengthy battle, worth a story. The cleaning up of the big defaulters in the NBFC and cooperative bank sectors will also be a lengthy and tedious process. Indian banking is today in a state of turmoil. The frauds will not stop just because the banking reforms have started. The leaks are still happening and will continue for some time. The plugging of leaks is an ongoing process. The regulators have to be skilful and fleet-footed in their approach if they have to stop the bank frauds from ballooning. Thereafter, the repair process will be long. This is especially because the effect of the Coronavirus lockdown will be additionally felt. So, reforms will need patience and persistence.

It will also require the understanding that it is very difficult to run any plant or machinery when major maintenance is on. This is why the economy is slowing down. This is largely due to the banking crisis, which is affecting the credit flow, especially from the PSB sector. The credit lines must be redrawn. But this time it must be credit with safety. It must not be due to a ministry directive, but because the bankers feel that giving credit is a good business proposition. That will eventually happen as PSBs adapt to the current-day challenges and initiate organizational reforms. The first reforms have begun. The mergers and structural changes in the banks have started to happen. If all things go well, the next decade for Indian banking could be transformative. Let us hope that happens.

BIBLIOGRAPHY

Chapter 1

1. Amol Agarwall, 'Banking Crisis: An Indian History', Live Mint, 26 February 2019, https://www.livemint.com/Sundayapp/fjheowjLjiFNsGcjzVZXsO/Banking-crises-An-Indian-history.html, Accessed 10 May 2020
2. 'This Smaller PSU Bank Was Founded 90 Years before State Bank of India', *Financial Express*, 29 March 2018, https://www.financialexpress.com/industry/banking-finance/this-smaller-psu-bank-was-founded-90-years-before-state-bank-of-india/1114624/, Accessed 10 May 2020
3. D.N. Ghosh, *No Regrets*, Rupa Publications, 2015
4. Reserve Bank of India, 'History of Reserve Bank of India', RBI Museum, https://www.rbi.org.in/scripts/ms_anecdotes.aspx, Accessed 10 May 2020
5. Reserve Bank of India, 'Brief History of RBI', https://www.rbi.org.in/scripts/briefhistory_demo.aspx, Accessed 10 May 2020
6. M.S. Sriram, 'Bank Nationalisation Stands the Test of Time', Live Mint, 21 July 2019, https://www.livemint.com/industry/banking/bank-nationalization-stands-the-test-of-time-1563730076513.html, Accessed 10 May 2020
7. Sandip Sen, '50 Years On: PSBs Need More Autonomy to Fulfil Role', 2 August 2018, https://www.dnaindia.com/analysis/column-50-years-on-psbs-need-more-autonomy-to-fulfill-role-2644469, Accessed 10 May 2020
8. P.N. Haksar, *The Haksar Papers*, NMML, 1980
9. K. Srinivasa Rao, 'How Bank Nationalisation Contributed to Bank Outreach', *Financial Express*, 19 July 2019, https://www.financialexpress.com/opinion/how-a-move-to-nationalise-banks-contributed-towards-robust-banking-outreach/1649081/, Accessed 10 May 2020
10. Sandip Sen, *India Emerging: From Policy Paralysis to Hyper Economics*, Bloomsbury, 2019

Chapter 2

1. TNN, 'Co-operatives get IFFCO control as Govt cuts stake to 41%', *Economic Times*, 2 July 2003, https://economictimes.indiatimes.com/co-ops-get-iffco-control-as-govt-cuts-stake-to-41/articleshow/53965.cms?from=mdr, 10 May 2020

2. FE Bureau, 'Govt eyes premium on co-operative equity buy back', *Financial Express*, 30 August 2006, https://www.financialexpress.com/archive/govt-eyes-premium-on-co-op-equity-buybacks/175828/#, 10 May 2020
3. DOF, Annexure -2A Excerpts from Annual Report of Department of Fertilizer of 2011-12 showing year by year subsidies on imported and indigenous fertilizer
4. DOF, Annexure -2B Department of fertilizers annual report 2012-13, year wise consumption of indigenous and imported fertilizer\
5. DOF Annexure 2C Annual Report 2008-09 Chapter 1.Cl. 1.8 showing sharp rise of international price of fertilizer during 2007-2009
6. DOF, Annexure V, Year wise nutrient wise consumption, production and import of fertilizer 1981-82 to 2012-2013
7. IPL, 10 yrs Annual Reports 2002 to 2011 Years Operating Results 1997-2008 of IPL
8. CAG, Performance Audit of Fertilizer Subsidy, Excerpt of CAG Audit Report of IPL of 2008-09
9. Sandip Sen, *Neta, Babu and Subsidy: Economic Roundup 2000-2014*, Vitasta, 2014
10. Sandip Sen, 'Why No Make in India for Urea', *Hindu Business Line*, 14 December 2014, https://www.thehindubusinessline.com/opinion/columns/why-no-make-in-india-for-urea/article20929930.ece, Accessed 10 May 2020
11. D.O. Letter of Dr J.S. SARMA Secretary D.O.F to chief Secretaries of State Governments in May 2007
12. American Antitrust Institute Reports, Reports under US Webb-Pomerene Act

Chapter 3

1. Pragya Shrivastava, 'India's bad loans: Here is the list of 12 companies constituting 25 per cent of the total NPA's', *Financial Express*, 23 October 2017, https://www.financialexpress.com/industry/banking-finance/indias-bad-loans-here-is-the-list-of-12-companies-constituting-25-of-total-npa/903396/, Accessed 10 May 2020
2. K. Radhika, Maureen Nandini Mitra, Sponge Iron Industries are Killing fields, Down To Earth, 7 June 2015, https://www.downtoearth.org.in/coverage/sponge-iron-industries-are-killing-fields-8328 Accessed 10 May 2020
3. PTI, 'Essar Steel ramps up Hazira Steel unit capacity to 10MTPA', *Economic Times*, 4 January 2012 https://economictimes.indiatimes.com/industry/indl-goods/svs/steel/essar-steel-ramps-up-hazira-steel-unit-capacity-to-

10-mtpa/articleshow/11365861.cms, Accessed 10 May 2020

4. Nicky Mirchandani, 'What Essar Steel Brings to the table for ArcelorMittal', *Bloomberg Quint*, 24 October 2018 https://www.bloombergquint.com/business/what-essar-steel-brings-to-the-table-for-arcelormittal, Accessed 10 May 2020
5. Sambit Saha, 'Electrosteel to be reported to BIFR', *The Telegraph*, 10 August 2015, https://www.telegraphindia.com/business/electrosteel-to-be-reported-to-bifr/cid/1455385, 10/5/20
6. Advait Rao Palepu, Aditi Diwekar, 'NCLT approves JSW Steel - Aion resolution plan for debt laden Monnet Ispat', *Business Standard*, 20 July 2018, https://www.business-standard.com/article/companies/nclt-approves-jsw-steel-aion-resolution-plan-for-debt-laden-monnet-ispat-118072000039_1.html, Accessed 10 May 2020
7. PTI, 'Urjit Patel admits RBI was slow to take timely measures for bad loan mess', *Hindu Business Line*, 4 July 2019 https://www.thehindubusinessline.com/money-and-banking/a-mess-urjit-patel-admits-rbi-was-slow-to-take-timely-measures-for-bad-loan-mess/article28281774.ece 04/07/19
8. Jayashree P Upadhyay, 'Inside the Audit lapsed that led to the IL&FS crisis', Live Mint, 21 May 2019, https://www.livemint.com/companies/news/inside-the-audit-lapses-that-led-to-il-fs-crisis-1558456079750.html, Accessed 10 May 2020
9. BS Bureau, 'What is the IL&FS crisis?', *Business Standard*, https://www.business-standard.com/about/what-is-il-fs-crisis, Accessed 10 May 2020
10. Tarun Sharma, 'Grant Thornton audit report reveals how rating agencies played along even as IL&FS time bomb ticked', MoneyControl, 20 August 2019, https://www.moneycontrol.com/news/business/companies/grant-thornton-audit-report-reveals-how-rating-agencies-played-along-even-as-ilfs-time-bomb-ticked-4224211.html, Accessed 10 May 2020

Chapter 4

1. Vivek Kaul, 'Narrow Banking: Why banks have shifted focus to retail loans', Live Mint, 7 August 2018, https://www.livemint.com/Industry/tiUvqj6gawtzkyaTtXMqcJ/Narrow-Banking-Why-banks-have-shifted-focus-to-retail-loans.html, Accessed 10 May 2020
2. Vivek Kaul, 'Why retail loans continue to grow amid a slowdown', Live Mint, 4 August 2019, https://www.livemint.com/industry/banking/why-retail-loans-continue-to-grow-amid-a-slowdown-1564930881240.html, Accessed 10 May 2020
3. Economic Times BFSI, 'A snapshot of RBIs trend and progress of banking

in India', *Economic Times*, https://bfsi.economictimes.indiatimes.com/news/banking/a-snapshot-of-rbis-trend-and-progress-of-banking-in-india/72957020, Accessed 10 May 2020

4. Ashwin Manikandan, 'NBFC loan growth in FY 20 to hit a 10 year low: Crisil', *Economic Times*, https://economictimes.indiatimes.com/industry/banking/finance/nbfc-loan-growth-set-to-hit-a-decadal-low-of-6-8-report/articleshow/72475297.cms?from=mdr, Accessed 10 May 2020
5. Saloni Shukla, 'Slumps real, NBFC Credit falls 31% Over to RBI, govt', *Economic Times*, 26 June 2019, https://economictimes.indiatimes.com/markets/stocks/news/slumps-real-nbfc-credit-falls-31-over-to-rbi-govt/articleshow/69951535.cms?from=mdr, Accessed 10 May 2020
6. Bloomberg, 'NBFC crisis has been averted says Aditya Puri', *Hindu Business Line*, 3 May 2019, https://www.thehindubusinessline.com/money-and-banking/nbfc-crisis-has-been-averted-says-hdfc-bank-md-aditya-puri/article27021677.ece, Accessed 10 May 2020
7. PTI, 'Housing Finance Company market share in reality loans doubled since 2016', *Economic Times*, 29 December 2019, https://economictimes.indiatimes.com/industry/banking/finance/banking/housing-finance-companies-share-in-realty-loans-doubles-since-2016-rbi/articleshow/73016523.cms?from=mdr, Accessed 10 May 2020
8. 'SBI's card growth rate higher than market leader: Sidharth Purohit', *Economic Times*, 26 February 2020, https://economictimes.indiatimes.com/markets/expert-view/sbi-cards-growth-rate-higher-than-market-leader-sidharth-purohit/articleshow/74320491.cms, Accessed 10 May 2020
9. HBL Bureau, 'Rated exposure of bank loans to NBFCs to be risk weighted', *Hindu Business Line*, 7 February 2019, https://www.thehindubusinessline.com/money-and-banking/rated-exposure-of-banks-to-nbfcs-to-be-risk-weighted/article26206254.ece, Accessed 10 May 2020
10. Mona Lisa, Khushboo Narayan, 'SC directs Sahara firms to hand over ₹20,000 crore title deed to SEBI', Live Mint, 29 October 2013, https://www.livemint.com/Politics/ZvOcouGsFIw6Ycu3jjLRIN/SC-directs-Sahara-firms-to-hand-over-20000-crore-property.html, Accessed 10 May 2020

Chapter 5

1. Bimal Jalan, *India Ahead: 2025 and Beyond*, Rupa, 2018
2. Y. Venugopal Reddy, *Advice and Dissent: My Life in Public Service*, Harper Business, 2017
3. Economic Times Bureau, '₹389 crore loans at the centre of ED probes

of Kochhar', *Economic Times*, 7 March 2019, https://economictimes.indiatimes.com/industry/banking/finance/banking/rs-389-crore-loans-at-centre-of-eds-probe-of-kochhars/articleshow/68295866.cms?from=mdr Accessed 10 May 2020

4. Anirudh Laskar, 'RBI widens ICICI Bank probe after whistle-blowers complaints', Live Mint, 26 June 2018, https://www.livemint.com/Money/ntZisjW8b3spPAuDblkfNJ/RBI-widens-ICICI-Bank-probe-after-whistle-blower-complaints.html, Accessed 10 May 202020
5. Vishwanath Nair, 'Bankers expect NPA crisis to worsen in the next few years', Live Mint, 9 September 2015, https://www.livemint.com/Industry/xPuLSOoxWckzmLk8RhnrGJ/Bankers-expect-NPA-crisis-to-worsen-in-next-few-years-EY-su.html, Accessed 10 May 2020
6. RBI, RBI data on credit growth and industrial credit growth 2006-2018
7. RBI, RBI data on restructured loans as % of Advances 2010-2018
8. RBI, RBI data on Gross NPA's as % of Advances 2009-2018
9. Anand Adhikari, 'The Big Credit Freeze', *Business Today*, 11 August 2019, https://www.businesstoday.in/magazine/cover-story/the-big-credit-freeze/story/366556.html, Accessed 10 May 2020
10. Saloni Shukla, 'RBI's gradual shift from transparency to forbearance', *Economic Times*, 28 February 2020, https://economictimes.indiatimes.com/industry/banking/finance/banking/rbis-gradual-shift-from-transparency-to-forbearance-towards-stressed-sectors/articleshow/74310581.cms?from=mdr, Accessed 10 May 2020

Chapter 6

1. Dipanjan Roy Chaudhry, '72 financial scamsters have fled since 2015: Ministry of External Affairs', *Economic Times*, 7 February 2020, https://economictimes.indiatimes.com/news/politics-and-nation/72-scamsters-have-fled-since-2015-ministry-of-external-affairs/articleshow/73998660.cms?from=mdr, Accessed 10 May 2020
2. Arup Roy and Dev Chatterjee, 'Banks wrote off ₹68,607 crores debt of top 50 wilful defaulters: RBI', *Business Standard*, 29 April 2020, https://www.business-standard.com/article/finance/banks-wrote-off-rs-68-607-cr-debt-of-top-50-willful-defaulters-rbi-120042801692_1.html, Accessed 10 May 2020
3. RBI, RBI data on Rise in bank frauds 2010-2019
4. Sunthar Rajagopal, 'RBI reveals banks are taking nearly 5 years to even detect cases of large frauds', CNBC TV 18, 30 August 2019, https://www.cnbctv18.com/finance/rbi-reveals-banks-are-taking-nearly-5-years-

to-even-detect-cases-of-large-frauds-4267561.htm, Accessed 10 May 2020

5. Kiran Kabatta Somvanshi, 'Whistle-blowers complaint on the rise in India Inc', *Economic Times,* 8 November 2018, https://economictimes.indiatimes.com/news/company/corporate-trends/whistle-blower-complaints-on-the-rise-in-india-inc/articleshow/66540004.cms?from=mdr, Accessed 10 May 2020
6. CVC, CVC analysis top 100 bank frauds, 16/10/18 https://pib.gov.in/newsite/PrintRelease.aspx?relid=184226, Accessed 10 May 2020
7. Economic Times Bureau, 'Probe NPA's above ₹50 crores, Make plans to combat risks: Finance Ministry', *Economic Times,* 28 February 2019, https://economictimes.indiatimes.com/industry/banking/finance/banking/probe-npas-above-rs-50-crore-report-fraud-to-cbi-finance-ministry-to-psbs/articleshow/63097118.cms?from=mdr, Accessed 10 May 2020
8. PTI, 'CVC sets up panel to examine bank fraud above ₹50 crore', *Economic Times,* 25 September 2019, https://economictimes.indiatimes.com/industry/banking/finance/banking/cvc-sets-up-panel-to-examine-bank-fraud-above-rs-50-cr/articleshow/70827816.cms?from=mdr, Accessed 10 May 2020
9. BT, 'Nirav Modi's Firestar Diamonds challenges money laundering case in Delhi HC', *Business Today,* 6 March 2018, https://www.businesstoday.in/current/economy-politics/pnb-fraud-nirav-modi-firestar-diamond-challenges-money-laundering-case-delhi-high-court/story/272049.html, Accessed 10 May 2020
10. Pavan C Lal, *Flawed: The Rise and Fall of India's Diamond Mogul Nirav Modi,* Hachette, 2019

Chapter 7

1. Rahul Tripathi, 'Will Expand probe to cover all kingfisher airlines deals: CBI director Anil Sinha', *Economic Times,* 14 March 2016, https://economictimes.indiatimes.com/news/politics-and-nation/will-expand-probe-to-cover-all-kingfisher-airlines-deals-cbi-director-anil-sinha/articleshow/51386264.cms?from=mdr, Accessed 10 May 2020
2. PTI, 'CBI moves extradition request for Vijay Mallya', *Deccan Chronicle,* 21 November 2016, https://www.deccanchronicle.com/business/in-other-news/211116/cbi-moves-extradition-request-for-vijay-mallya.html, Accessed 10 May 2020
3. Vidya, Vijendra Singh Ghunawat,' CBI chargesheet against Vijay Mallya, Kingfisher Airlines and IDBI Bank loan default case', *India Today,* 24 October 2017, https://www.indiatoday.in/india/story/cbi-chargesheet-vijay-mallya-kingfisher-airlines-idbi-bank-loan-default-

case-956862-2017-01-24, Accessed 10 May 2020

4. Raghav Ohri, 'O.P. Bhatt, Other SBI staff under CBI lens', *Economic Times,* 12 October 2018, https://m.economictimes.com/industry/banking/finance/banking/op-bhatt-other-sbi-staff-under-cbi-lens-for-loans-to-vijay-mallya/articleshow/66172610.cms, Accessed 10 May 2020
5. Pranab Dhal Samanta, 'CBI to probe UPA finance secretary angle in loans to Vijay Mallya',
6. *Economic Times,* 14 September 2018, https://economictimes.indiatimes.com/news/politics-and-nation/cbi-to-probe-upa-finance-ministry-angle-in-loans-to-vijay-mallya/articleshow/65802795.cms?from=mdr, Accessed 10 May 2020
7. PTI, 'CBI files chargesheet in Nirav Modi case names PNB ex-chief, senior officials', *New Indian Express,* 14 May 2018, https://www.newindianexpress.com/nation/2018/may/14/cbi-files-charge-sheet-in-nirav-modi-case-names-pnb-ex-chief-senior-officials-1814549.html, Accessed 10 May 2020
8. Moneycontrol, 'DHFL Financials 2015 to 2019', https://www.moneycontrol.com/financials/dewanhousingfinancecorporation/balance-sheet/DHF, Accessed 10 May 2020
9. Jayashree P Upadhyay, 'ED arrests DHFLs Kapil Wadhawan in Iqbal Mirchi money laundering case', Live Mint, 27 January 2020, https://www.livemint.com/news/india/ed-arrests-dhfl-s-kapil-wadhawan-in-iqbal-mirchi-money-laundering-case-11580126559311.html, Accessed 10 May 2020
10. PTI, 'PMC Bank has over ₹6500 crore exposure to HDIL: Ex MD Thomas', *Times of India,*, 30 September 2019, https://timesofindia.indiatimes.com/business/india-business/pmc-bank-has-over-rs-6500-crore-exposure-to-hdil-ex-md-thomas/articleshow/71368445.cms, Accessed 10 May 2020
11. IANS, 'RBI affidavit details how it was cheated by scam hit PMC Bank', *Times of India,* 20 November 2019, https://economictimes.indiatimes.com/industry/banking/finance/banking/rbi-affidavit-details-how-it-was-fooled-by-scam-hit-pmc-bank/articleshow/72129797.cms?from=mdr

Chapter 8

1. Express Web Desk, 'Full text of Raghuram Rajan's note to the parliamentary estimates committee', *Indian Express,* 9 November 2018, https://indianexpress.com/article/business/banking-and-finance/full-text-of-raghuram-rajans-note-to-parliamentary-estimates-committee-on-bank-npas-5351153/, Accessed 10 May 2020
2. Tamal Bandopadhyay, 'Indian bankers are on overdrive to clean up books',

Live Mint, 15 January 2018, https://www.livemint.com/Home-Page/GvGaS75Z7ABOTRCJWtF1YK/Why-Indian-bankers-are-on-overdrive-to-clean-up-books.html, Accessed 10 May 2020

3. MCA, Insolvency and Bankruptcy Code 2016, Government of India, http://www.mca.gov.in/MinistryV2/insolvency+and+bankruptcy+code.html, Accessed 10 May 2020
4. Bureau, 'NPA Mess: Govt asks banks to reveal asset quality review impact', *Hindu Business Line*, 14 December 2017, https://www.thehindubusinessline.com/money-and-banking/npa-mess-govt-asks-banks-to-reveal-asset-quality-review-impact/article9994138.ece, Accessed 10 May 2020
5. BQ, 'RBI Overhauls Stressed Asset Framework with Emphasis on Bankruptcy Code', *Bloomberg Quint*, 12 February 2018, https://www.bloombergquint.com/business/rbi-overhauls-stressed-asset-framework-with-emphasis-on-bankruptcy-code, Accessed 10 May 2020
6. Veena Mani, 'Govt plans to set up special insolvency benches under NCLT by November', *Economic Times*, 12 September 2018, https://economictimes.indiatimes.com/news/economy/policy/12000-cases-filed-since-implementation-of-insolvency-law-setting-up-of-nclt-says-official/articleshow/68563213.cms
7. Aashish Aryan, 'Challenges for IBC lack of operational NCLT benches, low approval rate', *Indian Express*, 1 December 2018, https://indianexpress.com/article/business/economy/challenges-for-ibc-lack-of-operational-nclt-benches-low-approval-rate-of-resolution-plans-6144774/, Accessed 10 May 2020
8. Suman Layak, 'The challenges facing.the insolvency and bankruptcy code', *Economic Times*, 9 June 2019, https://economictimes.indiatimes.com/industry/banking/finance/banking/the-challenges-facing-the-insolvency-and-bankruptcy-code/articleshow/70108989.cms?from=mdr, Accessed 10 May 2020
9. Jay Mazoomdaar, 'Paradise Papers, Via offshore firms Khaitans managed Ruia family trust', *Indian Express*, 8 November 2017, https://indianexpress.com/article/india/paradise-papers-shashi-ravi-ruia-essar-khaitan-appleby-black-money-4927419/, Accessed 10 May 2020
10. Ashish Gupta, Kush Shah, Prashant Kumar, 'House of Debt', Credit Suisse Asia Pacific/ India, 21 October 2015, https://plus.credit-suisse.com/rpc4/ravDocView?docid=V4pSWN1AF-WElY95 Accessed 10 May 2020

Chapter 9

1. Tamal Bandopadhyay, 'Finally RBI cracks the Da Vinci code of Indian banking', Live Mint, 29 May 2017, https://www.livemint.com/Opinion/MrHUkHobcTRc389OKVk62N/Finally-RBI-cracks-the-Da-Vinci-code-of-Indian-banking.html, Accessed 10 May 2020
2. Renu Yadav, 'PMC Bank shows why dual regulation doesn't work', Live Mint, 4 December 2019, https://www.livemint.com/money/personal-finance/pmc-case-shows-why-dual-regulation-doesn-t-work-11575398109144.html, Accessed 10 May 2020
3. Gayatri Naik, 'No banking regulator can catch or prevent frauds', *Economic Times,* 14 March 2016, https://economictimes.indiatimes.com/industry/banking/finance/banking/no-banking-regulator-can-catch-or-prevent-frauds-rbi/articleshow/63303634.cms?from=mdr, Accessed 10 May 2020
4. Sugata Ghosh, 'It's time to reform India's co-operative banks', *Economic Times,* 1 October 2019, https://economictimes.indiatimes.com/news/economy/policy/view-its-time-to-reform-indias-cooperative-banks/articleshow/71382171.cms?from=mdr, Accessed 10 May 2020
5. Ravi Shankar, 'The great bank robbery', *New Indian Express*, 7 April 2018, https://www.newindianexpress.com/magazine/2018/apr/07/the-great-bank-robbery-1797532.html
6. Financial Express Bureau, 'PNB net falls 11%, net provisioning rises 257%', *Indian Express*, 27 October 2012, http:/archive.indianexpress.com/news/pnb-net-falls-11.6--npa-provisioning-rises-257-/1022611/, Accessed 10 May 2020
7. Joel Rebello, Gayatri Nayak, 'The collapse of exposes the fault lines in the financial system', *Economic Times*, 2 October 2019, https://economictimes.indiatimes.com/industry/banking/finance/banking/the-collapse-of-pmc-exposes-the-fault-lines-in-the-financial-system-/articleshow/71402139.cms?from=mdr, Accessed 10 May 2020
8. Rishi Ranjan Kala, 'Aircel founder Sivasankaran used IFIN to sanction loans', *Financial Express*, 8 June 2019, https://www.financialexpress.com/industry/ilfs-scam-aircel-founder-sivasankaran-used-ifin-to-sanction-loans/1601285/, Accessed 10 May 2020
9. Tarun Sharma, 'Grant Thornton Audit Report Reveals How Rating Agencies played along even as IL&FS time bomb ticked', 20 August 2019, Money Control, https://www.moneycontrol.com/news/business/companies/grant-thornton-audit-report-reveals-how-rating-agencies-played-along-even-as-ilfs-time-bomb-ticked-4224211.html, Accessed 10 May 2020
10. Shayan Ghosh, 'RBIs DHFL takeover took banks by surprise', Live Mint,

22 November 2019, https://www.livemint.com/companies/news/rbi-s-dhfl-takeover-took-banks-by-surprise-11574362092389.html, Accessed 10 May 2020

Chapter 10

1. Shreya Sinha, 'Before heading to the graveyard NBFCs will damage many banks', *Economic Times*, 28 June 2019, https://bfsi.economictimes.indiatimes.com/news/nbfc/before-heading-to-graveyard-nbfcs-will-damage-many-banks-fis/69983685, Accessed 10 May 2020
2. Hindu Business Line Bureau, 'Defaults, frauds making banks wary of lending', *Hindu Business Line*, 24 December 2019, https://www.thehindubusinessline.com/money-and-banking/defaults-frauds-making-banks-wary-of-lending-rbi/article30390799.ece, Accessed 10 May 2020
3. Amol Dethe, 'Banks say will lend to industry, but few takers for loans', *Economic Times*, 27 January 2020, https://bfsi.economictimes.indiatimes.com/news/banking/banks-say-willing-to-lend-to-india-inc-but-few-takers-for-loans/73650541, Accessed 10 May 2020
4. Financial Express Bureau, 'Private banks maintain credit growth of 20% for the 5th straight quarter', *Financial Express*,
5. 21 March 2019, https://www.financialexpress.com/industry/banking-finance/private-banks-maintain-credit-growth-of-20-for-5th-straight-quarter/1522881/, Accessed 10 May 2020
6. Saloni Shukla and Ashwin Manikandan, 'Turmoil in the banking landscape, year of reckoning for PSU banks', *Economic Times*, 1 January 2020, https://economictimes.indiatimes.com/industry/banking/finance/banking/turmoil-in-the-banking-landscape-year-of-reckoning-for-psu-banks/articleshow/73053716.cms?from=mdr, Accessed 10 May 2020
7. Atmadip Ray, 'BoB shuts all Mumbai zone regional offices to go for vertical structure', *Economic Times*, 11 June 2019, https://economictimes.indiatimes.com/markets/stocks/news/bob-shuts-all-mumbai-zone-regional-offices-to-go-for-a-vertical-structure/articleshow/69734176.cms?from=mdr, Accessed 10 May 2020
8. Anand Adhikari, 'The Big Credit Freeze', *Business Today*, 11 August 2019, https://www.businesstoday.in/magazine/cover-story/the-big-credit-freeze/story/366556.html, Accessed 10 May 2020
9. Vivek Kaul, 'Narrow Banking: Why banks have shifted focus to retail loans', Live Mint, 7 August 2018, https://www.livemint.com/Industry/tiUvqj6gawtzkyaTtXMqcJ/Narrow-Banking-Why-banks-have-shifted-focus-to-retail-loans.html, Accessed 10 May 2020

10. Sandip Sen, 'What will RBI do to stop the domino effect of debt defaults', *Economic Times*, 14 May 2020, https://economictimes.indiatimes.com/blogs/Whathappensif/what-will-the-rbi-do-to-stop-the-domino-effect-of-debt-defaults/, Accessed 15 May 2020
11. Shayan Ghosh, 'Lenders to focus on corporates as retail loans expected to drop', Live Mint, 1 May 2020, https://www.livemint.com/industry/banking/lenders-to-focus-on-corporates-as-retail-loans-expected-to-drop-11588270932135.html, Accessed 10 May 2020

Chapter 11

1. Moneycontrol News, 'FM Nirmala Sitharaman announces mega public sector bank merger 10 banks amalgamated into 4 entities', Moneycontrol, 30 August 2019, https://www.moneycontrol.com/news/business/companies/fm-nirmala-sitharaman-announces-mega-public-sector-bank-merger-10-banks-amalgamated-into-4-4390911.html, Accessed 10 May 2020
2. PTI, 'Merger can't tackle issues of low capital higher NPAs : Analysts', *Economic Times*, 30 August 2019, https://economictimes.indiatimes.com/news/economy/policy/merger-cant-tackle-issues-of-low-capital-higher-npas-analysts/articleshow/70915028.cms?from=mdr, Accessed 10 May 2020
3. Vishwanath Nair, 'SBI merger with five associate banks from 1 April', Live Mint, 24 February 2017, https://www.livemint.com/Industry/mf507dGEvv1gCGRknnY9GM/SBI-merger-with-five-associate-banks-from-1-April.html, Accessed 10 May 2020
4. Anand Adhikari, 'SBI associate banks merger : 5 key challenges ahead', *Business Today*, 24 February 2017, https://www.businesstoday.in/sectors/banks/sbi-associate-banks-merger-five-key-challenges-ahead/story/246939.html, Accessed 10 May 2020
5. Anand Adhikari, 'Bank of Baroda's merger with Vijay Bank, Dena Bank: 4 key challenges', *Business Today*, 20 September 2018, https://www.businesstoday.in/sectors/banks/bank-of-baroda-merger-dena-vijaya-npa-merged-entity/story/282499.html, Accessed 10 May 2020
6. Atmadip Ray, 'IT and HR synergy are key challenges for PNB OBC UBI merger', *Economic Times*, 14 September 2019, https://economictimes.indiatimes.com/industry/banking/finance/banking/it-and-hr-synergy-are-key-challenges-for-pnb-obc-ubi-merger/articleshow/71127815.cms?from=mdr, 10/5/20
7. K Ram Kumar, 'Post mega merger Union Bank to add a layer of Chief General Manager', *Hindu Business Line*, 28 April 2020, https://www.

thehindubusinessline.com/money-and-banking/post-mega-merger-union-bank-to-add-a-layer-of-chief-general-managers/article31453943.ece

8. Mithun Dasgupta,' United Bank says it's valuation low largely due to lower net worth', *Financial Express*, 7 March 2019, https://www.financialexpress.com/industry/banking-finance/united-bank-says-its-valuation-low-largely-due-to-lower-net-worth/1891539/, Accessed 10 May 2020
9. Nichiket Kelkar, 'Mega Merger Impact. How Things Will Stack up Post Consolidation of Public Sector Banks', *The Week*, 2 April 2020, https://www.theweek.in/news/biz-tech/2020/04/02/mega-merger-impact-how-things-stack-up-post-consolidation-of-public-sector-banks.html, Accessed 10 May 2020
10. PTI, 'Allahabad Bank, Indian Bank merger delayed amid 21 days lockdown', *Business Today*, 28 March 2020, https://www.businesstoday.in/sectors/banks/allahabad-bank--indian-banks-merger-delayed-amid-21-day-lockdown/story/399498.html, Accessed 10 May 2020

Chapter 12

1. Vishwanath Nair, 'India's unbanked population halves to 233 million', Live Mint, 14 October 2015,
2. https://www.livemint.com/Industry/v4zrym0BCjNvXg3qcUD30K/Indias-unbanked-population-halves-to-233-million.html, Accessed 10 May 2020
3. G Sridhar, 'Jan Dhan accounts in one week total balance surges by ₹1272 crores', *Hindu Business Line,* 20 April 2020, https://www.thehindubusinessline.com/money-and-banking/jan-dhan-accounts-in-one-week-total-balance-surges-by-1272-crore/article31300792.ece, Accessed 10 May 2020
4. C.K. Prahalad, 'The Market at the Bottom of the Pyramid', Wharton School Publishing, 25 August 2004,
5. https://knowledge.wharton.upenn.edu/article/the-fortune-at-the-bottom-of-the-pyramid-eradicating-poverty-through-profits/, Accessed 10 May 2020
6. Vishnu Padmanabhan, Sneha Alexander, 'Are MSMEs adding to our lending woes?', Live Mint, 4 December 2019, https://www.livemint.com/industry/banking/are-msmes-adding-to-india-s-npa-problem-11575455448410.html, Accessed 10 May 2020
7. PTI, 'Nearly 3% Mudra loans turn into bad loans: Government', *Economic Times*, 3 December 2019, https://economictimes.indiatimes.com/news/

economy/finance/nearly-3-per-cent-of-mudra-loans-turn-into-bad-loans-government/articleshow/72348215.cms?from=mdr, Accessed 10 May 2020
8. PTI, 'Mudra loan disbursal stake a hit due to demonetisation', *Economic Times*, 7 January 2017, https://economictimes.indiatimes.com/news/economy/finance/mudra-loan-disbursals-take-a-hit-due-to-demonetisation/articleshow/56391892.cms?from=mdr, Accessed 10 May 2020
9. PTI, '2313 frauds reported in Mudra loan accounts', *Economic Times*, 1 July 2019, https://economictimes.indiatimes.com/industry/banking/finance/2313-frauds-reported-in-mudra-loan-accounts/articleshow/70024528.cms?from=mdr, Accessed 10 May 2020
10. Mayur Shetty, 'HDFC Bank unsecured loans exceed ₹1 lakh crore', *Times of India*, 29 November 2019, https://timesofindia.indiatimes.com/business/india-business/hdfc-bank-unsecured-loans-cross-rs-1-lakh-crore/articleshow/72285785.cms, Accessed 10 May 2020
11. Economic Times Bureau, 'HDFC Bank likely to sustain its growth momentum improve ratios - brokerages', *Economic Times*, 8 January 2020, https://economictimes.indiatimes.com/markets/stocks/news/hdfc-bank-likely-to-sustain-its-growth-momentum-improve-ratios-brokerages/articleshow/73148252.cms?from=mdr, Accessed 10 May 2020
12. ICICI, Artificial Intelligence in loan assessment, ICICI, 1 January 2020 https://www.icicibank.com/blogs/personal-loan/artificial-intelligence-in-loan-assessment-how-does-it-work.page?, Accessed 10 May 2020

Chapter 13

1. Dina Fine Maron, 'Wet Markets likely launched the Coronavirus, Here is what you need to know', *National Geographic*, 15 April 2020, https://www.nationalgeographic.com/animals/2020/04/coronavirus-linked-to-chinese-wet-markets/, Accessed 10 May 2020
2. Sinead Baker, 'Everything we know about the mysterious deadly Wuhan virus sweeping across China', *Business Insider*, 21 January 2020, https://www.businessinsider.in/science/news/everything-we-know-about-the-mysterious-deadly-wuhan-virus-sweeping-across-china/articleshow/73495648.cms?utm_source=contentofinterest&utm_medium=text&utm_campaign=cppst, Accessed 10 May 2020
3. Sean Clark, 'Traffic data shows the road into and out of COVID lockdown', *Guardian*, 27 April 2020, https://www.theguardian.com/world/ng-interactive/2020/apr/27/the-traffic-data-that-shows-the-road-into-and-

out-of-covid-19-lockdown, Accessed 10 May 2020

4. Stephanie Nebehay, 'WHO Chief says widespread travel bans not needed to beat China virus', Reuters, 3 February 2020, https://www.reuters.com/article/us-china-health-who/who-chief-says-widespread-travel-bans-not-needed-to-beat-china-virus-idUSKBN1ZX1H3, Accessed 10 May 2020
5. R Suryamurthy, 'Small businesses not happy with collateral free loans', *The Telegraph*, 14 May 2020, https://www.telegraphindia.com/india/economic-package-for-coronavirus-lockdown-kick-off-with-package-for-small-businesses/cid/1772808, Accessed 20 May 2020
6. Express Web Desk, 'Full breakup of all 5 tranches of economic relief package announced by Nirmala Sitharaman', *Indian Express*, 17 May 2020, https://indianexpress.com/article/india/economic-relief-package-break-up-five-tranches-6414076/, Accessed 20 May 2020
7. Samrat Sharma, 'Narendra Modi's 21 lakh crore special economic package actually costs the Govt only this much', *Financial Express*, 18 May 2020, https://www.financialexpress.com/economy/narendra-modis-rs-21-lakh-cr-special-economic-package-actually-costs-the-govt-only-this-much-nirmala-sitharaman-relief-package/1962288/, Accessed 20 May 2020
8. Vivek Kaul, 'Narrow Banking : Why banks have shifted focus to retail loans', Live Mint, 07 August 2018, https://www.livemint.com/Industry/tiUvqj6gawtzkyaTtXMqcJ/Narrow-Banking-Why-banks-have-shifted-focus-to-retail-loans.html, Accessed 10 May 2020
9. Sandip Sen, 'What will RBI do to stop the Domino effect of Debt Defaults?' *Economic Times*, 14 May 2020, https://economictimes.indiatimes.com/blogs/Whathappensif/what-will-the-rbi-do-to-stop-the-domino-effect-of-debt-defaults/, Accessed 20 May 2020
10. Daniel Flatley and Benjamin Bain, 'Senate passes Bill to delist Chinese Companies from Exchanges', Bloomberg, 20 May 2020, https://www.bloomberg.com/news/articles/2020-05-20/senate-passes-bill-to-delist-chinese-companies-from-exchanges, Accessed 20 May 2020

Chapter 14

1. 'Staff and agencies, UK and territories are greatest enabler of tax avoidance study says', *Guardian*, 28 May 2019, https://www.theguardian.com/world/2019/may/28/uk-and-territories-are-greatest-enabler-of-tax-avoidance-study-says, Accessed 10 May 2020
2. Imam Haque, 'Brexit could make UK the money laundering capital of the world', *The Independent*, 10 January 2019, https://www.independent.co.uk/voices/brexit-europol-money-laundering-crime-terrorism-

trafficking-a8720551.html

3. Deepti George, 'An alternative to privatisation of public sector banks', Live Mint, 23 Aprirl 2018, https://www.livemint.com/Opinion/uNFFjr8ijNfTC42uB6t9LI/An-alternative-to-privatization-of-public-sector-banks.html, Accessed 10 May 2020
4. Sandip Sen, *India Emerging : From Policy Paralysis to Hyper Economics*, Bloomsbury, 2019
5. Shayan Ghosh, 'PSB branches bear brunt of circulars', Live Mint, 27 April 2020, https://www.livemint.com/industry/banking/under-fire-for-poor-credit-pickup-psu-bank-officials-in-a-catch-22-situation-11587901772406.html, Accessed 10 May 2020
6. Shawsati Das, 'CVC report suggests tough measures to curb banking frauds', Live Mint, 17 October 2018, https://www.livemint.com/Politics/rB2pdCB6I0RkLUocPyj2zK/CVC-shares-report-on-top-100-bank-frauds-with-RBI-ED-and-CB.html, Accessed 10 May 2020
7. RK Pattnaik, 'Good Start to NBFC Regulation', Live Mint, 5 July 2019, https://www.thehindubusinessline.com/opinion/good-start-to-nbfc-regulation/article28299065.ece,, Accessed 10 May 2020
8. PTI, 'Govt proposes credit guarantee on debt in crisis hit NBFCs/HFC', *Business Standard*, 1 February 2020, https://www.business-standard.com/article/pti-stories/govt-proposes-guarantee-on-debt-to-tide-over-liquidity-challenge-in-nbfc-hfc-sector-120020101537_1.html, Accessed 10 May 2020
9. Agencies, 'Where the law stands on the whistle-blowers in India', *Economic Times*, 29 October 2019, https://economictimes.indiatimes.com/news/company/corporate-trends/where-the-law-stands-on-whistle-blowers-in-india/nhai-scam-paved-way-or-whistle-blowers-law/slideshow/71770899.cms, Accessed 10 May 2020
10. HT Correspondent, 'Chanda Kochhar is just the tip of the iceberg, Whistle blower in the CBI FIR in the Videocon loan case', *Hindustan Times*, 25 January 2019, https://www.hindustantimes.com/india-news/chanda-kochhar-is-just-the-tip-of-the-iceberg-whistle-blower-on-cbi-fir-in-icici-videocon-loan-case/story-HUJkNGI8kzx8bIfprF9iXI.html, Accessed 10 May 2020

INDEX